# Contemporary
# American Society

**By the same author**

Henry Ford: Ignorant Idealist

A History of the Youth Conservation Corps

Catalogue of the General Electric Photographic Archives (ed.)

The Invented Self: An Anti-Biography of Thomas Edison

American Studies in Transition (ed. with Christen Kold Thomsen)

Image Worlds: Corporate Identities at General Electric

Inventing Modern America (with Niels Thorsen and Carl Pedersen)

Electrifying America: Social Meanings of a New Technology
(Dexter Prize; Abel Wolman Award)

Consumption and American Culture (ed. with Carl Pedersen)

American Technological Sublime

American Photographs Abroad (ed. with Mick Gidley)

Consuming Power: A Social History of American Energies

Narratives and Spaces: Technology and the Construction of American Culture

Technologies of Landscapes (ed.)

# Contemporary American Society

Fourth Edition

## David E. Nye

AKADEMISK

**Contemporary American Society**
© Academic Press/Akademisk Forlag A/S, Copenhagen 1990

1. udgave, 1. oplag 1990, 2. oplag 1991, 3. oplag 1992
2. udgave, 1. oplag 1993, 2. oplag 1994, 3. oplag 1995
3. udgave, 1. oplag 1997, 2. oplag 2000
4. udgave, 1. oplag 2001

Omslag: Christensen Grafisk ApS, København
Forlagsredaktion: Carsten Jørgensen
Sats: Christensen Grafisk ApS, København
Tryk: Nørhaven A/S, Viborg

ISBN: 87-500-3629-7
Printed in Denmark 2001

*Dedicated to
Grace Swift Nye*

# Preface to the Fourth Edition

The fourth edition of *Contemporary American Society* appears eleven years after the first. There have been many small revisions and adjustments made for this edition, without fundamentally changing the fabric of the whole. Most obviously, the new edition includes the remarkable presidential election of 2000, welfare reform, the growing importance of the Internet in society, and the development of a federal budget surplus. Less obviously, many facts and figures have been updated and many short passages revised. I have also updated the bibliography and guide to American studies on the Internet, so that this book can continue to serve as a gateway to learning more about the United States.

The intended readers are European undergraduates at business schools and universities. As before, this volume outlines the nation's geography, population, politics, economic organization, class structure, racial divisions, religion, educational system, social services, and values. Chapters can be read independently, but there is a logic underlying the book. It begins with the relationship between the United States and Europe, and then takes up basic geography, because I have found that students have seen many places in films or read about them in novels, without knowing where they are. A sketch of the population is also needed, to help clarify how different the multi-racial United States is from most other nations. With this background, it is easier to understand the political system, since the system of representation is based on geography and inflected by racial and ethnic differences. Domestic politics in turn provides the framework needed to understand foreign affairs and the economic system. Economics leads to a discussion of class, race, and gender. All of these early chapters help the student to understand the subjects of the final chapters: the media, religion, welfare, and American values. The book is both a survey and a general essay on the condition of the United States at the end of the American century and the beginning of a new millennium.

Of the many that have helped me with this book over the years, I particularly want to thank – again – Dale Carter, Carl Pedersen, Clara Juncker, Helle Porsdam, Robert Baehr, and Randy Strahan.

Center for American Studies, University of Southern Denmark, February, 2001

# Contents

Tues    1 - 3
Wed    1 - 3

# Inhabiting America

"The reality of America is selective, optional, fantastic: there is an America for each of us." – Peter Conrad, 1980.

"I dare to state it: the discovery of America was an evil. Never can the advantages it brought about (no matter how one considers or depicts them) compensate for the harm it has caused." – Joseph Mandrillon, 1784.

## I. Europe and America

People imagine America before discovering it. Ever since 1492 visitors have arrived with preconceptions that shaped their vision. What they saw tells us about them. Columbus imagined America as India, and for the later explorers it was first an idea – cities of gold, a primitive utopia, a vast Garden of Eden, a heathen world where the Devil ruled, a mysterious realm of lost civilizations – and then a disconcerting reality, full of hardships, disappointments, unexpected sublimities, and racial confrontations. Some concluded, like Mandrillon, that the discovery of America had been an evil, causing wars, plagues, the depopulation of Europe, and the destruction of the Native Americans, who would have been better off undiscovered.

It is always hard to see a new place correctly, and the New World proved especially difficult. Its inhabitants were an unknown race. Its plants were not like those of Europe. Its wildlife differed enormously from anything previously seen. Who could believe that in America there were snakes with rattles in their tails, which they shook before striking? But the rattlesnake did exist. What was one to think of other explorers' reports, that frogs weighed as much as fourteen kilograms and bellowed like bulls, that Native-American men had milk in their breasts, that some American mosquitoes had wings a meter wide, that in the mountains were cities whose streets were paved with gold, that one of the lost tribes of Israel had been found there, that some American mountains were fifteen thousand meters high? From the first, everything about America was strange. Who could understand how to cultivate, how to cook, or how to eat its many new foods: tomatoes, potatoes, corn, beans, bananas, oranges, and grapefruit? More difficult still, how could one understand the many Native-American cultures? Half a millennium after Columbus, Indian languages still remain undeciphered on the walls of abandoned palaces and pyramids.

*The Mayflower II, a replica of the ship that brought the Pilgrims to America in 1620.*
*– Plimoth Plantation.*

Indeed, Europeans generally failed to understand these first Americans very well. Virtually all of the tribes who met the invaders died out completely in a short time, victims of war, slavery, and disease. Those who survived did so only at the cost of adapting and changing their cultures beyond recognition. The Indians originally had no horses, for example, so the horse must be considered one of the most successful exports from Europe to the New World. In adopting the horse, some tribes that previously had been agricultural became semi-nomadic. In adopting the gun and working in the fur trade, Native Americans destroyed the balance between themselves and the wildlife in regions they had traditionally inhabited. In accepting Christianity many tribes also lost much of their cultural identity. From their viewpoint, America was not discovered, but invaded and changed beyond recognition.

In these transformations the European was changed as well. If America is not as exotic today as it was in 1492, neither is it a copy of Europe. Brazil scarcely resembles Portugal. Quebec is not like France, nor Mexico like Spain. The United States was the first colony openly to declare this difference by rebelling against England's rule. Since 1776 it has held European attention, at first because of its novel democratic form of government, later because of its economic success and cultural dynamism, and today because of its military and economic power. More than most countries, America is preceded by its images, and, like Columbus, Europeans still imagine America, but they often do so in terms supplied by the United States, through Hollywood films, popular songs, television, and consumer goods. They still imagine they can get rich there and are often disappointed. They imagine a land of hamburgers, missiles, racial injustice, CIA conspiracies, shopping malls, circus-like elections, violence, gangsters, and oil tycoons in Dallas.

Europeans often see the United States as an anti-Europe, and, ironically, Americans are quick to agree, so that both accept a series of oppositions such as the following:

> America is new; Europe is old.
> America is naive; Europe is experienced.
> America is uniform; Europe is diverse.
> America is turbulent; Europe is calm.
> America is wild; Europe is civilized.

These notions turn out to be half false. In fact, the United States has an older continuous government than most countries, as the majority of the European constitutions – Germany, Austria, Italy, Spain, France, and Denmark for example – are much newer. Likewise, the notions that Americans are inexperienced or innocent on reflection prove to be extremely problematic. Finally, the country is neither as homogeneous nor as turbulent as many imagine. There are great regional variations, and some areas change very little from one decade to the next.

Both Americans and Europeans also make over-simplified contrasts that favor America. They may say that the United States is dynamic and innovative, Europe is conservative and slow; that it is the future, Europe the past; that it is open, Europe closed. For the most part, these clichés give no more idea of the lived reality of America than did the explorers' reports five centuries ago.

## 2. How Americans Inhabit Their Country

The landscape of the United States has acquired new meanings since Europeans first conquered it. To the Native Americans, space was not uniform and land was not a commodity to be bought and sold. Each tribe viewed certain areas as sacred, and private ownership of land was not possible in the European sense. Whole tribes possessed lands, but they in turn felt possessed by the earth. In contrast, the invaders fenced off individual lots for personal use. While the Native Americans sought to live in harmony with the natural world, the white men and women viewed the land in terms of development. Many English settlers came as part of investment ventures by private companies. Those who emigrated to Virginia in 1607 were not only supposed to set up a colony, they were to make a profit, too. Failing to find gold or precious stones, they instead developed tobacco as an export. Growing much more than they required for their own needs, they traded tobacco to Europe for manufactured goods, setting a pattern that changed little for hundreds of years. America remained an undeveloped nation selling raw materials to other countries until the middle of the nineteenth century, and it would be a debtor nation until the First World War.

Although the United States began as a group of rural colonies, this did not mean that the settlers lived in harmony with nature. Quite the contrary. They developed an intensive, one-crop agriculture of tobacco, sugar, and cotton. They trapped or slaughtered animals for their pelts, particularly the beaver. They cut down forest lands and drained swamps to increase the amount of arable land. In Europe, their former countrymen pursued the same policies, expanding the area of cultivated lands in most of the nations in Europe during the seventeenth century. But the scale of expansion differed. The original thirteen colonies, settled before the American Revolution (in 1776), are larger than England, France, and Germany combined. Yet none of these original thirteen is today among the largest thirty states. Indeed, the settlement of the United States has still not ended, as almost one million (legal and illegal) immigrants enter the country each year. The center of the nation's population even now continues to move westward. In 1980, that center crossed the Mississippi River for the first time.

Yet while the United States has been filling up with people for the past 350 years, the immigrants have not seen their activity as a simple extension of European civilization. Instead, they have conceived of their resettlement as an escape from Europe. To most of them America has seemed to be the opposite of the Old World, opposing its civilization with nature, its aristocracy and class interests with egalitarian democracy, its state churches with privately supported religions, and its corruption with New World innocence. Many American writers have seen the emerging United States as a vast garden where men and women could reverse the Biblical story of the expulsion of Adam and Eve from Eden. In America, they thought, lay a chance to escape from the errors of the past into a Utopian, agrarian world. The corruption, class divisions, and sinfulness of the Old World would be forgotten in the New. While such a view was strongest in the nineteenth century, it has scarcely disappeared today. Many classic works in American literature, such as Henry David Thoreau's *Walden* and Mark Twain's *The Adventures of Huckleberry Finn*, suggest that the essence of Americanness lies in the natural landscape. Most American readers still identify themselves with the boy Huck as he floats down the Mississippi with the runaway slave, Jim. On the river they have escaped from society into nature, where they can avoid employers, judges, parents, owners, clergymen, teachers, and other agents of civilization. Advertising often makes good use of this theme of escape into a more primitive landscape. Cars in particular are sold by putting them on top of a mountain or out in the deserts of the far west.

The same idea of escape from society appeared in the classic western films, particularly those made before 1950. In them, the hero usually lives in the wilderness and only goes into the towns and settlements to solve problems that he cannot deal with himself. Afterwards he rides back into the incorruptible wilderness. Many of America's characteristic heroes have emerged from (or have claimed to emerge from) rural or uncivilized conditions. Close association with nature seemed to ensure a political candidate's virtue, and a long line of politicians claimed they were born in log cabins. Presidents Andrew Jackson (1829-1837) and Abraham Lincoln (1861–1865) are only two of the most famous examples. Even in the twentieth century politicians nurture associations between themselves and the natural world. Jimmy Carter presented himself in TV commercials as a successful farmer, walking through his fields wearing blue jeans. Ronald Reagan often posed for photographers with axe in hand, cutting down small trees and brush on his California ranch. Bill Clinton continually stressed his small town origins in Hope, Arkansas. In short, white Americans see the rural landscape and wilderness as sources of good morals and strong character.

In contrast, most Americans view their cities as centers of moral and political problems. An American today might prefer to think of Copenhagen or Paris as a symbol of sophistication and style, rather than New York, which for many suggests crime and danger, as well as expensive theater, fine museums, and a vibrant musical life. For a long time Americans have not particularly liked their cities. President Thomas Jefferson (1801–1809) expressed a national consensus when he declared that, "The mobs of great cities add just so much to the support of pure government, as sores do to the strength of the human body." While he wrote these words shortly after the American Revolution, most Americans today would apparently agree. They still prefer not to live in cities, in contrast to Europeans who often prefer apartments in the urban center. Even in the case of New York, which offers many fine apartment complexes, executives often commute an hour or more each day from distant suburbs rather than remain in the city. Generally speaking, in the US the poorest groups live quite near the commercial heart of the city, as foreign travelers on the Greyhound Bus system quickly discover. The middle classes live outside the city in concentric circles of suburbs, with the wealthiest living in the outermost ring. Since 1960 the fastest growing areas of the United States have been "edge cities" formed at the intersections of two or more interstate highways. An "edge city" contains at least six million square feet of office space and 600,000 square feet of shops and services. It can only be reached by car, and consists of several giant shopping malls, light industry, hotels and new office towers. Half of all commercial sales now take place in the 28,000 shopping malls. Travelers who only visit American cities see an area in decline, with sharp contrasts between areas of poverty and a core of expensive shops and skyscrapers. They do not see the vast suburban tracts where the middle class lives or the edge cities where they work and shop. To the casual visitor, therefore, the US may seem like a land of far more pronounced class differences than in fact is the case.

Although most Americans live in or near cities and work for large companies, they retain vestiges of their rural past. The suburban house appeals to the American homeowner not merely because it is outside the noise and congestion of the city. That home also requires some of the skills and preserves some of the structures of earlier American life. A geographer once observed: "A typical suburban house lot recreates in miniature the farm of the past. The front lawn, frequently fenced and always carefully mowed, assumes the role of the meadow. . . . Behind the house lies the yard, again often enclosed, but serving as both farmyard and pasture. The backyard provides privacy . . . but most importantly offers an outdoor workplace." The garage substitutes for the barn. Dogs and cats are livestock; the garden serves as a miniature field. The ever popular American station-wagon replaces the farm wagon. The American homeowner spends evenings and weekends painting the house, rolling the lawn, refinishing the basement, pruning bushes, and performing other chores that require a variety of skills in carpentry and husbandry. Visitors from countries such as Spain and Italy are often amused at this incessant work on the home, whose owners never seem to have time to relax. The US pattern seems more familiar to Northern Europeans.

## 3. Organization of Space

It is difficult for anyone from outside the United States to grasp the American sense of space. For Americans, the world seems to have few boundaries. Canada to the north and Mexico to the south are separate countries, but they have seldom posed a threat to the security of the United States, and one does not need a passport to visit them. Canada in particular is often thought of as a vast 51st state that will one day become part of the country. For centuries the width of the Atlantic and the Pacific oceans made a sea invasion of the country virtually impossible. This long experience of open, unbounded space gives Americans an expansive sense of physical mobility, as they feel free to move thousands of kilometers in any direction over an entire continent.

To organize the land mass of the United States, government surveyors early created a system of rectangular dividing lines. If one flies over the Middle West or Far West today the results are easily discernible. Roads usually run in straight lines east–west or north–south, creating a giant checkerboard pattern. In the Rocky Mountains, where one might expect the impressive natural land formations to determine boundaries, one finds instead that entire states take the form of squares and other geometrical figures. (See the shapes of Colorado, Wyoming, and Utah, for examples.) Similarly, most American cities display a grid pattern so severely logical that a complete stranger can often find his or her way around a new city. Visitors to New York can locate Fifth Avenue and 37th Street or move from there to Second Avenue and 21st Street with little trouble. No such regularities organize London, Paris, or Hamburg. As a result, Americans move freely about their continent and find their way without much difficulty. A cynic might complain that all places in the United States are as interchangeable as hamburgers, but this is only a superficial truth. While the grid pattern does recur in most of the country, along with such standardized restaurants as Howard Johnson's, McDonald's, and Burger King, the nation nevertheless displays great regional differences, particularly if one leaves the main highways. The variety stems not only from climatic differences, that make California a more outdoor culture than Michigan, but also from industrial and cultural differences.

Consider industrial differences first. An area south of San Francisco has become internationally known as "Silicon Valley," named after the silicon computer chip which so many of its companies use or produce. The rapidly growing computer industry has attracted a highly trained, aggressive group to this one site, giving the area a technological sophistication and wealth in stark contrast to some other industrial areas, such as Detroit, whose automobile industry has performed erratically over the last 30 years. Most American regions are stamped by their industries, which impart a particular rhythm of life to a company town or a glitter of sophistication to a white-collar neighborhood.

*Los Angeles city center. The flat suburbs beyond are built on farmland. – Nordfoto.*

These differences, combined with climatic variations and considerable ethnic diversity, make every region of the United States distinctive. The large Cuban population in Miami makes it unlike any other Southern city. Coming mostly from middle-class, urban backgrounds, the Cubans have less in common with Mexican-Americans than their common language might suggest. A visitor to San Antonio, Texas, will find that its Spanish-speaking majority has created a cultural ambiance quite unlike Miami's, while the Puerto Rican sections of New York will reveal a third, equally distinctive form of Hispanic culture. As these examples suggest, American immigrants have never spread out evenly to all parts of the country, but have concentrated in particular regions. Swedes and Norwegians often went to Wisconsin, Minnesota, or other parts of the upper middle west. Italians settled in the urban Northeast, in large cities of the interior such as Chicago, and in California. The ethnic mix is never quite the same from one place to the next. Indeed, in some areas, there is no mix. Certain towns in Minnesota remain almost entirely Norwegian. The Mennonites, a German Protestant sect, cluster in a few tightly knit communities. Once off the major highways, the traveler can stray into quite varied ethnic enclaves: Scotch-Irish in the mountains of the Old South, French-speaking Cajuns in Louisiana, or Koreans on the West Coast. America is not the homogeneous world that its pattern of roads and boundary lines might suggest. If its inhabitants feel free to wander over the face of the continent, one reason that they travel is to see the country's enormous variety.

Indeed, a whole literary genre explores the cultures and landscapes of North America, and not a decade passes without the appearance of at least one excellent book of this sort. The student can learn a good deal about the country rather painlessly by reading one of these. *Blue Highways* recounts the experiences of its author, Least Heat Moon, as he circled the United States in a small truck, choosing to drive the whole way on back roads. Other notable examples of the genre are Jack Kerouac's *On the Road* and John Steinbeck's *Travels with Charley*. All three were best sellers.

Like the narrators of these books, Americans inhabit their land restlessly, moving from place to place more than most other peoples. It is not unusual to commute more than fifty kilometers to work each day, nor do people find it strange to drive an hour or two to eat in a restaurant. The American love of movement began long before the present century, but since 1900 the ability to move about has been greatly increased by the automobile. Virtually no one owned a car in 1903 when Henry Ford started his automobile company; twenty-five years later there was one car for every six Americans, and half of these were Fords. The organization of contemporary American life is unthinkable without a car for every family. Stores, banks, movie theaters, and essential facilities of every kind are located on systems of freeways. Dependence on automobiles even causes structural unemployment, as some jobs are inaccessible to those without cars. Homes, shopping areas, and workplaces are segregated from one another and separated by automotive distances. As a result, the population density is generally so low in all but the largest American cities that mass transportation proves impractical and expensive.

These characteristics, evident in all parts of the nation, become more pronounced as one moves toward the western cities developed largely after the coming of the motor car. Los Angeles, California, is the best example, a city with no center in the traditional sense, a city crossed by hundreds of miles of expressways, a city where walking from place to place would literally be impossible, a city where virtually no one uses buses and where a commuter rail line introduced in 1992 has few passengers. Within this enormous grid of freeways lies an astonishing diversity of ethnic enclaves: Mexican Americans, African-Americans, Chinese, Koreans, Filipinos, and other groups, each preserving some cultural distinctiveness. The vast city cannot be understood as a geometrical design filled with identical communities. Rather, Los Angeles is a series of ethnic worlds within a landscape designed for the automobile.

Most Americans prefer to define themselves not by where they have been, but by where they are going. They live not in the past and only tenuously in the present, focusing instead on the future. As early as the 1780s visitors noted that Americans moved to new places far more often than people in Europe. As a result, the population seldom remains the same in any location for long. Today, the average American family moves about twice in each decade. In many cases these moves are short, from one part of a metropolitan region to another. Americans live in an age-graded society, and communities tend to be somewhat homogeneous by age. The young couple or single person lives in an apartment complex or urban area heavily populated by similar people. When children are born, the family moves to a small suburban home. Should the family prosper, the money invested in this first house will help provide the capital needed to purchase a series of larger homes. Finally, with old age and retirement, some couples make yet another move to an old age community. Of course, not all remain married. The divorce rate in the US is approximately 50%, with a high rate of remarriage. Corporate employers further increase this continual change of address, as they often ask managers to transfer from one office to another. The impersonal forces of economic cycles likewise force many workers to find new jobs in other cities.

Looked at from the child's point of view, this sequence of moves begins very early in life, with several occurring before age 18, when most take a first job or attend the university. While Europeans usually prefer to remain in the area where they grew up, young people in the US try to get away from home, and usually they do not resist but rather welcome the chance to go far away. Later, if they want to come back home, it often proves to be a rather pointless return. Many strangers now live in the place that once was home, and the old community no longer exists. Even the shape of towns changes rapidly, as new highways, shopping malls, urban renewal programs, and other changes can make the "hometown" almost unrecognizable after only a few years. As a result, Americans often stop saying that they are "from" the place where they were born or the place where they grew up.

The early experience of continual change leaves a strong mark on the American, who cannot be defined in terms of family or location as easily as the European. Mainstream American culture emphasizes the individual rather than the group, and personal experience rather than collective experience. As a result, life in the United States has several unique characteristics: (1) a tendency toward anarchic individualism, (2) a fragile sense of community, and (3) an openness to new experience and new friendships. These three topics suggest the importance of American geography to understanding the culture of the United States. Without first knowing how Americans have conceived of and organized space, it is impossible fully to comprehend much of American literature and politics. For American culture is marked by contradictions: its politics are intensely regional yet the country has a weak sense of community; its spatial organization is repetitious and emphasizes national commonalities, and yet the population is extremely individualistic.

The European invasion of North America has resulted in a rather abstract pattern of spatial relationships, in which the country as a whole appears to be a vast interlocking system of straight lines. But within this grid lie diverse regional and ethnic communities, each preserving some of its cultural traditions. The Native Americans themselves offer the best example, as they struggle to preserve their cultures on so-called "reservations." Most of them continue to reject the European definition of the earth as property, retaining a collective spiritual relationship to their lands. As a result, they still find themselves in conflict with whites, who wish to use their reservations to build highways, mine coal and mineral wealth, or pursue other kinds of "development." From the Native-American point of view, the European conquest of the United States has gone too far, and the rationalization of its landscape will hopefully never be complete. Indeed, judging by the lack of enthusiasm white Americans had for the five hundredth anniversary of Columbus's voyage, native voices are being heard.

## 4. American History

After this brief description of American space, it is also useful to have a sense of how Americans see their history.

The centuries before 1492 are usually called the pre-Columbian period.

1492-1607 is a time of exploration and discovery.

1607-1770 is the colonial period, when North America was settled by the Spanish, French, Dutch, and English. These powers battled each other and Native Americans for territory. English dominance was only assured in 1763, when the French surrendered in Canada.

1770-1789, the revolutionary period. The nation was founded, embodied in three central documents, The Declaration of Independence, The Constitution, and The Bill of Rights.

1789-1828 was the early national period. During these years leadership came from the men who had guided the Revolution. The first President was the former commander of the army, George Washington. Until 1824 all the Presidents who came after him had either signed the Declaration of Independence or the Constitution. The economy remained largely agricultural. The country tried to remain neutral during the French Revolution and the Napoleonic Wars, and was only drawn into that conflict on the French side in 1812. After that, the United States remained neutral until 1917.

1828-1865 was defined by the sectional crisis. North and South each rapidly developed their quite different economies. The plantation South relied on slavery for power and produced wealth in the form of raw materials: cotton, tobacco, sugar. The industrial North relied extensively on water-powered factories. Each region was dynamic, sending settlers west. The Civil War (1861-1865) was about state's rights, about the moral abomination of human slavery, and about which system would dominate the West.

1865-1877 the North occupied the defeated South, while the nation as a whole continued its rapid expansion and industrialization. Most Native-American resistance was snuffed out. Immigration increased rapidly, with most coming from Northern Europe. The rail system reached from coast to coast in 1869. Tensions between capital and labor grew, culiminating in bloody railroad strikes in 1877.

1877-1917, a period of high rates of immigration from southern and eastern Europe, rapid industrialization, the formation of monopolies in key industries, and the concentration of economic power in the city. This was a particularly turbulent period for socialists and unions, which met with less success than their European counterparts. Farmers formed powerful movements to protest the power of trusts and to demand political reforms. Women also organized, demanding the vote. The two major political parties adapted enough to reabsorb these groups. In contrast, African-Americans, Native Americans, and new Asian immigrants were marginalized and had little voice. The majority of Americans were united by a new vibrant popular culture.

1917-1941 After entering World War I in a burst of idealism that later many thought had been misguided, the nation returned to neutrality in foreign affairs. In 1920 the United States had the world's largest economy, and it was rapidly adopting mass production methods. Both the prosperous

1920s and the Great Depression of the 1930s were marked by a long-term shift toward a white-collar economy, by the rapid adoption of the automobile and electricity in daily life, and by the public's full immersion in national events by means of advertising, film, and radio.

1941- The Japanese attack on Pearl Harbor pushed the United States into World War II, beginning a period of global engagement. During the Cold War, America reached its greatest economic hegemony, marked by the world-wide spread of its capitalist business methods and its popular culture. At home, marginalized groups increasingly demanded the rights guaranteed by the Declaration of Independence. African Americans led the way with the Civil Rights movement, followed by women, Native Americans, Hispanic Americans, and gays. Their demands were yet another reminder that the struggle to achieve life, liberty, and the pursuit of happiness unleashed in the American Revolution continues to this day.

# Peopling America

## I. America before Columbus

Humanity reached North America relatively recently, coming from northern Asia and crossing into present-day Alaska about 30,000 years ago. While much remains to be learned about the many Native-American cultures, a few generalizations are possible. When Columbus arrived in 1492 the first Americans were more heterogeneous than Europeans. Their languages were more diverse, and the forms of their cultures quite varied. Some, like the Aztecs in Mexico, had built cities as large as any in Europe, while others were small bands of hunter-gatherers. Long before Europeans arrived, most tribes had developed systems of agriculture. The earliest evidence found until now is from 7,000 years ago in Mexico. This means that people were no longer nomadic, as they had to remain near their crops. It also meant a larger population than hunting could support. Estimates vary considerably, but at least 10 million people lived within the present-day United States, and quite possibly many more. There are no written records, but physical evidence and the survival of some tribes permit a fragmentary reconstruction of some of these pre-Columbian cultures.

The Iroquois confederation, for example, united five tribes in what is now New York State and parts of Canada. The Iroquois do not correspond well to Hollywood's representation of Native Americans. The Iroquois were not roving bands, but settled, agricultural people. They lived in a heavily forested region and built log lodges, not tepees. Iroquois men were fierce warriors, but they did not have the highest positions of leadership. Rather, both family structure and political organization were focused on women. In the Colonial period the Iroquois sided with the Americans and British against the French, and they established their right to the lands in New York and Canada which they still hold. In language, religion, and culture, the Iroquois belong to the eastern Woodland group of tribes. They are not at all like the Hopi in the deserts of the Southwest, the Sioux in the western plains, or the Tlingits of southern Alaska.

While Europeans usually met a friendly reception on first arrival, this did not stop them from seizing the lands they encountered. Their imperialism was assisted by microscopic allies. Native Americans had no resistance to the diseases that Europeans brought with them, and even a common cold could be deadly. In some cases, ships carrying new settlers to America came to empty lands, whose inhabitants had died off en masse, victims of diseases they received during a casual encounter with earlier explorers. The early history of the colonies was not one of growth, but one of replacement. In 1700 the number of people in New England was about the same as it had been a century before. But the dominant complexion had changed, primarily through immigration but also through intermarriage.

## 2. Population Growth

In 1700 there were 250,000 people in the colonies that would become the United States. The number roughly doubled every twenty-five years, reaching 2.5 million in 1775. Colonial women normally bore between five and ten children. It was a young population. Over half of all Americans were under the age of sixteen. (Today about one-third of the population is that young.) Of course immigration also played a role. The biggest surge in early immigration came between 1750 and 1775, when 220,000 people arrived. Of these, 100,000 were slaves, brought involuntarily. While a few were sold in the North, most were put to work in the South. The majority of the rest of the immigrants were men from the British Isles and from Germany, travelling alone.

Immigration was by no means constant. It was interrupted by both the Revolution and the wars of the French Revolution. Yet the American population continued to grow rapidly. By 1810 it had reached 7.2 million, by 1860 31 million, and by 1900 76 million.

While the birth-rate for women fell slightly in every decade after 1800, improved infant mortality and longer life expectancy compensated. The population remained young. In 1880 over half the American people were under 21, and they married earlier in life than people do now. As the population became more urbanized, the number of children declined. On a farm each child represents additional labor, and it is an asset to have many. But people living in cities usually cut back family size, because there children become an expense. Most urban families chose to provide well for a few children.

The life-cycle also changed. In Colonial times it was rare for both parents to live long enough to see all their children reach adulthood. By the end of the nineteenth century, however, people were living longer. It became common for parents to survive into old age together. Having children increasingly became only one stage of life, rather than the chief occupation of adulthood. In the twentieth century, birth-control technologies improved, and women gained more control over family size. Fertility continued to drop until the end of World War II, when a surprising thing happened: the baby boom. In 1946, one million more children were born than in the year before, and for the next decade female fertility reversed the downward trend of the previous 150 years. As a consequence, the population began to grow more rapidly again, but the change was not evenly distributed across the nation. The increase was modest in the Northeast and Midwest; however, they were almost stagnant between 1970 and 1990. In contrast, the South and West attracted many new residents. Indeed, the West more than doubled in population between 1950 and 1985 alone.

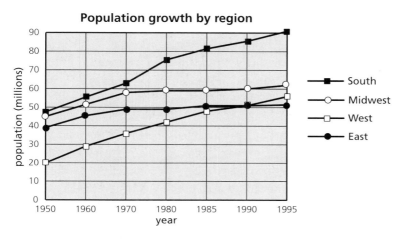

**Population growth by region**

On January 1, 2001, the estimated population of the United States was 276,601,000. The Census Bureau estimated that one person was born every eight seconds, or seven-and-a-half per minute, while someone died every fourteen seconds. By comparison, immigration was less important, as one person arrived every forty-two seconds. Once all factors were taken into account, including Americans returning from abroad and foreigners returning home, there was a net gain in population of one person every fourteen seconds. The nation was hardly static, but in one sense matters were much as they have been for centuries: natural increase still accounted for most of the growth.

## 3. Nineteenth-century Immigration

American immigration was little regulated, in contrast to much tighter Spanish controls in Latin America, which did not have an early influx of northern Europeans. Immigration was shaped by both "push" and "pull" factors. Those who came often had been displaced by European industrialization and land enclosures. Other "push" factors were religious persecution, food shortages (such as the potato famine in Ireland), and overpopulation of some regions. But not all were pushed to leave. Many also were pulled toward the United States by the promise of inexpensive land, democratic political institutions, and higher wages.

Since the mid-nineteenth century the United States has managed to assimilate immigrants while at the same time defining its own culture. As Europeans have learned since guest workers arrived in the 1960s, assimilation cannot be taken for granted. Immigrants do not want to give up their cultural identity. Today, some Europeans seem particularly sensitive to the value of cultural diversity within their borders, but others demand that new immigrants and refugees immediately learn a new language and act like long-term residents. Right-wing political groups in Germany and France go even further, making racist attacks on immigrants and demanding that they go home. Such insensitivity was once common in America, too, when waves of immigrants arrived during the nineteenth century. At that time, many old stock Americans feared that the new arrivals would never assimilate, but would establish permanent ghetto communities where they would remain more loyal to a foreign culture than to their adopted land. The problem seemed less acute when most immigrants came from northern Europe, and shared with the earlier settlers the Protestant religion, experience with industrial culture, and a high rate of literacy. Just as important, Germans, Dutchmen, and Scandinavians looked much the same as Americans of British descent.

European immigrants were often attracted to the new land by fellow countrymen. In Johan Bojer's novel *The Emigrants* a Norwegian returns to his native village after seven years in America. His old acquaintances are surprised at his self-assurance and his refusal to take off his hat to local dignitaries, because, he explains, in America there are no class distinctions, and he only doffs his hat to personal acquaintances.

> He had worked as a railroad navvy and as a farm laborer, and had himself owned a farm for three years; then the railway came along, prices went up, and he sold out. Now he wanted to go farther west, to the Red River Valley, where the land could still be had for nothing and was very easy to put under cultivation, because the soil of the prairie was free from stones and tree stumps, and you had only to put in your plow and start plowing at once. If any of them cared to join him, they could go in company.

Immigrant groups often went to America from the same towns, especially before 1890 when agricultural land was more easily available. Ethnic groups also clustered together in the cities. In the 1860s Germans in New York City had created a neighborhood called Kleindeutchland, where a resident did not need to know English to make a living. This practice spread to the southern and eastern Europeans who began to arrive in large numbers after 1890. They quickly became the most numerous immigrants after 1900, during a period when the number of newcomers rose to over one million a year. Most crowded together in cities, particularly New York, Detroit, Chicago, and Philadelphia.

*Home of an Italian ragpicker in New York photographed by the Danish immigrant Jacob Riis in the 1890s. – Nordfoto.*

In the 1890s the Danish immigrant Jacob Riis photographed the poor in New York, intentionally shocking the middle class with images of poverty and overcrowding in dark tenements. His images called out for reform – not only for improved housing and sanitation, but for the Americanization of these immigrants, whom Riis described as potential threats to political and economic stability. In 1908 a play entitled *The Melting Pot* caught the popular imagination and provided an image of what immigration meant. If America was heterogeneous, the play asserted that this condition was temporary, and that the United States was in the process of merging the good qualities of all races into a new people uniquely suited to lead the world. The ideal American would exist in the future, not the present. The belief that the American was to be produced out of the dynamic of immigration and settlement was not new, and could be traced back at least to the eighteenth century. But the phrase, "The Melting Pot," condensed this

## Two phases of immigration

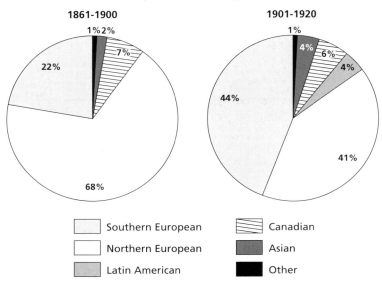

1861-1900

1901-1920

Southern European     Canadian

Northern European     Asian

Latin American     Other

idea into a single phrase at a time when more immigrants were arriving than ever before.

Despite the persuasive rhetoric of the melting pot, old-stock Americans began to demand legislation that would restrict immigration. They also looked for ways to assimilate those who had already come. One obvious way to unify social life was to define standards of dress, education, and behavior, to draw a line of acceptability. Many customs from the Old World found no favor in the New. Mothers who arrived in New York wearing black clothing and wooden shoes and hiding their long hair from public view under kerchiefs, either adopted American fashions or watched their daughters do so against their wishes. Despite such adaptations, however, the desire to restrict immigration grew, and laws were passed just after World War I that reduced by two-thirds the number of immigrants who could enter the country each year. There were two quota laws. The first, in 1921, limited immigration to only 357,000 people each year, with places available for up to 3 percent of the number of each nationality represented in the Census of 1910. An even more severe law in 1924 cut this quota in half and favored northern Europeans over southern Europeans, while virtually excluding Asians. Canadians and Latin Americans were favored by the new laws, however. The combination of restrictive legislation and the Great Depression slowed immigration to a trickle. In the entire decade of the 1930s fewer immigrants arrived than in the single year of 1914, when 1.2 million came.

*Immigrant just arrived at Ellis Island, New York harbour, 1905.*
*– George Eastman House.*

## 4. The New Immigrant Majority:
## Hispanics and Asians

While traditionally the great mass of immigrants were Europeans, this situation began to change rapidly in the 1960s. By then, western Europe was prosperous, and only east European refugees came to the United States in any numbers. Instead, taking advantage of liberal immigration laws, starting in 1965 immigrants poured in from Latin America and Asia.

In 1950 there were less than four million Hispanics; today, there are more than twenty-six million. Their average age is only 23 compared to 31 for the population as a whole. Many Hispanics are mulattos, suggesting one way out of the Black–White polarities of American culture. Hispanics define themselves through culture and language rather than race, and may be White, Indian, Black, or a blend of the three races. Hispanics are not, of course, a single group, and they are in America for quite different reasons. The Puerto Ricans are not immigrants, but became American citizens when the Spanish lost their island to the United States in the War of 1898. On the mainland they have long preferred to live in the New York area. Cubans, mostly refugees from Fidel Castro's government, have relocated in Florida or large cities on the east coast. Colombians and people from Central America have not concentrated in single regions, but often prefer to live in Hispanic communities in the larger cities. The largest group of all, two-thirds of the Hispanic population, are Chicanos, who are concentrated in the Southwest where the major cities were founded during 300 years of Spanish-Mexican rule. More than two million live in Los Angeles.

Unlike nineteenth-century immigrants, who usually left Europe forever on a sailing vessel, Hispanics come from neighboring countries, and are able to return home more frequently, often by plane. They can keep their culture alive not only through Spanish language newspapers, but through their own radio and television stations. Furthermore, Chicanos can quite literally declare themselves at home in the Southwest, to which they sometimes give its Aztec name, Aztlan. Chicano writers also refer back to the Mayans, laying claim to their Indian heritage as the original settlers of America. Compared with the European immigrants, Hispanics are closely tied to their home countries, able to retain their language and culture, and prepared psychologically to maintain their traditions rather than assimilate to the dominant Anglo-American society. About 250,000 Hispanics legally immigrate to the United States every year; a large number also enter illegally.

People illegally enter the United States from other countries as well, and while no one knows how many have slipped across the border, estimates range between two and four million. Illegal immigrants have no legal right to work, and so get the worst jobs, often receiving less than the minimum wage. They seldom have sickness insurance or a pension plan. Thousands nevertheless attempt to come across the border every week, in small boats from the Caribbean islands and on foot across the long border with Mexico. Russell Banks described the fatalistic determination of French-speaking Haitian illegal immigrants who take passage on a boat for Florida: "They risk everything to get away from their island, give up everything, their homes, their families, forsake all they know, and then strike out across open sea for a place they've only heard about." Many die in the attempt.

More than half of all immigrants arriving in the 1980s and 1990s have come from Asia, and a disproportionate number of them have settled on the west coast, sharpening its difference from the east coast, where European immigration has long been predominant. This is the second tide of Asian immigrants, who first came in the nineteenth century. The early generations endured a hundred years of second-class status, in which they were caricatured as mentally inferior, treacherous, and cowardly. One of the most widely accepted stereotypes about the Chinese was the figure of Dr. Fu Manchu, an asexual, evil man who had mastered the science of the West without grasping western morality. Other racist stereotypes were the despot, the heathen, the amoral dragon lady, and the foolish but loyal servant. Taken together, Asians were seen as the "Yellow Peril," a vast horde blindly loyal to emperors and war-lords who would overwhelm American society. This paranoia was fed by the large number of Chinese and Japanese who settled in California, and soon led to special immigration laws passed in 1882 that prohibited further Chinese immigration.

*A Vietnamese refugee family outside their family-run grocery store. – USIA.*

Early Asian immigrants faced discrimination, and until World War II they were not allowed to apply for citizenship. In addition, most of the states with a large Japanese or Chinese population passed laws making it a criminal offence for them to intermarry with whites. Their isolation was completed by job discrimination, which confined Chinese to laundries, res-

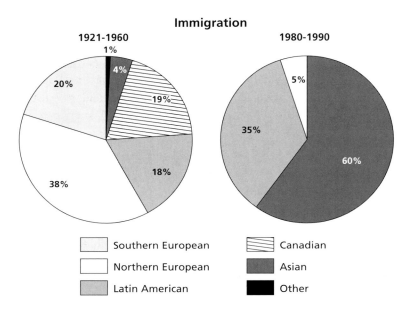

**Immigration**

1921-1960

1%
4%
20%
19%
18%
38%

1980-1990

5%
35%
60%

Southern European | Canadian
Northern European | Asian
Latin American | Other

taurants, and other menial occupations. What made Chinese isolation all the worse was the extreme imbalance of the sexes. Most Chinese immigrants were young men who intended to return to their villages; they often had a wife and family to support back home. As late as 1940 Chinese men outnumbered Chinese women by a ratio of three to one.

The Japanese experience was different, fitting more closely the southern European pattern, though their immigration was cut off sooner, lasting from the 1870s until only 1906. In the early years they were slightly more successful in being assimilated to American society than the Chinese, though California limited their right to own land in 1913. Any early success was destroyed with the outbreak of World War II, however, when the Japanese-Americans were rounded up and forced to live in remote camps for the duration of the conflict. The Americans feared that, given the chance, they might become spies or assist invaders from Japan on the Pacific coast. This injustice was only officially recognized in the 1980s, when Japanese families were voted compensation by the United States Congress, because their rights had been violated and they had been incarcerated without trial.

As the new immigration law went into effect at the end of the 1960s, Chinese and Japanese Americans had not achieved equality, but most of the worst injustices had been removed. Intermarriage with whites was legal, discrimination on the job was illegal though it still took place, and Asian immigrants could become citizens on the same terms as others. Yet in 1970 Chinese men on average still earned only 55 percent as much as white men, while Japanese males earned 81 percent as much. In the following decades, both groups rapidly closed the gap, particularly because Chinese and Japanese families lay heavy stress on education. As a result, they are over-represented at the best universities and they are rapidly making their way into the professions. Like well-educated Blacks and women, they benefit from Affirmative Action programs in hiring. Today, Japanese and Chinese Americans have higher average incomes than white Americans.

Between 1970 and 1980 the number of Asian Americans increased by 142 percent to 1.6 percent of the total population, with even more arriving in the next decade. Overall, in 1989 there were more than one million immigrants, a number further swelled by many illegal aliens, who, under the Immigration Reform and Control Act of 1986, could register and attain immigrant status. Since 83 percent of those who now arrive each year come from Asia and Latin America, the relative size of these minority groups is changing dramatically. New Asian immigrants seldom come from prosperous Japan, but from nations that are industrializing rapidly, leading to the same kinds of displacements that sent Europeans to America a century ago. Instead of the old contrast between whites and Blacks, the United States increasingly might be characterized by what Jesse Jackson imaginatively called a "rainbow" of races and ethnic groups. Jackson has recognized the chance to forge a new political coalition inside the Democratic party that includes white liberals, Blacks, Hispanics, and minorities. Immigration from Asia and Latin America means that the United States is becoming more pluralistic than ever before. But adding more racial groups to the United States does not necessarily lead to greater racial harmony. As a third-generation Chinese American found after the Rodney King verdict, when Los Angeles erupted with violence, "Suddenly, I was scared to be Asian."

## 5. Assimilation?

Any culture receiving immigrants must find a way to assimilate its new citizens. The problem of creating a unified culture is suggested by the Statue of Liberty. The words carved on its base read, "Give me your tired, your poor, your restless masses yearning to be free." America has long understood itself to be an asylum for those rejected by other lands. Each ethnic group is to have full freedom of speech, the right to practice its religion, and to maintain its customs. Yet the United States is also to be a single nation, welding together these many ethnic groups in a common culture. How can this be done? Since Americans had rejected the traditional unity of a common state church, another possibility was to insist on acceptance of a common political culture, articulated in the *Constitution* and the *Declaration of Independence*. Some immigrants have been far more interested in adopting new ways than others. The Chinese who came to America usually kept their traditional clothing and long hair, hoping to return to their ancestral villages. The Japanese, in contrast, "had their hair cut in modern European styles and attempted to dress like Americans as much as possible. Japanese picture brides told of being whisked from the ships by their new husbands directly to the dressmaker's, where they would be outfitted in Western clothing, including hats, corsets, high-necked ruffled blouses, long skirts with bustles, high-laced shoes, and, for the first time in their lives, brassieres and hip pads." Many Japanese also converted to Christianity. Most immigrants lie somewhere between these extremes of Chinese traditionalism and Japanese accommodation.

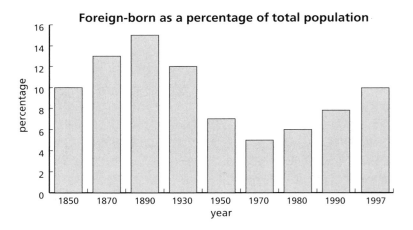

**Foreign-born as a percentage of total population**

Europeans today are taking new interest in how Americans assimilate more than 800,000 new citizens a year. When 75 percent of all Frenchmen fear the loss of national identity from immigrants, believing that the threshold of tolerance has been reached, when some Danes mutter about a tiny influx of outsiders, the American experience may be instructive. In response to the waves of immigrants arriving before 1914, Americans created many institutions of assimilation. Most obvious were the public schools. There, children began each day by standing at attention, saluting the flag, and saying: "I pledge allegiance to the flag of the United States of America, and to the Republic for which it stands: one nation indivisible, under God, with liberty and justice for all." The daily assertion that the United States was "one nation indivisible" did not square with the reality of the schoolroom itself. Often half the students were the children of immigrants and did not speak English at home. In most public schools, however, instruction was given only in English. Outside of school, immigrant youths were attracted to other institutions of assimilation. They could join the Young Men's [or Women's] Christian Association, the boy scouts, or the girl scouts. Their parents could spend leisure time at "settlement houses," which were neighborhood community centers, where they could learn English, study art, discuss politics, and engage in other activities that would bring them into the mainstream of American life. Europeans generally have been slow to establish such mediating institutions that open a dialogue between immigrants and their new culture.

After 1910, large corporations such as International Harvester, General Electric, and the Ford Motor Company pressed their employees to attend special classes, both in language and culture, so that they could qualify for American citizenship. At the Ford plants, graduates acted out the metaphor of the melting pot in ritual: after the students had completed the course, they appeared on stage in the costumes of their homelands, entered a large symbolic melting pot, and emerged wearing American style

| Ancestry of Euro-American population | Figures in 1,000s | | |
|---|---|---|---|
| Austrian | 865 | Lithuanian | 812 |
| British | 1,119 | Norwegian | 3,869 |
| Croatian | 544 | Polish | 9,366 |
| Czech | 1,296 | Portuguese | 1,153 |
| Danish | 1,635 | Russian | 2,963 |
| Dutch | 6,227 | Scandinavian | 679 |
| English | 32,652 | Scots-Irish | 5,618 |
| European | 467 | Scottish | 5,394 |
| Finnish | 659 | Slovak | 1,883 |
| French | 10,321 | Swedish | 4,618 |
| German | 57,947 | Swiss | 1,045 |
| Greek | 1,110 | Ukranian | 741 |
| Hungarian | 1,582 | Welsh | 2,034 |
| Irish | 37,736 | Yugoslavian | 258 |
| Italian | 14,665 | | |

suits, carrying briefcases, and waving American flags. While the Ford ceremony is an extreme case, it suggests how insistently many old-stock Americans tried to assimilate immigrants. Today, some European politicians have similar ideas, demanding that newcomers learn to speak their new country's language and that they give up their cultural identity. Worse yet, neo-Nazi rioters in Germany have called for the expulsion of immigrants.

The American experience suggests that such demands are ethnocentric and unrealistic. In practice, adult immigrants usually do not fully assimilate and seldom learn to speak the English language flawlessly. In contrast, immigrant children absorb American culture from birth. If the first generation almost invariably retains a good deal of the old culture, their children more often than not reject the old ways and consciously choose to integrate themselves into the new culture. By the third generation most have forgotten the original language, and the original clothing survives only in chests in the attic. This is not to say that no ethnic distinctiveness remains, but what survives is not a transplant of another nation's culture but a creolized culture, a mixture of the old and the new, that often is most obvious in cuisine, but may also find expression in festivals, architecture, sports, clubs, and religious organizations.

| National backgrounds of Spanish-speaking Americans, 1990 | |
| --- | --- |
| Mexico | 11,587 |
| Spain | 2,024 |
| Puerto Rico | 2,000 |
| Dominican Rep. | 506 |
| Cuba | 860 |
| El Salvador | 500 |
| Other Hispanic | 1,113 |

The most effective agents of assimilation in American proved to be not government or corporate programs, but the new forms of mass culture that emerged at the end of the nineteenth century. One was cheap popular newspapers catering to the working class. The twentieth century brought with it two even more compelling media: film and radio. The movies became a practical possibility when Thomas Edison and Eastman Kodak collaborated on designing a compatible projector and film, both available after 1895. Silent movies were popular with the working classes and could be understood whatever one's native language. They immeasurably widened visual experience, so that soon anyone might see moving pictures of the streets of Paris, the latest invention, or the newest celebrity. Film created "stars" in a way that theater never had, making the same performance available everywhere, projecting enlarged close-ups of the actor's face across the large screen, and giving the illusion of beings who were "bigger than life." Not all stars embodied old stock Anglo-Saxon character, like Douglas Fairbanks. Rudoph Valentino was of Italian background, and he legitimized a Latin form of male beauty other recent immigrants could identify with. While Valentino often played the aristocrat, Charlie Chaplin was the working class "tramp" who aspired to respectability. One of his most popular early films was "The Immigrant." In later years stars like Mae West, John Wayne, Humphrey Bogart, Lauren Bacall, and Woody Allen created images that were indisputably American. Movies not only provided role models for immigrants, but also created a new common culture for all Americans.

In the 1920s radio was added to the powerful illusions of film. By 1935 even poor families had radios, and networks of stations carried regular shows to millions of listeners. Before radio, much of musical culture had been local, consisting of vaudeville performances, amateur singing groups, and dance orchestras. Immigrants had preserved their language and customs through these institutions and through their own theaters, newspapers, and other cultural activities. But radio was a force for homogeneity, where Americans heard a few stellar performers like Louis Armstrong, Benny Goodman, or Judy Garland. Such star entertainers established the repertoire and the styles for local musicians, and their great talent undercut the appeal of local and ethnic cultural activities. Likewise, by the 1930s most accepted radio news as "the" news, and followed national sporting events through the new medium. The drama of radio made national events seem more central to daily life. Politicians seized upon the medium, and political culture became intertwined with the media in a new way.

To hear or see the new popular culture required knowledge of English. The immigrant child was assimilated at least as much by the media (newspapers, advertising, film, radio, and television after 1946) as by schools or other formal institutions. Indeed, the assimilation was so effective that in retrospect many present-day Americans wish that they had retained more of the culture of the old country. By the 1960s and 1970s many proclaimed pride in their roots, and sociologists studying New York City announced that the melting pot had proven a myth. Yet measured in terms of language, dress, and daily habits, the melting pot idea contained some truth. Few fourth and fifth generation immigrants retain an active engagement with the culture of the old country, but most do take an interest in their ethnic community. Intermarriage between ethnic groups also becomes more likely over time, especially if children attend university, as 60 percent of the population now does. Yet the power of ethnicity remains important. For example, ethnic background is often crucial to getting elected to local office. On the whole, American experience suggests that after a century immigrant families become integrated into the culture, even if their old identities do not entirely melt away. Europeans who worry about immigrants as the unassimilated "other" perhaps ought rather to worry about retaining the cultural diversity immigrants bring.

## 6. The Question of Multiculturalism

It has become a cliché to say that the United States is a multicultural nation. This is certainly true if one means to say that there are people from many immigrant cultures and racial groups, each with distinctive traditions. But the United States is not multicultural in the same way as Canada or Belgium. Such nations have distinct cultural regions (Quebec, for example) in which the majority of the local population speaks one language and shares other important characteristics (religion, for example). In contrast, racial and ethnic groups are jumbled together in the United States, there are far more groups, and the space they occupy is often not well defined. In 1990 the Census Bureau tried to count how many white Americans come from different European national backgrounds. However, in many cases it could not discover what nation people had come from, and it had to resort to terms such as European, British, Yugoslavian, and Scandinavian. The confusion only begins there. Many people have multiple backgrounds. The author of this textbook has ancestors who were French, German, Dutch, and English immigrants, as well as at least one Native American. The figures on page 37 clearly do not take such cases into account. Yet the longer a family remains in the United States, the more unusual it is to have blood lines that lead back to only one nation. And when an immigrant comes from Germany or Austria, what does that really mean? The size and make-up of both nations have changed tremendously between 1700 and today. Statistics about cultural origins can obscure something obvious to any foreign visitor: those of European background born in the United States share more with each other than with their previous homelands. The nation may not be a melting pot where previous national characteristics disappear, but as far as white people are concerned it is hardly a balkanized nation of tiny ethnic fiefdoms.

There are wider divisions, however, between Whites, African Americans, Hispanics, Asians, and Native Americans. These are not five internally coherent groups, of course. Native Americans may have a national organization, the American Indian Movement (AIM), but their tribes are quite distinctive. Asians are just as obviously a heterogeneous group. Even African Americans cannot be said to be a single group, since they were captured from many different tribes and sent to the New World. Black immigrants from Haiti or Jamaica cannot be lumped together with the great-grandchildren of African-American slaves. Hispanics are by no means one cultural unit either, but take pride in distinctive national backgrounds.

The United States is multicultural in the sense that people come from and take pride in a great many different cultures. Ethnic and racial organizations nurture these traditions. Yet few Americans master foreign languages, and there is little talk of racial purity, because too much intermarriage takes place. While it is common to take pride in one's ethnic and racial origins, cultural identities within the United States are not as consistently maintained or as rooted in tradition as in Europe or Asia.

**Population projections, by race, 1995-2025**

|  | 1995 | 2000 | 2010 | 2025 |
|---|---|---|---|---|
| White | 218,000,000 | 226,000,000 | 240,000,000 | 262,000,000 |
| African American | 33,000,000 | 35,500,000 | 40,700,000 | 47,500,000 |
| Hispanic | 26,700,000 | 31,400,000 | 41,100,000 | 58,900,000 |
| Asian | 9,700,000 | 11,200,000 | 15,200,000 | 22,000,000 |
| Native American | 2,300,000 | 2,400,000 | 2,700,000 | 3,300,000 |

## 7. Current Trends

The American population continues to change and develop, and shows no sign of becoming fixed in size or rooted in place. People are living longer, and the median age is 35.2, twice has high as in the Colonial period. Life expectancy apparently will continue to rise, to seventy-eight for men and eighty-one for women by 2010. The population is also increasing rapidly. By 2010, demographers expect the United States to have 300 million people, double the population of 1950. Most growth still comes from natural increase, with four million births each year and 900,000 immigrants, offset by 2.3 million deaths.

Growth is not evenly distributed among racial groups. Both Native Americans and African Americans are increasing at double the rate of the white population; Hispanics are increasing at quadruple the white rate; and Asians even faster. The result will be a more multi-racial society than the United States has had in the past. The Census Bureau projects that Hispanics will become the largest minority group sometime early in the twenty-first century.

As this population ages, increases in size, and becomes more multiracial, it is also shifting location. The American people as a whole are moving toward the west and the south, and have been doing so since 1790. Between 1940 and 1980 the mean center of population moved entirely across the state of Illinois and crossed into Missouri, south of St Louis. Since then the speed of movement has not slowed. The Census Bureau expects the western third of the United States to grow at a rate of 15-20 percent during the next decade. The settlement of the nation is far from over.

To understand this growth and mobility more clearly, it is time to examine the geography of the United States in detail.

# Geography

"My own quarrel with America, of course, was that the geography is sublime but the men are not." – Ralph Waldo Emerson

To the tourist, America often appears to be a land of natural wonders, such as Niagara Falls, the Grand Canyon, Yellowstone, and the inland seas called the Great Lakes. Aside from these natural phenomena, the United States may seem  to be the same everywhere. Yet, to the native, each place is unique, with its own landscape, foods, traditions, and ethnic mix. For a basic orientation, one can divide the country into seven parts: (1) New England, (2) Middle Atlantic, (3) South, (4) Midwest, (5) Southwest, (6) Mountain, and (7) Northwest. Such a division does not do justice to distinctive areas, such as the state of Louisiana with its French background, and it leaves out Alaska and Hawaii, which will be treated separately at the end. But these seven regions provide a starting point for understanding differences in climate, landscape, history, ethnic background, and customs.

**Regions of the United States**

## 1. New England

Englishmen began the conquest of New England in the early 1600s, when tension between Protestants and Catholics was increasing. Virtually all of the early settlers were Protestants who found the Church of England too much like the Catholic Church to suit their consciences. New England long maintained its Protestant homogeneity, and only in the middle of the nine-

*Typical church in Vermont landscape, New England. – Nordfoto.*

teenth century did it begin to acquire its present diversity, as first the Irish and then many other immigrant groups arrived. The landscape retains many features of the first English settlement, particularly in the layout of smaller towns, arranged around village greens. Likewise, the place names often sound English: New London, New Britain, Plymouth, Cambridge, Northampton, and Exeter to name but a few.

The regional center is Boston, with a metropolitan population of about four million. The city serves as an educational center for the nation, with more than 100,000 students at many different universities, including Harvard, Massachusetts Institute of Technology, Boston University, Boston College, Tufts, Northeastern University, Wellesley, and many others. Nearby, New England's universities include some of the most prestigious and expensive schools in the nation, such as Yale, Amherst, Trinity, Dartmouth, Brown, and Wesleyan. This concentration of highly educated people has made the region a center for computer companies, publishing, and high-technology industries. It is hardly self-sufficient agriculturally, importing most of its food, but it does export fish, lumber, potatoes, tobacco leaves, and maple sugar.

New England gave birth to the American industrial revolution. Here were the first United States textile mills, the early machine tool industry, and the first arms industry. In New England were the first semi-automated flour mills and the first factories producing interchangeable parts (originally used in guns). In New England the insurance business developed, and still finds its national center in Hartford, Connecticut. The region, with its highly skilled work force, usually has a relatively low unemployment rate and is a center of innovation and light manufacturing, as well as a supplier of high-tech military technology. Connecticut alone has major manufacturers of jet engines, helicopters, and nuclear submarines. Advanced computers are produced in Boston, and machine tools are an area specialty.

In the context of the United States, New England is old, traditional, and sophisticated. Americans view it as a venerable place with a long history. This may seem strange to Europeans, but recall that there are some parts of the United States that have been settled by whites for only one hundred years. To inhabitants of these newer regions, where it is difficult to find a building constructed before 1900, New England's three hundred

## New England

| State | Population | Sq. miles | Capital |
|---|---|---|---|
| Connecticut | 3,300,000 | 4,862 | Hartford |
| Maine | 1,200,000 | 30,920 | Augusta |
| Massachusetts | 6,000,000 | 7,826 | Boston |
| New Hampshire | 1,100,000 | 9,027 | Concord |
| Rhode Island | 1,000,000 | 1,049 | Providence |
| Vermont | 580,000 | 9,267 | Montpelier |
| Region | 13,200,000 | 62,951 | |

New England is roughly twice the size of Austria.

year old houses are ancient. Tourists also go to Boston to see "the birthplace of the American Revolution," for it was here that local farmers armed themselves and formed a local militia that fired the first shots against the

British. New England has also long served as a center of literary culture. In Massachusetts alone Americans can visit the homes of Ralph Waldo Emerson, Henry David Thoreau, Nathaniel Hawthorne, Herman Melville, and Emily Dickinson. Mark Twain and Harriet Beecher Stowe lived in Hartford. Likewise, many contemporary writers have chosen to live in the region.

Within the United States, New England serves as a center of traditions and a suitable location for educational institutions. New England has not suffered greatly because of the general move of the population to the South and West. Its great strengths – skilled workers and world class educational institutions – are precisely what is needed to compete in the post-industrial economy.

## 2. The Middle Atlantic States

The middle of the eastern seaboard, which stretches from New York City to just north of Washington, D.C., was first settled primarily by immigrants from Holland, England, Germany, and France, with smaller groups from other countries. Colonists from Holland came to present-day New York in 1624, and cities more than 200 kilometers inland still bear Dutch names, such as Rotterdam and Amsterdam. The British came in the middle of the seventeenth century, seizing the Dutch lands by force in 1664. King Charles II of England granted individuals the right to foster settlements in Maryland (whose proprietor was a Catholic, Lord Baltimore) and Pennsylvania (owned by the Quaker, William Penn). Because of these mixed ethnic

*An Amish Farmer's buggy crossing Maryland countryside, 1972.*
*– National Geographic Society.*

and religious beginnings, the middle colonies soon turned into a haven of religious toleration. Many German Pietists emigrated to Pennsylvania, where the Quakers were particularly tolerant. Scots Presbyterians settled much of the inland Appalachian Mountain region. Originally more diverse in language and religion than New England, the Atlantic States proved to be a model of what the United States would become: a patchwork of ethnic settlements and a mix of religions living in mutual tolerance. Furthermore, in the city plans of New York and Philadelphia one can find the beginnings of the grid pattern of urban design that spread westward across most of the nation, along with many other cultural characteristics.

In Colonial times this region produced more foodstuffs than either New England or the South, and it remains important agriculturally, as New York and Pennsylvania possess some of the best farmland in the nation, with more regular rainfall than most areas farther west. Today, the region remains a center of commerce, with four of the fifteen largest urban centers: New York, Philadelphia, Pittsburgh, and Baltimore. It retains a remarkable economic diversity, including coal-mining and steel-making, shipyards, every conceivable kind of light industry, and of course the culture industry in New York: music, fashion, theater, publishing, painting, dance, television, radio, advertising, and public relations. Since the late nineteenth century New York has been the literary capital of the United States and a great deal of American literature deals with the city, from Washington Irving to the Harlem Renaissance writers of the 1920s, from Henry James to contemporary writers such as Norman Mailer, Philip Roth, E. L. Doctorow, and Tom Wolfe.

### The Middle Atlantic States

| State | Population | Sq. miles | Capital |
|-------|-----------|-----------|---------|
| Delaware | 700,000 | 1,980 | Dover |
| Maryland | 5,100,000 | 9,890 | Annapolis |
| New Jersey | 7,900,000 | 7,520 | Trenton |
| New York | 18,200,000 | 47,830 | Albany |
| Pennsylvania | 21,100,000 | 44,970 | Harrisburg |
| Region | 53,000,000 | 112,190 | |

The Middle Atlantic States cover an area slightly smaller than Germany.

Many Europeans assume that New York City must be the center of American life. But Americans often feel otherwise. The cost of living there is very high, and the undeniable advantages of being in such a center have been somewhat undercut in recent years as the population has shifted south and west. Most of the major urban centers of the Atlantic region have been losing population. Smaller cities such as Scranton, Pennsylvania, or Schenectady, New York, display little new construction and many signs of decay, such as depressed housing prices. Local industries have left for warmer climates, where energy costs are lower, where labor is less organized, and where pollution control is at times more relaxed. The Atlantic area was the industrial center of the nation from 1830 until roughly 1910. Today, it remains populous and prosperous, but it has gradually lost ground to other regions with newer industrial plants and less fully exploited resources. Many of the largest corporations in the United States are located in New York City, but a number have moved away. One symptom of the trend: in 1989 Exxon, the world's largest oil corporation, announced it would move its headquarters from New York City to Dallas.

## 3. The South

Since 1950 the South has been the most populous region of the United States. It has always been an important region. Virginia was the first area the British settled; colonists arrived in 1607. By the time of the American Revolution, the South stretched along the Atlantic seaboard from Maryland to Georgia. English Protestants were the largest group of settlers in the seventeenth and eighteenth centuries, establishing a vigorous agricultural system based on tobacco, sugar, and cotton. They imported Africans and made them slaves to provide the brute labor needed to clear the land and plant these cash crops. While every American colony permitted slavery, fewer Africans were purchased in the North, where the climate did not lend itself to production of these crops. Most slaves lived on the southern coastal plain, and even today very few live in the southern mountains.

The psychological division of the United States into a distinct North and South took place primarily during the first half of the nineteenth century. The North was rapidly industrializing and developing large cities, while the South remained agricultural and relied upon slave labor. The North needed the cotton produced in the South for its textile mills, and the nation as a whole received the bulk of its foreign exchange from agricultural exports. This regional specialization was functional economically, but had its human price: the slave system. Indeed, before this specialization the South was sympathetic to the idea of abolishing slavery, and it was openly

*Migrant worker from Mexico harvesting tobacco in Kentucky. – Nordfoto.*

debated in the Virginia State legislature during the 1830s and defeated by only a single vote. Thereafter, slavery was accepted as part of a distinctive way of life, which Southerners justified in a variety of ways. They said it was moral, because Blacks in Africa were heathens, who under slavery would have the chance to become Christians. They argued that slavery is mentioned in the Bible. Doctors offered medical "proof" that slaves were less intelligent. And the cleverest justifications contrasted the lives of Northern mill workers under capitalism with the slave master's responsibility for his human "property." Justifications of the slave system contributed to stereotypes: the Northerner as the calculating and cold Yankee industrialist, the Southerner as a kind-hearted but tempermental aristocrat. Contrary to these myths, most Northerners were farmers, and few slave-owners lived in large white mansions surrounded by lovely gardens. Most held less than twenty slaves and, contrary to the fantasies of Hollywood, lived in only modest comfort.

In the nineteenth century the South and its slave system expanded westward. The Federal Government purchased Florida from Spain in 1819, and more states (often called the New South) were added to the region as settlers moved toward the Mississippi River. The expansion of the slave system troubled the North and created sectional conflict. Slavery was not a particularly efficient form of agricultural production, since African Americans obviously had nothing to gain for their pains. Moreover, because of the plantation economy, the South did not develop large cities until the twentieth century, with the exception of New Orleans. Its canals, roads, railroads, and industries were in every way inferior to those of the North until after World War II, and this discrepancy helps to explain why the South lost the Civil War (1861–1865). After the war, won as much by Northern factories and numerical superiority as by the strategies of battle,

## The South

| State | Population | Sq. miles | Capital |
|-------|-----------|-----------|---------|
| Alabama | 4,300,000 | 51,609 | Montgomery |
| Arkansas | 2,500,000 | 53,104 | Little Rock |
| Florida | 14,200,000 | 58,560 | Tallahassee |
| Georgia | 7,100,000 | 58,876 | Atlanta |
| Kentucky | 3,800,000 | 40,395 | Lexington |
| Louisiana | 4,400,000 | 48,523 | Baton Rouge |
| Mississippi | 2,600,000 | 47,716 | Jackson |
| North Carolina | 7,200,000 | 52,586 | Raleigh |
| South Carolina | 3,700,000 | 31,055 | Columbia |
| Tennessee | 5,200,000 | 42,244 | Nashville |
| Virginia | 6,600,000 | 40,817 | Richmond |
| Washington, D.C. | 560,000 | 20 | – |
| West Virginia | 1,800,000 | 24,181 | Charleston |
| Region | 64,000,000 | 549,686 | |

The South has as many people as France, but is twice as large.

the South entered a long period of stagnation. Only in the past fifty years has the region begun to industrialize rapidly, with the result that at present it is one of the most dynamic regions of the nation. The so-called "sun belt," a broad zone of economic development, begins in Florida and stretches through Texas across the country to Southern California. Since 1963 every Democratic President has come from the South: Lyndon Johnson, Jimmy Carter, Bill Clinton, and both candidates in the deadlocked 2000 election.

Atlanta, the capital of Georgia, is the major city in the region. Headquarters of Coca Cola and CNN, it has become an international center, and hosted the 1996 Olympic games. In Florida, both Miami and Tampa have mushroomed to over two million people. Memphis, Tennessee, and New Orleans, Louisiana are also important cities. In North Carolina a major research and industrial park has grown up near Chapel Hill, drawing on the rich resources of three nearby universities.

As a result of urbanization and industrialization the South has come to resemble the North far more than it did fifty years ago. The portrayal of Black–White relations in Richard Wright's autobiographical *Black Boy* or in the fiction of William Faulkner and Eudora Welty no longer describes Southern reality. Today, African Americans vote in great numbers, the mayors of many Southern communities are Black, segregation in public places has been abolished, and the incidence of inter-racial violence has diminished. Indeed, some African Americans have moved from the North back to the South, because they feel that racial relations are better there. For the Black middle class, Atlanta is a preferred location. Overall, the South remains more conservative both politically and socially than the North, though it is far more ethnically and racially diversified than a half century ago.

## 4. The Midwest

The Midwest is 823,210 square miles of flat or gently rolling countryside, extending a thousand miles from the Appalachians to the Rocky Mountains. It includes the area drained by the northern half of the Mississippi River and its two major tributaries, the Ohio and the Missouri. It is one of the richest agricultural areas in the world, and is the source of American exports of corn, wheat, soybeans, and other agricultural products. The Midwest also contains much of the heavy industry of the United States, including steel mills, chemical works, and factories for automobiles and farm equipment. Most of its important cities are located on the Mississippi river system or on the Great Lakes – the largest freshwater lakes in the world – which border Canada. The biggest city, Chicago, connects these two great water systems of lakes and rivers. Detroit, center of the automobile indus-

*The Midwest is America's cattle and wheat country yet it is more urban than rural. – Nordfoto.*

try, lies at the point on the Great Lakes where entry into Canada is easier than anywhere for hundreds of miles in either direction. Minneapolis and St. Paul, the so-called "Twin Cities," sit on either side of the Mississippi River at its most northerly navigable point. A map will show that the other major cities (St. Louis, Kansas City, etc.) stand at strategic points on water routes. Railroads and highways later connected these cities in additional transportation networks, reinforcing their importance.

Military defense was only briefly a consideration in the settlement of this region, which has never been invaded by a foreign power. The entire area was settled quickly. It took the first colonists 150 years to reach the Appalachian mountains that form the region's eastern edge. Then, between 1800 and 1860 the settlers poured west, creating the midwestern states in a single lifetime. Characteristically, one man was born in the East, moved several times to the West, and along the way had a son, Abraham, who in 1860 was elected President from the new state of Illinois. Like Lincoln, many Presidents have come from the Midwest. Not only is the region populous and powerful, but its citizens combine the qualities of North and South, East and West. For most Americans, the Midwest seems to typify the nation, and indeed the ideal commentator on American television ought to have a Nebraska accent.

Many twentieth-century American writers came from and wrote about the Midwest, and a social history of the region could be constructed by reading fiction and autobiography. The autobiography of a Native-American holy man, *Black Elk Speaks*, describes the coming of the white man and the near-destruction of Indian cultures; Willa Cather's *My Antonia* recounts the harsh lives of the first settlers. Sinclair Lewis's *Main Street* and Sherwood Anderson's *Winesburg, Ohio* describe the life of the small town, while Theodore Dreiser captures the diversity of Chicago in *Sister Carrie*. Ernest Hemingway, F. Scott Fitzgerald, and T. S. Eliot also came from the Midwest, which arguably produced more important writers than any other region in the first half of the twentieth century.

### The Midwest

| State | Population | Sq. miles | Capital |
|---|---|---|---|
| Illinois | 11,900,000 | 56,400 | Springfield |
| Indiana | 5,800,000 | 36,291 | Indianapolis |
| Iowa | 2,900,000 | 56,290 | Des Moines |
| Kansas | 2,600,000 | 82,264 | Topeka |
| Michigan | 9,600,000 | 58,216 | Lansing |
| Minnesota | 4,600,000 | 84,068 | St. Paul |
| Missouri | 5,300,000 | 69,686 | Jefferson City |
| Nebraska | 1,600,000 | 77,227 | Lincoln |
| North Dakota | 640,000 | 70,665 | Bismarck |
| Ohio | 11,200,000 | 41,222 | Columbus |
| South Dakota | 730,000 | 77,047 | Pierre |
| Wisconsin | 5,100,000 | 56,154 | Madison |
| Region | 62,000,000 | 823,210 | |

The Midwest is the size of Western Europe, excluding Scandinavia.

In the 1970s and early 1980s the region suffered economically, and even today Detroit has only partially recovered from the challenge of European, Japanese, and Korean automobiles. Likewise, the heavy steel industry virtually collapsed under competitive pressures from abroad, and the area briefly was known as the "rust belt" in contrast to the growing Southern "sunbelt." But not every part of the Midwest has been so hard hit. If Detroit has high unemployment and shows in its physical appearance the ravages of foreign competition, Minneapolis is developing rapidly into a major cultural center. And Chicago is the third largest metropolitan region in the United States, and lies in the heart of the country. Indeed, in the last decade, this area has prospered more than either coast. In the fall of 1996 Omaha had such low unemployment that it held job fairs, where there were more recruiters than applicants. A historian who looked in out of curiosity had a difficult time getting away.

## 5. The Southwest

First explored by the Spanish at the end of the sixteenth century, the Southwest was part of Mexico until the United States conquered the region in the Mexican–American War of 1848. The area seized included the present states of Texas, Arizona, New Mexico, Oklahoma, Colorado, and most of Nevada and California. In this arid country the Spanish had found Native-American tribes with sophisticated cultures, particularly the Hopi, Navajo, and Apache, all of whom survive in the region today. Since 1848 millions of newcomers have migrated into this region from both the rest of the United States and from Mexico, with a very large influx since World War II. Today, ten million Hispanics live here.

Many know something about this region from John Steinbeck's *The Grapes of Wrath* or the songs of Woody Guthrie. The Southwest has risen from the poverty of the Great Depression and the Dust Bowl to be the most dynamic market in the United States. Six of the largest American cities are now in this area: Los Angeles, San Diego, Phoenix, San Antonio, Houston, and Dallas, with a seventh, San Francisco, at the border with the Pacific Northwest. These cities have all more than doubled in population during a single generation, while those of the East have stagnated. In 1997 both Austin and Phoenix were growing at an annual rate of more than 5.5 percent spurred by high-tech firms and small manufacturing. The population increase in this region has given it more political power, with most states voting for conservative candidates, such as Dole and Bush. However, in 1992 and 1996 California strongly supported Clinton, who also carried Nevada and New Mexico. Los Angeles, now the second largest metropolitan area in the country, is undoubedly the best-known of these cities. The presence of the film industry in nearby Hollywood has suggested to many that Los Angeles is the place where dream and reality become indistinguishable, the place where the American dream imperceptibly can become a nightmare.

## The Southwest

| State | Population | Sq. miles | Capital |
|-------|-----------|-----------|---------|
| Arizona | 4,000,000 | 113,909 | Phoenix |
| California | 32,400,000 | 158,693 | Sacramento |
| New Mexico | 1,700,000 | 121,666 | Santa Fe |
| Oklahoma | 3,300,000 | 69,919 | Oklahoma City |
| Texas | 18,600,000 | 267,338 | Austin |
| Region | 60,000,000 | 731,525 | |

The Southwest equals the combined areas of England, Germany, France, Italy, and Spain.

The Southwest has grown for many reasons. Extensive irrigation projects opened up new lands to agriculture and made it possible for cities to grow in the desert. The warm dry climate has attracted both retired people and many light industries, which have selected the area for new factories. The defense industries are also strong in this area, partly because the Federal government has built many airfields, testing sites, and ports in the region. The area also has extensive mineral wealth, particularly oil, coal, copper, uranium, natural gas, and potassium salts. Texas, of course, has long been a world center of the oil business, while the aircraft industry has built many plants in California. Today, however, both Southern California and Texas have so many different industries that they are not as affected by sudden

*Canyon de Chelly, National Monument, Arizona. – Nordfoto.*

changes in the oil market or the aircraft industry as they were forty years ago. The Southwest now has a rich mix of industries, and it continues to be one of the most dynamic areas in the United States.

One myth about this region, reinforced by many films, is that it is mostly desert. Yet New Mexico, one of the driest states in the nation, has over eighteen million acres of timberland and more than two million head of cattle or other livestock. Nor is the Southwest necessarily hot. For every change in elevation of one thousand feet (310 meters), the temperature changes by five degrees fahrenheit (c. two degrees celsius). Those who descend five thousand feet into Arizona's sweltering Grand Canyon quickly find out how important this information can be, as do hikers in the mountains, who are sometimes caught in summer snow storms. Tourists visit the region summer and winter to see its many National Parks, to escape the cold, to go skiing, and to see the stark contrasts of the landscape.

## 6. The Mountain States

Few people live in the Mountain states. Montana, a third larger than Italy, has less than one million inhabitants. Wyoming, slightly smaller than Germany, has less than 1 percent of its population. The story is similar for Idaho, Utah, and to a lesser degree, Colorado. In each, the climate is too dry for intensive farming without irrigation, and water rights are bought and sold like property itself. Land that cannot be irrigated is usually used for cattle ranching or forestry. This is an important mining region, with large reserves of coal, oil, zinc, lead, and other minerals. Mining was central to the region's early development, as discoveries of gold, silver, lead, and copper drew many settlers and investors to Colorado, Montana, and Nevada. Mines created most of the early urban centers: Virginia City, Nevada; Butte, Montana; Deadwood, South Dakota; Leadville, Colorado. They first stimulated the regional economies and made many railroad lines economically feasible. They attracted outside investment. The Comstock Lode in Virginia City alone produced silver worth $300 million in a twenty-year period. Without the income such mines created and the settlers they attracted, development would have been slow. The region's two major cities, Denver and Salt Lake, drew much of their early wealth from proximity to gold and silver mines.

Resource development is complicated today by the Federal Government's extensive land holdings. These states have some of the most spectacular mountain scenery in the country, as well as vast canyon lands. Not only are many of the National Parks here, including Yellowstone, the Grand Tetons, Mesa Verde, Glacier, and Rocky Mountain National Parks, but the Department of the Interior controls other lands that amount to as much as one-third of some states. Forest reserves, wilderness areas protect-

**The Mountain States**

| State | Population | Sq. miles | Capital |
|---|---|---|---|
| Colorado | 3,700,000 | 104,247 | Denver |
| Idaho | 1,200,000 | 83,557 | Boise |
| Montana | 900,000 | 147,138 | Helena |
| Nevada | 1,500,000 | 110,540 | Carson City |
| Utah | 2,000,000 | 84,916 | Salt Lake City |
| Wyoming | 490,000 | 97,914 | Cheyenne |
| Region | 9,850,000 | 621,310 | |

The Mountain States are four times the size of Germany.

*The Grand Teton Mountains and Jackson Lake, Wyoming. – Dnon Knight.*

ed from development, wildlife refuges, and Native-American reservations (also administered from Washington) fill large sections of the map, collectively protecting the ecology. Despite the tourism brought in by this landscape, however, many residents want more exploitation of the protected lands. They resent the fact that Washington controls much of their land, and tend to vote Republican. All these states except Nevada voted for Dole in 1996.

With a metropolitan population of over two million, Denver is the regional center. Its economy reflects the rapid growth that the entire area has experienced since the 1970s. The Census Bureau expects the population of these states to grow by about 20 percent between 1990 and 2000. Greater Las Vegas has grown to over one million people, based largely on the city's enormous gambling casinos, hotels, and convention centers. More people (22 million) visited Las Vegas in 1995 than went to London. In 1996, Boise, Idaho had an annual growth rate of 5 percent, focused in white-collar work, and high-tech industry. There was virtually no unemployment. Salt Lake City, Utah, the second largest city in the region, grew even faster, at 5.5 percent a year, with much of that in bio-technology and construction, suggesting even stronger future development. Named after the nearby lake, which is five times saltier than the Atlantic Ocean, Salt Lake City was settled by Mormons seeking to escape from persecution in the nineteenth century. It remains the world headquarters of this remarkable sect, which had already become so well established by 1870 that Mark Twain parodied their scriptures in his early work, *Roughing It*. More recent literary works dealing with the mountain states include Norman Maclean's *A River Runs Through It* and Edward Abbey's *Desert Solitaire*.

# 7. The Northwest

By any standard, the Northwest is one of the most beautiful areas of the United States. In terms of climate, it is split by mountains that run from north to south. The western side has heavy rainfall, cool summers and moderate winters. To the east it is drier, with more climatic extremes. Geologically, the whole area is new. The mountains are still rising, and volcanic eruptions and earthquakes are common. Before the white man came, the Native-American peoples lived comfortably here, because the heavy rainfall, abundant seafood, and temperate climate made existence easier than in many other parts of North America. White men were slow to enter the region. In the eighteenth century Russian explorers probed south from Alaska (which they then controlled), but established no colonies. They made brief contact with Hispanic settlers who were moving up from Spanish controlled Mexico, but the region lay so far from both centers of power that neither empire took much interest in it. The United States sent an expedition to the area in the early nineteenth century, but few settlers came before the California Gold Rush of 1849.

As Anglo-Americans displaced the Native Americans after 1850, they developed an enormous logging industry, soon accompanied by a strong

**The Northwest**

| State | Population | Sq. miles | Capital |
|-------|-----------|-----------|---------|
| Oregon | 3,100,000 | 96,981 | Salem |
| Washington | 5,500,000 | 68,192 | Olympia |
| Region | 8,600,000 | 165,173 | |

These two states are as large as Greece and Italy combined. (California's statistics are listed with the Southwestern states.)

agricultural sector that today includes the famous California wine vineyards and the apple orchards of Washington. Yet the area has not been over-developed. In the days of the wagon trains the position of the mountains made it easier to migrate to central and southern California than to Washington, Oregon, and northern California. By the time the railroad had come, so had national interest in preserving parks, wilderness areas,

*Barley harvest in the Palouse Hills of southwest Washington. – Nordfoto.*

and forest lands. As a result, in Oregon and Washington the Federal government owns land equivalent to Austria and Switzerland combined.

With the exception of Spokane, Washington, all the larger cities lie on the Pacific coast: San Francisco at the border with the Southwest, Portland on the Columbia River, and Seattle at the Canadian border on Puget Sound. Like much of the West, which is the most heavily urbanized region in the United States, all three cities have grown rapidly since World War II, spurred in part by their aircraft construction corporations and other high-tech concerns, notably Microsoft. Including suburbs, each city now has a population of over one million. Indeed, growth has been so rapid that Oregon and Washington actively discourage in-migration, hoping to keep the present balance between agriculture and industry, nature and civilization, which makes this such an attractive area. Politically, this region is distinctly more liberal than the Southwest. Its climate and its lifestyle resemble those of Denmark or Norway more than other areas of the United States.

San Francisco has been the literary capital of the West since 1865, thanks to the works of Bret Harte and Mark Twain, who immortalized the mining camps. Shortly afterward came the nature writer, John Muir, and, later, Frank Norris (*McTeague: A Story of San Francisco*) and Jack London. Most of John Steinbeck's work is set in central California, as is the poetry of Robinson Jeffers, and the fiction of William Saroyan. In the 1950s came the explosion of west coast poetry: Lawrence Ferlinghetti, Kenneth Rexroth, and Gary Snyder. Many of the Beat poets from New York also found a second home at the famous City Lights Bookstore. Two important recent writers from the Northwest are Ken Kesey, whose *Sometimes a Great Notion* evokes the Oregon logging industry, and Ursula K. Le Guin, whose science fiction (*The Lathe of Heaven*) draws upon the eco-system mutations easily imaginable in this region of volcanos and earthquakes.

## 8. Alaska and Hawaii

Bought from the Russian Czar in 1867 for $7 million, Alaska remained a territory until 1959, when it became the largest state. Its national parks alone are larger than the entire state of California. However, Alaska has a tiny population of only 630,000, most of whom live along the state's southern rim, where the ocean keeps temperatures moderate. Lying at about the same latitude as Norway, but more than four times its size, Alaska has similar geographical features: many offshore islands, long fjords, and snow-capped mountains. The two regions also resemble each other economically, with large fishing and logging industries and huge oil reserves. The difference is that Alaska's oil has been found not at sea but far north of the Arctic Circle. Only the original Eskimo inhabitants and a few scientists lived in the north until the oil companies arrived, drilled for oil, and built

a pipeline from Proudhoe Bay in the Arctic Ocean to Valdez in Prince William Sound in the south. While this pipeline undoubtedly has its ecological drawbacks, for the state as a whole oil development has produced so much wealth that income taxes have been abolished. Instead, residents actually receive an oil dividend that is usually close to $1000 a year per person. Despite such direct personal benefits, however, Alaskans have gradually become more attentive to the pleas of conservationists, who want to protect the state from too much development. After the wreck of the tanker Exxon Valdez spilled millions of gallons of oil on Alaskan coasts in 1989, fishermen, the Eskimos, and those in the tourist industry joined forces against the giant oil companies. Many Americans see Alaska as the last frontier.

*Pipeline for transport of oil crossing Alaska. – Nordfoto.*

Hawaii was annexed as a United States territory in 1898. Before then, although independent, it had already been colonized unofficially by Americans with interests in shipping and tropical agriculture. Hawaii became a state virtually at the same time as Alaska and is so unique that it can hardly be compared with any other American region. A cluster of volcanic islands several time zones away from the West Coast in the midst of the Pacific, Hawaii is actually somewhat larger than most people realize, about the size of Connecticut and Rhode Island combined. Its climate varies little from month to month. Hawaii has not only a unique geographical location but an entirely different population composition than the mainland. Fully 25 percent of its 1.2 million people are Japanese Americans, descended from immigrant laborers brought in to work the sugar and pineapple plantations. An additional 20 percent of the population comes from other Asian countries. Only 2 percent of the population is African American, and 8 percent is Hispanic. The resulting mix is unique to the islands, where Whites constitute little more than a third of the one million inhabitants. Agriculture is still important here, but increasingly the land has been used for other purposes. Hawaii is a strategic air and naval base and extremely popular with tourists, not only from the United States and Canada but also from Japan and other countries of the Far East.

## 9. Landscape

Understanding regional variations is only a bare beginning in understanding the United States. As one cultural geographer has noted, "Every landscape of any size or age has a style of its own, a period style such as we discern or try to discern in music or architecture or painting." Likewise, every social and ethnic group has its own mental geography, as it separately conceives the space where it lives. The farmer in the Midwest sees himself at the center of the universe, in a vast flat country that stretches for thousands of miles on every side. The oceans, the mountains, and the cities are all distant, and the landscape is formed by the sky and a few man-made landmarks that stand out against it in the distance. The experience of living in such a world is far different from that of living in a port on the Gulf of Mexico, like Galveston, with its hurricanes, searing heat, tropical nights, and waterfront bars frequented by foreign sailors. Cultural geographers do far more than merely measure the physical world; they examine the landscape as a social construction, seeking to understand space as it is lived in and experienced. Men and women continually map the world in their minds. They seek to transform the world according to preconceived ideas, and they adjust these ideas to new economic, political, and physical circumstances.

The poet Robert Frost wrote, "The land was ours before we were the land's." Taking possession of the American continent required more than journeys in covered wagons, cutting down trees, plowing fields, or building railroads and cities. Such individual acts themselves were part of a larger design, an imagination of what a place might be. Thus the first settlers in New England saw their settlements as attempts to create a more perfect version of British society in the wilderness, to make a City on a Hill. Their towns were carefully laid out in the English fashion, giving each family parcels of woodlot, pasture, and farmland, with all the houses clustered around a village green with its church. In contrast, the Mormons journeyed into a desert, erected an elaborate irrigation system, and created a garden in the wilderness of Utah, not merely as a matter of economic development, but in accord with a religious vision. The American landscape was created through such continual acts of the imagination, and the study of American culture reveals several powerful geographical myths.

This mythology, like that of ancient Greece, provided explanations for the movement of history, and it helped to motivate the original settlers. Most prominent was the frontier myth, primarily a male fantasy of continual conquest and renewal through contact with the virgin land of the New World. The frontier myth claimed that the wilderness regenerated Europeans, stripping away centuries of decadent culture and returning them to a natural state, and thus it explained the development of Americans as a separate people. Some of its central heroes were Daniel Boone, who led settlers over the Appalachian mountains; Davy Crockett, a frontiersman who died in the war against Mexico, a war that increased the size of the nation; and, more ambiguously, General Custer, who died at Little Big Horn in 1876, the last general to lose a battle with the Native Americans.

In 1894 the historian Frederick Jackson Turner presented his famous frontier thesis, which gave formal expression to this geographical myth and persuaded a generation of historians that American history and character had been shaped by the westward moving frontier. Today, scholars have disputed this myth at every point, showing that the western movement was not a colorful and romantic story of a return to nature but one of repeated despoilation. The conflict with the Native Americans was not a glorious tale of manly valor, but one of racial warfare, in which broken treaties, disease, alcohol, and deceptive practices collectively dispossessed the Indians. Railroads and speculators, not private individuals, first owned most of the western lands, selling them to settlers who remained in debt for years. Farmers were not self-sufficient, but produced cash crops whose price was set by international markets. Nor were western states more democratic than those of the east. Rather, they copied their laws and institutions from the original thirteen states, notably in their constitutions. In short, the east shaped and dominated the west, rather than the reverse, and Turner's thesis, rather than explaining American development, articulated the mythology required to move settlers westward.

An equally powerful geographical image was the closely related idea of America as a vast garden. Focusing on the farmer rather than the frontiersman, it explained the nation's history in terms of agricultural expansion, as Americans made the unproductive wilderness into the world's richest farmland. Politically, the farmer was not a dependent European serf, but an individualist whose spirit was purified by continual contact with the soil. He rejected all forms of absolutism and demanded democratic institutions. According to this myth, the central crisis in American history was the Civil War, pitting individualistic farmers against the Southern slave system, which was an expression of European decadence, a remnant of feudalism. Only after the South was defeated could the west be settled by free farmers, who transformed the empty prairies of the Midwest into a garden of democracy, and who made the western desert bloom through vast irrigation projects.

Persuasive as this myth of the garden was in the nineteenth century, it too, like that of the frontier, was a male fantasy. In contrast, women did not imagine the west as a virgin land to be taken in an erotic fantasy, but more modestly saw it as a place for an idealized home and community, whose domestication was symbolized by their flower and vegetable gardens. Where male fantasies of conquest had focused on the woodland that could be cleared and transformed, women eventually found the prairie an ideal landscape, where the garden and the home merged. For them the frontier made possible an extended family, and the west became an idealized domestic space.

As these examples suggest, the west has been many things in the American imagination, and the same could be said of each of the seven cultural regions discussed here. Landscape is a symbolic construction, a social creation, and the experience of the world varies according to whether one is Hispanic, Asian, African American or white, male or female, rural or urban. The study of landscape is thus central to cultural studies, as it focuses on the point where fantasy and the tangible world intersect. And just as contrasting images of western development contributed to both the treatment of Native Americans and the outbreak of the Civil War, it should not be surprising that American politics is built up on the basis of geography.

# The American Political System

## I. Historical Origins of American Politics

When watching American politics from abroad on television, it may seem that the President is like a Prime Minister, that the two large parties are internally unified groups, and that presidential elections are the key process to be understood if the system as a whole is to be grasped. Yet, at the heart of the presidential election, one finds that the voters do not select the President. Rather, it is a strange institution called the "Electoral College" that makes the decision. This "college" has no permanent location, and not one American in 10,000 can name any of its members. These confusions arise because outsiders do not understand that geography, more than ideology, determined the structure of American government when it was formed in the late eighteenth century. As the name implies, the United States came into existence as a union of thirteen diverse states which might be compared to the countries of the European Union, which today are moving toward a federal system of government. The Americans confronted the same questions: How much power should be centralized? What governmental functions should be left in local hands? Should there be a single currency? Can states with diverse interests conduct a single foreign policy? The American answers to these questions have changed somewhat over the past two centuries, but the federal system of government they created in the late eighteenth century has proven remarkably durable.

The division of power between the states and the federal government was a consequence of the American Revolution. After 1783, each state had an independent government, with its own legislature, courts, and local laws. State and local governments came first, the federal government evolved later. Because of this circumstance, today many rights and powers are not centered in Washington. Indeed, most of the things that directly touch the lives of Americans are controlled at the state and local level. The states build the vast majority of the highways, they collect their own income taxes, they run all of the public schools and most of the universities, they license all automobiles, and they regulate the sale of alcohol and tobacco. The states issue marriage licenses, building permits, and birth certificates. They have their own police, their own forests, and their own environmental agencies. They administer justice for virtually all crimes, and they pass laws concerning gambling, hunting, firearms, fishing, and censorship. In practical terms, most businesses deal far more with state governments than with the federal government in Washington. Each of the fifty states establishes its own laws, writes its own business regulations, sets the maximum interest rates that banks may charge, and supervises most commercial affairs. Because the states have distinct legal systems, few lawyers are qualified to work in more than one state, because each of them combines English common law with rulings made by local courts and statutes passed by the state legislature.

Because of these legal variations, some states are far more favorable to businesses than others. Corporate taxes in the United States vary greatly from one place to the next, as do the laws for incorporating a business, with the result that many large companies have their headquarters in what may seem to be unlikely locations. For example, the tiny state of Delaware, between Philadelphia and Washington, is headquarters for many corporations, because its laws make incorporation particularly easy. Western Connecticut is also an attractive site for many large corporations, because it is quite near New York City but has low personal income tax. Local governments are also surprisingly powerful. Each town controls its school system and levies rather sizable property taxes to support it. Towns own and control their fire departments, recreational areas, libraries and other cultural institutions. Towns can also charge sales taxes (VAT), and they can exempt new industries from property taxes for a start-up period of time. They can build special facilities that will attract new business or they can pass laws that will prevent or discourage certain kinds of companies. In short, because the tax system is not uniform, towns compete for attractive companies, and inner cities usually lose such competitions. One study found that typically a company could save $800 per employee per year by building a new plant in the suburbs where taxes are lower, instead of remaining in the central city.

## 2. Elections and Political Parties

Americans vote in three quite different sets of elections: local, state, and federal. Locally, they elect members of the school board, a town council, a mayor, and other officials, often including the chief of police, the district attorney, and local court judges. At the state level, they select members of the legislature, the governor, the treasurer, and others. In federal elections they select a Representative to Congress, a Senator, and presidential electors, of which more later.

State and local elections also include another feature almost unique to American politics, the referendum. Any citizen or group can propose that a particular matter be decided by referendum, provided they can amass enough signatures from voters in the area involved. For example, in Berkeley, California, where the largely student population faced severe prosecution for possession of marijuana, a law was passed by referendum that reduced penalties to a minimum. In this case, the town could not overturn the state law making possession of the drug a crime, but it could reduce the penalty for that crime. In 1992, twelve propositions were presented to the voters of California, who chose to lift taxes on soft drinks and snack foods but turned down a proposal to increase state income taxes on the very wealthy, rejected a $1 billion bond issue for passenger rail service, and rejected a proposal to legalize physician-assisted euthanasia. In 1996, Californians voted to allow the use of marijuana for medicinal purposes. As these examples suggest, such propositions can deal with extremely important issues. Far-reaching changes were sparked in 1978 when California voters decided by referendum to reduce their property taxes by more than 50 percent, much to the consternation of most politicians. The revolt against the state property taxes soon spread to many other states as well, with the short-term result that taxpayers were happy. By 1992, however, California had a huge deficit and could not meet its state payrolls. Briefly, it was reduced to the expedient of issuing IOUs to state employees.

The taxpayers' revolt was not at first the policy of either of the major political parties. Rather it was a grassroots movement. Neither the Democrats nor the Republicans are organized parties by European standards. Neither has a formal connection to labor unions, religion, or ideological theory. Often, their leaders fail to control the selection of presidential candidates. Party membership requires no dues, no voluntary work, and no active political involvement. It is simply a matter of declaring one's preference at the local courthouse, when registering to vote. Nevertheless, almost a third of the voters refuse to call themselves Republicans or Democrats and instead choose to be registered as "Independents." Their reluctance to join either of the major parties illustrates how casual party identification is for many Americans. Because membership in a political party is free, parties at the local level often have little money except for a few months around election time, when they establish temporary campaign headquarters, seek contributions, and look for volunteers to work. Yet if locally the two parties are not monoliths, but loose coalitions of shifting interests, at the national level, each is well-funded and strong.

Given these facts, it is tempting to conclude that there is little difference between Republicans and Democrats. Yet while the winner-take-all election system makes it prudent for each party to move toward the middle of the political spectrum, there are some tell-tale differences in their supporters. Democrats pushed through the major civil rights legislation, and they receive an overwhelming percentage of the Black vote, in Clinton's case 83 percent. If whites alone had voted in 1996, Dole would have been elected. Traditionally, Democrats also have had the support of urban ethnics, blue-collar workers, and Catholics, although these differences have eroded somewhat in recent decades. Republican Reagan won many votes from labor, in Michigan for example, and some Catholics have been attracted to the Republicans because both tend to oppose abortion. In terms of gender, a majority of women lean to the Democrats because of their support for social programs and for a woman's right to choose an abortion. In 1996, women voted for Clinton over Dole, 54 percent to 38 percent.

Regionally, Democrats today are strong in the northeast, the upper midwest, the northwest, and Hawaii, and they can generally count on carrying these areas. Democrats were long dominant in the South, but their support for civil rights cost them much support in that region, which has increasingly moved toward the Republicans since 1964. Republicans have long had the support of a majority of Protestants, and are usually strong in the farm states, the central midwest, the mountain states, and California. They enjoy considerable support from white-collar workers, and have long been regarded as the party of business. For example, one week before the 1992 election a poll of small businessmen found 51 percent supporting Bush, 18 percent for Perot, and only 15 percent for Clinton. Had only Americans with incomes over $75,000 voted in 1996, Dole would have won. Another important difference between the parties is the existence inside the Republican party of a vocal minority of religious fundamentalists. One of them, John Ashcroft was George W. Bush's selection for Attorney General in 2001. Anyone who thinks the parties are identical need only study the crowds of delegates at their national political conventions to see that they are quite different. Democratic delegates are more flamboyantly dressed and come from a wider variety of ethnic backgrounds. At the Republican convention, delegates are conservative in appearance and generally have assimilated the norms of the white middle class.

Republican and Democratic policies evolve from differences between their supporters. Since Democrats have more urban, African-American, and ethnic support, they are usually friendly to welfare programs. Historically, they have also embraced Keynesian economics, although during the Reagan years they were sharply critical of deficit spending, and in 1992 Clinton emphasized his ability to balance the Arkansas state budget. Yet the Democrats also gladly take credit for creating jobs programs, a social security pension in the 1930s, the civil rights laws, and the Medicare and Medicaid public health bills of the 1960s. Republicans, in contrast, are rhetorically committed to limiting federal regulation of business, holding down public expenditures, and balancing the budget, goals to be achieved by reducing welfare expenses, while emphasizing self-help and rugged individualism. In practice, however, when the Republicans gained a majority in both houses in the election of 1994 they proved unable to implement this philosophy in the face of President Clinton's resistance.

On presidential ballots there are other American parties besides the Democrats and Republicans, including extreme parties on the right and left. Yet while alternate parties are formally present in every election, voters usually ignore them, because Americans do not have proportional representation. Rather, a field of candidates contests for one office. Such a system only gives a party a chance if it can regularly muster support from 50 percent or more of the voters. In practice, there is only room in the system for two parties. Occasionally, third party movements have succeeded at the state and local level, but these cases are statistically rare and historically short-lived. In the spring of 1992 Ross Perot seemed able to overturn this system, as he briefly scored higher in the polls than Clinton or Bush. Yet it proved difficult to turn his general popularity into a coherent set of policies and a party organization, and by the end of July he was falling in the polls and withdrew from the race, leaving the election to the traditional party system. When Perot decided to rejoin the race a scant month before the election, his support rose rapidly, and he garnered a remarkable 19 percent of the popular vote. Yet he had no chance of victory in the winner-take-all system of voting, and in the 1996 election he received only 9 percent of the vote. In Germany, Italy, or Sweden, that many votes would have given Perot a good number of seats in the legislature, but in the US he received none.

If Americans can only realistically choose between two parties, they are given this choice with regard to every office contested in an election. Americans vote for individuals, not party slates or ideologies. In a single visit to a polling booth an American can vote for a Democrat for President, a Republican for Senator, an independent for the town council, and a write-in candidate for the local school board. About half of all voters engage in this practice of "splitting the ticket" between representatives of different parties. As a result, quite commonly a President or a state governor is from one party and a majority in the legislature is from the other. In 1996, Americans chose a Democrat (Clinton) as President, but gave control of Congress to the Republicans.

A federal election involves fewer choices than elections at the state and local level. At stake are only three offices: the Presidency, a representative, and a senator. Comparing these elections, the local one has the most importance for everyday life and involves issues and personalities that can readily be understood. The state elections often seem less important, but again there is a clear set of issues in most campaigns. In the federal election, however, the issues are seldom terribly clear. Candidates discuss problems that have caught the public imagination at that particular time, such as the morality of abortion, the best way to fight crime in the streets, the need for family values, and the like. They do not discuss foreign affairs much, because most of the public is not interested. Because most practical matters are regulated at the state and local level, politicians who aspire to the national stage often must find rather strange topics to animate the voters. For example, in 1988 George Bush emphasized respect for the flag. The more elevated the office, the windier the rhetoric becomes, until one reaches the presidential campaign, in which the candidate makes every effort to appear all things to all voters, blurring his stand on many controversial issues.

## 3. The Structure of National Government

The basic form of the federal government was worked out at a convention in 1787, where representatives from the states drew up the Constitution (reproduced in full at the end of the volume). When this document was ratified by the states, the United States became the first government in the world to have a written constitution which specified the powers and duties of its government. The idea of creating a written document of this sort has been widely imitated, but the specific form of the American government has not often been copied in its details. The Constitution defines three separate branches of government: the legislative branch, or the Congress; the executive branch, or the Presidency; and the judicial branch, headed by the Supreme Court. As conceived by the founding fathers, each of these

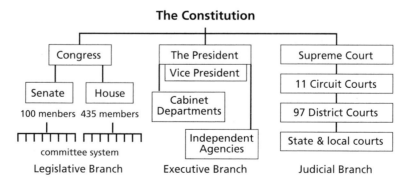

branches was intended to act as a check upon the other two, creating a system that could maintain its balance.

Europeans often criticize the American political system for being too restrictive, preventing the development of ideologically based parties. It also seems needlessly complex, with the executive separated from the legislature, and with two branches of the legislature instead of one, each with its own committees and sub-committees, and each besieged with lobbyists. But most Americans believe they have a simple and logical political order, and they are usually surprised to learn that anyone finds it hard to understand. Indeed, Americans often tacitly assume that the rest of the world is evolving toward a system like their own. They look at European politics and shake their heads at what seems a chaotic system. From their point of view, European politics has two drawbacks: power is splintered into too many political parties to allow decisive action and European elections arise unexpectedly.

## System of checks and balances

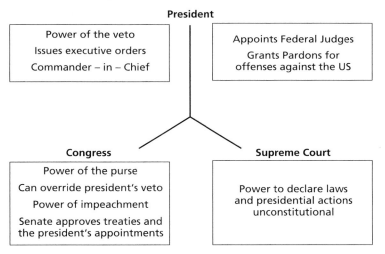

**President**

| Power of the veto<br>Issues executive orders<br>Commander – in – Chief | Appoints Federal Judges<br>Grants Pardons for<br>offenses against the US |

**Congress**

| Power of the purse<br>Can override president's veto<br>Power of impeachment<br>Senate approves treaties and<br>the president's appointments |

**Supreme Court**

| Power to declare laws<br>and presidential actions<br>unconstitutional |

Another important difference is that the three branches of American government – legislative, executive, and judicial – are all intentionally designed to restrict each other's activities. The authors of the Constitution wanted to prevent the concentration of power in any single branch of government. Their idea was to create a system of "checks and balances" in which each part of government could exert some control over the other parts. Thus Congress can refuse to pass legislation the President desires. The Senate can reject the President's appointments to the cabinet or to the courts. It can investigate the President, and on rare occasions it can impeach him from office. Most important of all, it has the "power of the purse" and can withhold money from particular projects. For example, in the fall of 1995 Newt Gingrich, the House majority leader, blocked passage of all money bills, because he disagreed with President Clinton on the budget.

For several months much of the national government had to shut down until they reached an agreement.

But the President has power over Congress as well. He can veto a bill outright. He can interpret the general guidelines of a law through administrative orders. He can campaign against those who oppose him. In the day-to-day power struggles of Washington the Supreme Court often appears to be a silent partner in government. But the Court has the ultimate power to declare unconstitutional any presidential action or executive procedure, and it can likewise invalidate any federal law. In doing so, it often makes law more effectively than the legislature.

In recent years the president has at times used the mass media to destabilize this system of checks and balances, by making direct appeals to the voters, helping to create what some observers call the "imperial Presidency." Yet the mass media can also be used by Congress, as in the Army–McCarthy hearings of the 1950s, the Watergate scandal of the 1970s, the Iran–Contra Affair of the 1980s, and the Monica Lewinsky investigation of the 1990s. If television was hardly envisioned in the Constitution, it nevertheless has not entirely disrupted the system of checks and balances envisioned by the founding fathers.

## 4. The Congress

The first article of the Constitution divides the legislative branch, or Congress, into two chambers: the House of Representatives and the Senate. No one elected to either chamber can be appointed to any other government job at the same time. In other words, legislators cannot serve in the President's cabinet or in any part of the executive branch, which is under the President's control. To further ensure their independence from the President, no member of Congress can be arrested while attending sessions or while traveling to and from their meetings. The greatest curb on the President's power, however, is the regional character of elections. Each of the members of the House of Representatives in Washington comes not from a state but from a district within a state, where he or she must seek re-election every two years. Representatives are the most immediate link between the region and the federal government, and people often turn to them for help. It is common to call or write them directly, and each receives hundreds and even thousands of letters a week. A large staff answers each letter and adds the correspondent to appropriate mailing lists. The staff also deals with complaints, such as the visa problems of foreign-born relatives or conflicts between constituents and federal agencies. The average citizen regards the representative as an ally in the struggle against Washington.

The representative, in turn, realizes that each time he aids one voter he strengthens his hold on the office. As time goes on, party affiliation becomes less and less important to re-election. The most important thing is to represent the region's citizens and interests in Washington. There are no legal limits to re-election of representatives, and many stay in office for more than thirty years.

Presidents have a shorter political life. They run for office every four years and they are limited to two terms. Thus Clinton could not run for President again in 2000. A representative may serve for decades, increasing control over a home district and power in Washington until he or she is virtually unassailable. Regardless of party affiliation, he or she will vote according to the home district's wishes or the dictates of conscience. Often no other leader can control him, because he has his own office staff and local organization. The party therefore has a weak hold over its representatives. A candidate for President needs their support to win; but the representatives do not always need or even want the presidential candidate's support in return. In fact, some Republicant congressmen avoided too close an association with Bob Dole in the 1996 election for fear that he would drag them down to defeat. Representatives generally do not lose elections. Indeed, one out of every seven is so popular that he faces no opponent at all, and in most years more than 90 percent of the representatives are re-elected. In 1992 the re-election rate was expected to be much lower, because of the scandalous behavior of many congressmen, who abused their check-cashing privileges. But when the election was over, most districts had returned the incumbent. The 1994 election was unusual, however. Led by Newt Gingrich the Republicans running for Congress launched a united platform under the slogan "Contract With America," and they managed to take over control of both the House and the Senate.

On the whole, American politics is regional politics. Candidates must be residents of the state districts where they run for office. Usually they are lawyers with extensive local connections. In Washington they represent not the nation, not the party, not the individual state, but their particular region. In the nation as a whole there are 435 such representatives. Each is the only elected candidate from a particular place, which is to say that each is the victor in a winner-take-all contest. Every state, no matter how small, has at least one Congressman, but otherwise the distribution of seats is based strictly upon population. The seven most populous states – California, New York, Texas, Florida, Illinois, Ohio, and Pennsylvania – send 196 representatives to Congress, while Wyoming, Vermont, Delaware, Alaska, Nevada, and North Dakota send but one each. On average, it is necessary to win between 80,000 and 120,000 votes to hold a seat in Congress. This is not such a large number, and it is quite likely that a congressman and his staff will have direct contact with many of these supporters during every two years.

Since World War II, politicians have adopted television as an ideal means by which to appeal to a plurality of the voters. At the local level, television is a less effective tool than it is nationally, because voters know the politicians and their reputation through personal contacts. Television is most effective on the national stage, where it can easily be used to project an intimate image. Carefully crafted political commercials that usually last no more than one minute cannot explain a candidate's views, but they can project a personality. Likewise, television news focuses on the short, colorful quotation, or "sound bite," that takes no more than 15 seconds. In contrast, Perot pioneered another use of television. He prepared 30-minute programs, where he presented a detailed analysis of the American economy. Holding up charts and graphs, he successfully presented himself as a teacher and concerned citizen. The 2000 campaign also witnessed many appearances by candidates on television. They frequented interview shows and MTV, as well as appearing in presidential debates.

Political Action Committees, or PACs, also have considerable impact on elections. Dedicated to protecting a particular interest or to passage of a particular law, they can donate up to $10,000 to a candidate, plus giving additional sums to political parties. One might be organized by groups against abortion, for example, or by those in favor of daily prayer at the start of each school day. In 1992, such PACs spent more than $180 million on the campaign. The largest PAC, more than $1.5 million, was set up by American Telephone and Telegraph and was used to support the majority of the congressional candidates. Since the telephone company is regulated by the government, the reasons for these donations are not obscure. Other companies take no chances and contribute an equal amount to both sides. With such sums being distributed, the cost of running for office tripled between 1978 and 1986, when running for the House cost $355,000, cheap compared to the $3.1 million then needed on average to run for the other legislative chamber, the Senate. A decade later it was possible to spend $8 million in a Senate campaign and lose. By 2000 campaign contributions became an important issue in the primary elections. John McCain (R) treated the problem as a central issue, and Bill Bradley attacked Al Gore, who in 1996 had used White House telephones to raise campaign money and invited the largest contributors to spend a night as a guest at the White House. Nevertheless, the 2000 election was by far the most costly in American history. Reform of the system does not appear to be high on Bush's agenda. After all, Republicans usually have been able to raise more money than Democrats.

If the most populous states dominate the House of Representatives, the smaller states play a larger role in the Senate. Regardless of population, every state elects two Senators, or 100 from the fifty states. Senators are usually former members of the House or former state governors, and for most politicians the Senate is the highest office they can hope to attain. Senators are elected for six-year terms, and once elected most manage to get re-elected, since while in office their names become better known in their home states than they were before. Because of their long terms and strong local power base, Senators may become independent of their parties and follow their own policies, often in response to local interests, but at times not. Senator William Fulbright served local interests well, but he also pioneered an international exchange program that was largely his own idea. A President cannot be sure of the Senate's support, and he must continually court its members with special attentions, such as private meetings and personal telephone calls.

Given its small size, the Senate has the atmosphere of an exclusive club more than of a debating society. Its members come to know one another well, and no matter how great their political differences they usually maintain friendly personal relations. They seldom treat one another as do the members of the British Parliament, where stormy debate and explosive interruptions are common. A senator usually addresses his fellows in cordial terms, such as "The Gentleman from Mississippi" or "The Honorable Senator" or "The Lady from California."

While debates can be important, the chambers of Congress are often half empty, and most of the work is done through the committee system, which forms the heart of the legislative process. Few proposed pieces of legislation are passed without first being sent to a committee. Both the House and the Senate have their own committees, dealing with major topic areas such as labor, education, agriculture, the armed services, the budget, foreign affairs, and finance. Usually a member serves on several committees, keeping the same assignments year after year and developing considerable expertise in these areas. Each committee in turn has sub-committees. Committees do not simply sit and discuss the merits of legislation; they hold public hearings to which they invite interested parties. The transcripts of these hearings are published, often running to thousands of pages. In addition, committees can request information from the Library of Congress, which maintains a permanent research staff of social scientists, historians, and lawyers who prepare reports for members of Congress on any topic they desire. Finally, each congressman has at least one staff person whose main responsibility is keeping up with the committee assignments.

Members seek to be on powerful committees, such as that on the budget, and on committees whose work affects their home district. Those from farm states seek the agricultural committee; those from industrial states prefer the labor committee, and so forth. The assignments to sub-committees illustrate this bias toward home districts most clearly. In 1985 all of the twelve members of the Tobacco and Peanuts Sub-Committee came from the South, three from North Carolina alone. The Wheat, Soybeans, and Feed Grain Sub-Committee was similarly dominated by mid-westerners, and so it went throughout the other sub-committees. Given this arrangement, little wonder that elected officials seek to extract as much money as possible from the public treasury for their home districts. This attitude and the spending it generates is called pork-barrel politics.

Because committees take months to hold hearings on each bill, those interested in its passage or defeat have time to present their point of view. They often write letters to newspapers or organize letter-writing campaigns directed at members of the committee. Moreover, powerful private associations seek to protect their special interests. Farmer groups lobby to keep price supports for their crops; manufacturers lobby in favor of tariffs; labor groups lobby for a higher minimum wage; and the American Medical Association lobbies against public supported healthcare. It must be emphasized that lobbying is a time-honored tradition. It is a regulated, accepted part of American politics. There are lobbies to protect gun ownership and for gun control, for construction of new dams in the west and for preservation of the wilderness. Indeed, there are many more lobbyists than senators and representatives, who often find themselves besieged with offers of "information" and invitations to lunch from those eager to expound their cause. There are also some populist lobbyists. Ralph Nader has organized a national organization based on contributions from thousands of students at 175 state universities. Yet, as might be expected, the majority of these lobbyists represent big business, which has the resources needed to hire people full time. The power of lobbyists is all the more obvious when one considers that neither the Republicans nor the Democrats are able to enforce much party discipline when it comes to voting on legislation, since each elected official has a personal power base.

In 1996–1997, the 104th Congress passed 333 bills that were signed into law. What is the process involved? In a sample year, 1970, no fewer than 20,500 bills were introduced in the House and referred to committee, of which only 1,319 were reported out of committee to be voted on. The disparity here is not as great as it seems. All members of Congress want to claim that they have introduced important legislation, and many propose quite similar bills. When sent to committees, the many bills are combined and reworked, until a compromise emerges that is acceptable to a majority. Of the 1,319 bills reported out of committee in 1970, more than 80 percent (1,133) were passed. Debate in the House is often nothing more than a series of prepared speeches by congressmen intent on having the record show that they supported a given piece of legislation. The Senate, with one fourth as many members as the House, introduced about a fourth as many proposals (4,199) in the same year, yet actually passed a few more. A bill can only become law, however, if it is passed in identical form by both chambers and then signed by the President. During each session conference committees meet to reconcile differences between House and Senate versions of bills. Sometimes they fail to agree, and no law is passed. Often the discussions occur in a last minute rush in the closing hours of each session, when many bills are passed and sent to the President. He can veto any one of them, but usually signs more than 90 percent into law. In this last minute rush of bargaining and legislating a good many special provisions and amendments are added to bills, changes which often are scarcely noticed, but which may well have been the chief object of a lobbyist for the previous year.

## 5. Presidential Elections

The Constitution specifies that the President is not to be elected by the people of the United States, but by representatives of the states meeting once every four years in the Electoral College. Each state has as many votes in this election as it has senators and representatives in Washington. This means that there are 535 electors in all (equal to 100 Senators plus 435 Representatives). In addition, the District of Columbia (or the City of Washington itself) has three votes. To win the Presidency a candidate

### Electoral Votes in each state

needs more than half of these 538 electoral votes, or 270. While the total number of electoral votes is fixed, the number given to each state is not. Every ten years the electoral votes allotted to each state are readjusted in accord with new census figures.

The most unusual aspect of this system is that, except for Maine and Nebraska, each state votes as a single block: a candidate either wins all of a state's electoral votes or none of them. A candidate who receives less than 50 percent of the popular vote in a state gets 0 percent of the electoral vote. This system shapes the way presidential candidates run their campaigns. If polls show that a majority of the popular vote in a given state will go to one candidate, his opponent stops campaigning there. It is simply abandoned. Thus Bush hardly campaigned in New York or Massachusetts in 2000, and Clinton made few campaign appearances in Wyoming or Montana. Presidential candidates always give a few large states special attention because they have so many electoral votes, particularly California (54 votes), New York (33), and Texas (32), but also Pennsylvania (23), Illinois (22), Florida (25) and Ohio (21). Indeed, most politicians believe that it is virtually impossible to win the Presidency without winning (or "carrying") at least one of the two largest electoral states.

**Presidential Election 2000**

Alaska
Hawaii

Bush, 271 electoral votes
Gore, 267 electoral votes

It is difficult to be elected president without winning at least one of the two largest electoral states, New York or California. Kennedy could not have won in 1960 without New York; Nixon needed California to win against Humphrey in 1968; Carter needed New York to beat Ford in 1976. In all of these cases California voted Republican and New York voted Democratic. In the 1990s, however, both California and New York moved firmly to the Democratic side, and George W. Bush pursued the unusual strategy of

*Senator Edmund Muskie campaigns for votes in the New Hampshire presidential primary, 1972. – New York Times.*

emphasizing the South and the smaller states of the West and Middle West. He lost the popular vote, but barely won enough electoral votes to become President.

The candidates for president and vice-president usually are balanced between regions, typically including one from the south and one from the north. Thus Al Gore from Tennessee chose a northern running mate, Joe

Lieberman, from Connecticut. John Kennedy, a northerner, selected Lyndon Johnson from Texas as his running mate. In 1992 the Democrats found an unconventional strategy, choosing moderate southern candidates for both president and vice-president. Together, they won, as they carried both New York and California, but they failed to carry most of the South. George W. Bush, from Texas, selected Dick Cheney from Wyoming, and this alliance of the South and West suggested the possibility of a new Republican axis that ignored liberal northern states.

Every American-born citizen over the age of 35 has the right to run for the Presidency, and beginning about one year before the election prominent men and women begin to announce their desire to run, usually as either Republicans or Democrats. Long party service or even membership in a party is not necessary, however. General Dwight David Eisenhower was extremely popular after the end of World War II, and since he had no clear affiliation with either of the major parties, both wanted him to run for President. On other occasions, party professionals want a particular candidate, but they cannot make him acceptable to the public.

By tradition, each party holds a national convention in the summer before the election, where delegates from every state gather to determine who should run for President. The delegates to these national party conventions are state and local politicians. The Constitution says nothing about national parties, national conventions, or selection of delegates, so each party is free to devise its own system to decide who will represent it. Some states have meetings, called caucuses, but most have elections, called Presidential Primaries. A book would be required to describe the different systems employed to select delegates and how these systems have been modified, but the end result is that every four years several thousand men and women descend upon a major city to hold a Republican Convention and an even larger group goes to another city to hold a Democratic Convention. Both are nationally televised, and both are increasingly media events, rather than decision-making meetings. Characteristically, although writing the party platform causes considerable internal debate, the convention focuses not on issues but on the candidates. Yet the outcome of the voting often is known in advance, because each convention delegate's vote is determined by the popular vote in the primary election or caucus back home. From February onwards the news media make it their daily business to count how many delegate votes are pledged to each candidate. Usually, well before the convention, one candidate manages to assemble a majority of the votes. However, after the first ballot is over, if no candidate has a majority, the delegates are free to vote as they please. Then virtually anything can happen. In 1924, the Democrats required more than one hundred ballots before they could agree on a candidate. Likewise, in 1960 no Democratic candidate won on the first ballot, and the nation watched with excitement as Kennedy gained supporters, and then offered the Vice-Presidency to Lyndon Johnson in exchange for his delegate support. Usually, there is no such drama, however, as one politician secures a majority of the delegates in primaries and caucuses and then plans the convention as a show of unity. This is precisely what Bush did in 2000, when he ran against Gore.

Since World War II most of the surprises at the party conventions have been the selection of vice-presidents. For example, in 1988 both George Bush and Michael Dukakis clinched their nominations as presidential candidates before the conventions. Interest focused on whether Dukakis would select Jesse Jackson as his running mate, and on Bush's choice.

### Sequence of Events in a Presidential Campaign

| | |
|---|---|
| Candidates announce they will run for President | c. 1 year before the election |
| State primary elections and caucuses | February to early June |
| National Conventions, one for each party | Late July and early August |
| The Campaign | September – November |
| Election Day | First Tuesday in November |
| Electoral College Votes (a formality) | December |
| New President takes office | January |

Dukakis selected a now forgotten Senator, and Bush chose Dan Quayle, who came as an unwelcome surprise to most, especially when attention focused on the question of whether he had used personal influence to dodge military service in Vietnam. In 1992 Clinton announced the week before the Democrats met in New York that he had selected as his running mate a man similar to himself, Senator Al Gore. Thus the convention became a predictable form of television entertainment, with the main events scheduled for the evening hours when the largest public could tune in. Also in pursuit of party unity, Dole pursued another strategy in 1996, as he selected a running mate from the conservative wing of the Republican party, Jack Kemp.

The electoral system of primaries, caucuses, and conventions costs millions of dollars. While the system developed because of popular demands for participation in selecting the candidates, the result is a long and expensive procedure that leaves the parties and the unsuccessful candidates hovering near bankruptcy. In 1996 the two parties together spent half a billion

*President-elect Bill Clinton photographed in St. Louis in September 1996 running for reëlection. – Nordfoto.*

dollars on the campaign. This astounding figure comes after attempts at reform. Because of the high cost of campaigning, in 1974 the Congress passed an Election Reform Act. It provides federal funds to the parties for their conventions, to the candidates in primaries, and to official party candidates for the final election campaign in the fall. To qualify for these federal funds the candidate must agree not to raise on his own more than a specified amount. The law also restricts individual contributions to no more than $1,000. In the presidential elections since 1974, all candidates have had this federal support, but huge sums continue to be raised, and many are still in debt at the end of the campaign.

Usually, the Electoral College has not played a visible role in selecting the president, although political scientists and thoughtful citizens have long known that it might do so in unusual circumstances. In theory, a third party candidate such as Ross Perot in 1992, George Wallace in 1968, or Ralph Nader in 2000 could receive enough electoral votes to prevent any candidate from having a majority when the Electoral College meets. In that case, the Constitution dictates that the final selection of the president shall take place in the Congress, with each state having a single vote. When Congress decided the 1824 election, it led to angry charges of corruption. Andrew Jackson had received a solid majority of the popular vote, but he lost the election in Washington months later. Something similar almost happened in 1968, when third party candidate George Wallace won 14 percent of the popular vote, and carried five southern states. Nixon, winner over

Humphrey, received only 43.4 percent of the popular vote. If Wallace had won two more states, or if Nixon and Humphrey had divided the remaining votes more evenly between them, no one would have won in the Electoral College. Congress then would have chosen the president. The possibility of an inconclusive election appeared even more likely in 1992, because of Perot's popularity, but he carried no individual states.

In addition to the possibility of inconclusive elections contested by three or more candidates, the American system in theory can be undemocratic even with only two candidates. In the hotly disputed election of 2000, Al Gore received 500,000 more votes than George W. Bush, who nevertheless won the election in the Electoral College. The vote was so close in Florida and the irregularities so widespread that Bush's slender lead of only a

| Presidential Popular Vote Since 1932 | | | | | |
|---|---|---|---|---|---|
| Year | Winner | % | Loser | % | Other (%) |
| 1932 | Roosevelt (D) | 57.4 | Hoover (R) | 39.6 | 3.0 |
| 1936 | Roosevelt (D) | 60.8 | Landon (R) | 36.5 | 2.7 |
| 1940 | Roosevelt (D) | 54.7 | Willkie (R) | 44.8 | 0.5 |
| 1944 | Roosevelt (D) | 53.4 | Dewey (R) | 45.9 | 0.7 |
| 1948 | Truman (D) | 49.5 | Dewey (R) | 45.1 | 5.4 |
| 1952 | Eisenhower (R) | 55.1 | Stevenson (D) | 44.4 | 0.5 |
| 1956 | Eisenhower (R) | 57.4 | Stevenson (D) | 42.0 | 0.6 |
| 1960 | Kennedy (D) | 49.7 | Nixon (R) | 49.5 | 0.7 |
| 1964 | Johnson (D) | 61.0 | Goldwater (R) | 38.5 | 0.4 |
| 1968 | Nixon (R) | 43.4 | Humphrey (D) | 42.7 | 13.9 |
| 1972 | Nixon (R) | 60.7 | McGovern (D) | 37.5 | 1.8 |
| 1976 | Carter (D) | 51.0 | Ford (R) | 48.9 | 0.1 |
| 1980 | Reagan (R) | 51.0 | Carter (D) | 41.2 | 7.8 |
| 1984 | Reagan (R) | 58.8 | Mondale (D) | 40.6 | 0.6 |
| 1988 | Bush (R) | 54.0 | Dukakis (D) | 45.5 | 0.5 |
| 1992 | Clinton (D) | 43.3 | Bush (R) | 37.7 | 19.0 |
| 1996 | Clinton (D) | 50.0 | Dole (R) | 41.0 | 9.0 |
| 2000 | Bush (R) | 48.2 | Gore (D) | 48.7 | 3.0 |

few hundred votes out of 6 million could easily have disappeared in a complete recount. One of the central problems in conducting a recount was that voting machines were not identical across the state, with the best (most accurate) machines concentrated in wealthier areas that voted for Bush, and the older (less accurate) machines concentrated in poor and black areas that voted overwhelmingly for Gore. Former President Jimmy Carter commented that the rate of error in Florida - nearly five percent - was so high that it could not meet international standards and made a fair election impossible. Gore's lawyers proved less adept than Bush's, who prevented either a full recount of the entire state's votes or a recount of particular districts where the voting machines had not worked well. Instead, after more than a month, the election was finally determined in the courts, ending in an appeal to the Supreme Court in Washington. It determined, by a vote of 5 to 4, that the recount that the Florida State Supreme Court had ordered was flawed and that it should be halted. Bush therefore retained his narrow victory in Florida, but it was a tainted victory that angered the national majority of voters who had, after all, preferred Gore.

In 1976 the electorate also split almost exactly in half, as Ford received 48.9 percent of the vote, and yet lost to Carter by a thin margin. Had the popular vote for Ford been distributed only slightly differently, he might have won the electoral votes of Ohio or Kentucky or New York. He might then, like Bush, have become President despite having fewer popular votes than his opponent did. Because Americans choose their president not through direct popular vote, but through the mediating institution of the Electoral College, the system can produce such a result. The present system assures that small states will not be overlooked, because they have slightly more influence in the election than their population warrants. Popular dissatisfaction with the unfair result of the 2000 election has produced proposals for a Constitutional amendment eliminating the Electoral College. At the local level, the problems experienced with Florida's voting machines should force an improvement in voting procedures.

## 6. The Executive Branch

The President is the head of the executive branch. He cannot be a member of the Congress, nor need he be a former member. Many come to the office from a state governorship, as did Jimmy Carter, Ronald Reagan, and Bill Clinton. Elected to a four-year term, the President's career moves at a different pace from that of either the representatives (two-year terms) or the senators (six years). In addition, a President can only be re-elected once, making the second term a time when he or she no longer need think of re-election at all. These differences loosen the connection between the executive and the legislature. The separation is accentuated by the fact that neither the President nor his cabinet have seats or votes in Congress.

Thus the American President is considerably less powerful than a European Prime Minister, whose position immediately implies that he or she commands a majority of the votes in any dealings with the legislature. American Presidents seldom control both Houses of Congress. For most of this century, the Democrats had a majority in the House (though not since 1994), yet even so internal party differences have made unity fragile on many issues. Democrats have been less successful in dominating the Senate, where control has shifted back and forth between the two major parties. At present, both chambers are controlled by the Republicans.

Even given a majority in each chamber, however, the President has no assurance of support from fellow party members, since they often vote with regional interests in mind. Most European parties that hold power automatically control both the executive and the legislative branches of government. In contrast, no President, not even one as popular as Ronald Reagan, can compel Congress to do his bidding. The representative is constantly thinking about the next election, which is never more than two years away. In half of these elections the Presidency is not contested, so the Congressman listens as much to the voters back home as to the President. Alexis de Tocqueville had already observed in the 1830s that in the United States, "faith in public opinion" was "a species of religion, and the majority its ministering prophet." This accounts for the importance of opinion polls in American political life. Polls, combined with letters, telephone calls, and e-mail keep the congressman alert to the electorate's changing moods. When Ronald Reagan suggested cut-backs in Social Security payments to the elderly, for example, both House and Senate members quickly discovered that this measure would be disastrous to them in the next election, and virtually the entire Congress voted against the idea. Similarly, Jimmy Carter was unable to pass his energy legislation during the oil crisis, despite the fact that in theory he had a majority in both houses.

The Constitution defines the President as the executive who puts into effect the laws Congress passes. Since Franklin D. Roosevelt, however, the President has increasingly tried to lead the Congress by proposing legislation. Yet, unlike a British Prime Minister, even if the President would like new legislation, he often finds that he cannot have it. The President can propose, but he cannot compel. Sometimes he cannot even get legislation onto the floor of the House or Senate for a vote. Nor has the President definitive power to prevent legislation he disapproves of from becoming law. He can veto any bill, but Congress can over-ride that veto if two-thirds of its members vote to do so. These limitations on the President were intentionally built into the office by those who wrote the Constitution. Written in 1787, it is the oldest constitution still in use in the world, and it bears the mark of the time when it was composed. The Americans had just defeated the British in the Revolutionary War (1776–1783). They were not about to create a strong executive power like that of the British king, whom they regarded as a dangerous despot, and they looked for ways to reduce the power of the executive as much as would be consistent with good government. Since that time the American Presidency has become more powerful, especially in the twentieth century when radio and television made it possible for him to communicate directly with the entire electorate, and when the rapid pace of events often made swift decisions necessary. The President is Commander-in-Chief of the armed forces, so that in times of war or crisis his power increases. Yet when a crisis is prolonged, such as the Vietnam War (which was never an officially declared war) or the Iranian hostage crisis, the President can soon seem to be weak. He becomes the focus of unfavorable media attention whenever he appears unable to use the power of his office to solve a problem quickly.

In all of his activities the President works with his cabinet, with a large White House staff, and with the administrators he appoints to government agencies (subject to Senate approval). The Cabinet is particularly important. The Constitution makes no mention of it, but even in George Washington's first administration it was clear that all the day-to-day work could not be done by one person, and he appointed several men to assist him, notably Alexander Hamilton (Secretary of the Treasury) and Thomas Jefferson (Secretary of State, i.e. Foreign Secretary). In the first year of his administration (1789), Washington began to consult with all department heads, and by the time he left office regular cabinet meetings were assumed to be a part of the governing process. The Cabinet is clearly subordinate to the President. It meets only at his request, and no vote is taken unless the President asks for one. Abraham Lincoln once said, when he found himself with little support from his Cabinet, that the only vote that matters is the President's. Since 1789 the Cabinet has grown to include so many departments that it is no longer a group of administrators who meet frequently. Nor are they necessarily party insiders, as they often come to Washington from the private sector or state government. As a result, cabinet members often do not know one another well, and they may become rivals for the President's attention and the Congress's money.

Members of the Cabinet play important roles in carrying out the President's policies. Ronald Reagan appointed an anti-environmentalist lawyer, James Watt, to run the Department of the Interior, which controls public lands. Watt aggressively moved to allow exploration for oil and mineral wealth in previously protected areas. Similarly, every President can choose administrators with strong commitments to particular goals, whether they be racial justice, a balanced budget, or restricting immigration. By selecting Madeleine Albright as Secretary of State, Clinton not only selected a strong figure, but the first woman to hold the office. Many of the more important changes that come with the election of a new President occur at the administrative level, as laws are interpreted and new regulations imposed. Under the Reagan

| Cabinet Department | Year created |
| --- | --- |
| State | 1789 |
| Treasury | 1789 |
| Army (now "Defense") | 1789 |
| Navy (now "Defense") | 1789 |
| Interior | 1849 |
| Agriculture (full status, 1889) | 1862 |
| Justice | 1870 |
| Commerce | 1903 |
| Labor (taken from Commerce) | 1913 |
| Defense (replaced Army & Navy) | 1947 |
| Health and Human Services (HHS) | 1953 |
| Housing and Urban Development | 1965 |
| Transportation | 1966 |
| Education (removed from HHS) | 1969 |
| Energy | 1977 |
| Veterans | 1987 |

administration, for example, rules concerning provision of free food to public schools were modified, with the number of items and the amounts available for distribution cut back. Because Europeans seldom hear about such changes at the administrative level, the major political parties may seem more alike than they are.

The President also oversees many independent agencies, such as the National Aeronautics and Space Administration (NASA) and the Central Intelligence Agency (CIA). These agencies do not have representation in the Cabinet, and at least in theory they are expected to be less political than those which do. The CIA, for example, was conceived as an information-gathering agency that would have no investigative powers inside the United States. In practice, however, it became involved in domestic politics, particularly during the Vietnam War period. As a commission headed by Vice-President Rockefeller later disclosed in 1975, during the Nixon years the CIA had infiltrated anti-war groups, tapped telephones, illegally opened mail, and kept files of information on several million citizens and aliens inside the United States. Under the Carter administration, Congress made many reforms with the intention of de-politicizing the CIA and removing it from domestic life. The CIA is a rather exceptional case, however, as most of the independent agencies perform the routine functions their names suggest.

| Independent Agencies (selected) | Date Created |
| --- | --- |
| Civil Service Commission | 1883 |
| Interstate Commerce Commission | 1887 |
| Federal Reserve System (banking) | 1913 |
| Federal Trade Commission | 1914 |
| Federal Power Commission (utilities) | 1920 |
| Securities and Exchange Commission | 1934 |
| Federal Communications Commission | 1934 |
| National Labor Relations Board | 1935 |
| Civil Aeronautics Board | 1940 |
| NASA (space) | 1958 |
| National Foundation for Arts & Humanities | 1965 |
| Energy R&D Administration | 1974 |

Most agencies were created in response to particular crises. After the great stock market crash of 1929 came the Securities and Exchange Commission of 1934. Worsening labor troubles in the 1930s forced creation of a National Labor Relations Board. Intensifying air traffic led to the Civil Aeronautics Board in 1940; the oil crisis of the 1970s led to the Energy Research and Development Administration of 1974, and so forth. In general, such agencies have come into existence during Democratic Presidencies. As the government took on new functions, the federal bureaucracy mushroomed from a mere 11,000 employees in 1831 to three million today, with the greatest growth taking place during the Roosevelt Presidency (1932-1945). As a percentage of the total population, however, the federal government has grown only slightly since 1960.

Nevertheless, the bureaucracy is vast, and has proven to be an unwieldy giant that often is slow to act. Once a law has been passed by Congress and signed by the President, it often takes years before the bureaucracy writes all the rules and regulations that will put that law into effect. Recent studies of the implementation of legislation suggest in fact that special interests are often able to effect significant changes in the administration of a law. Every federal agency has its clients. The Interstate Commerce Commission in theory regulates railroads, but in fact it often protects them. So-called "clientism" is an informal system of mutual aid between regulators and the groups regulated, in which each side helps the other. For example, the Department of Agriculture usually protects farm interests, and in return farmers lobby on behalf of that Department, protecting it from budget cuts. Over time, a system evolves in which bureaucrats, lobbyists, clients, and congressional committees work together. Congress, instead of acting as a watchdog for the people, can be gradually infiltrated by special interests from all sides. The President, instead of acting as the supreme administrator, often must battle this long-established network of specialists.

One small example of clientism from Richard Nixon's Presidency will illustrate how it works. Nixon wanted to prevent the creation of the Youth Conservation Corps (YCC) in the early 1970s, this being a summer job program for unemployed teenagers. Nevertheless, the YCC was started as a pilot program by Congress and ran for several years. Moreover, the legislation was originally drafted not in Congress but in the Department of Agriculture, at the request of a Senator from a heavily forested western state. The Senator then introduced the bill and held hearings, inviting the men who had in fact written the bill to testify. They came, and following President Nixon's orders they testified against their own idea. Under questioning, however, they confessed that it would be possible to launch a YCC program, and it just so happened that they had with them extensive information about how it might function. Environmental groups interested in the YCC were also asked to testify. The YCC was pushed through Congress, it came into existence as a pilot program, and then it grew in subsequent budget years. Thus the President was outwitted and defied by career bureaucrats who work together with Congress to create a "pet" program. While the YCC was undoubtedly a good thing, giving jobs on federal forest lands to otherwise unemployed urban youth, many other projects are not. But because of clientism and policy networks, the President often loses control over policy, and the budget tends to grow larger.

The federal budget for 2001 was estimated at $1.789 trillion, not including $1.4 trillion in state and local expenditures. For every federal employee there were four more working on state and local payrolls. California alone has 330,000 state employees. Transportation, education, police and fire protection, unemployment benefits, and health care are all financed primarily on the local level. Between 1960 and 1997, the United States had a surplus in the federal budget only twice, in 1960 and 1969. During the rapid growth years of the 1960s, however, the deficits were small, and they were considered justifiable according to a Keynesian economic policy. The situation worsened in the 1970s, when the deficit more than doubled in a single decade. During the Reagan years it more than doubled again, threatening the health of the economy by the early 1990s.

When President Clinton took office in 1993, the federal deficit had reached $290 billion. Then, in a startling reversal, the yearly deficit shrank year by year during the Clinton Administration. In 1998 for the first time in 29 years, the budget yielded a surplus. By the time Clinton stepped down he had paid off $600 billion of the national debt, lowered interest rates, and reduced unemployment to less than 4 percent. The budget surplus of the late 1990s was the result not only of the strong economy that grew at the rate of 4 percent a year, but also of a declining commitment to welfare benefits (discussed in chapter 9). In 2001 taxes were expected to produce a $236 billion surplus, and the presidential candidates agreed that a tax cut was needed. Bush wanted the majority of the deductions for the wealthy; Gore asked that tax relief focus on the poor and middle class. In 2001, however, a tax cut looked necessary for quite another reason: the Clinton economy, after the longest sustained period of growth in American history, was showing clear signs of slowing down.

**Federal Budget Projections, 2001-2005**

|  | 2001 | 2002 | 2003 | 2004 | 2005 |
|---|---|---|---|---|---|
| Receipts from taxes, etc. | 2,025.2 | 2,124.6 | 2,209.7 | 2,301.3 | 2,400.6 |
| **Discretionary:** |  |  |  |  |  |
| Defense | 295.0 | 303.7 | 306.7 | 321.1 | 331.0 |
| Non-Defense | 322.0 | 350.5 | 374.9 | 388.7 | 397.5 |
| Subtotal, discretionary | 617.0 | 654.1 | 681.5 | 709.8 | 728.5 |
| **Mandatory:** |  |  |  |  |  |
| Social Security | 406.0 | 431.4 | 451.3 | 473.6 | 498.7 |
| Medicare and Medicaid | 312.0 | 347.7 | 369.2 | 394.2 | 421.6 |
| Means-tested entitlements | 105.2 | 108.7 | 114.5 | 120.2 | 125.0 |
| Other mandatory | 125.5 | 116.2 | 124.2 | 122.8 | 129.3 |
| Subtotal, mandatory | 948.8 | 1,004 | 1,059.2 | 1,110.8 | 1,174.4 |
| **Net interest** (on national debt) | 223.2 | 210.2 | 192.0 | 173.8 | 154.6 |
| **Total Outlays** | 1,789.0 | 1,868.3 | 1,932.8 | 1,994.4 | 2,057.5 |
| **Total Surplus** | 236.2 | 256.3 | 276.9 | 306.9 | 343.0 |

# 7. The Judiciary and the Supreme Court

The third branch of the federal government is the judiciary, established under Article III of the Constitution. Each judge is appointed by the President, subject to approval by the Senate, which more than 90 percent of the time approves the selection. In recent years, appointments have become a center of contention, however. Two of Nixon's nominees and one of Reagan's were turned down, and in 1991 the hearings on Clarence Thomas's nomination became a national media event, as Americans tried to decide whether they believed Anita Hill, who accused him of sexual harassment. Thomas angrily fought back, calling the proceedings an "electronic lynching," and he was finally confirmed. Although the Constitution does not specify qualifications for the Court, all judges are lawyers, and few have been under 40 years of age. Unlike congressmen and members of the administration, federal judges serve for an unlimited period, and most of the 846 federal judges remain on the bench until retirement. They can only be removed for gross misconduct.

The federal court system is arranged as a hierarchy, with the Supreme Court at the top. It receives cases that have been appealed from the eleven circuit courts located around the country. These in turn review cases from 97 district courts. One can think of these courts as a series of sieves, each more refined that the next, with the Supreme Court receiving only the most refined and complex matters for review. The nine justices of the Supreme Court are arguably the most powerful individuals in the United States, since they can overturn presidential decisions and invalidate laws passed in Congress, with no appeal. Their power is all the more clear, when one realizes that the only justice who ever went to trial for impeachment was acquitted in 1805. Most Americans accept and respect the Supreme Court with an almost superstitious awe, and many assume that should they be wronged in the lower courts they could always appeal to the nine justices in Washington for justice.

In fact, few cases are eligible to come to the Supreme Court, whose primary function is to interpret the meaning of the Constitution, as applied to specific cases. While the question of jurisdiction is complex, basically there are only four types of cases that qualify to be considered in the federal courts:

1. Cases that involve Constitutional questions, for example, in which Constitutionally protected rights are threatened, such as the right to religious freedom, freedom of speech, or freedom of assembly.
2. Cases that involve federal laws concerning, or treaties made with, Native Americans or with foreign governments.
3. Maritime cases (ships at sea, etc.)
4. Conflicts between two or more of the 50 states, and/or citizens of more than one state.

Only a few hundred cases reach the Supreme Court each year, and, of these, many are dismissed because the Court finds either that it does not have jurisdiction over the matter, or that it agrees with the ruling of the lower court. The cases selected for review are usually complex and often controversial. They require long hearings, which result in published decisions, and, if there is disagreement, in published dissents. All of the Court's new decisions must agree with those that it has reached in previous years, another way of saying that every case is a precedent, setting guidelines for all future cases of the same type. In general, the Supreme Court plays a conservative role, maintaining a legal tradition. Since 1790 it has found only two hundred laws to be un-Constitutional.

Occasionally, the Court plays a major role in making social policy. This was the case in many instances from the middle 1950s until the 1970s. During these years an activist Court made a series of landmark decisions that dramatically affected American life. In 1954, when the Congress proved unable to act on problems of Civil Rights, the Supreme Court ordered an end to segregated schooling in the entire nation in its *Brown v. The Board of Education* decision. In 1962 in *Engel v. Vitale* the Court banned religious prayers in public schools, a decision that outraged many Christians, who were further incensed when the Court outlawed Bible-reading in school. Both practices, it found, violated the strict division between church and state laid down in the Constitution. In 1973 it was the Court, not Congress, that declared abortion to be a legal right, protected under the Bill of Rights. After Reagan's many conservative appointments to the Court, however, the right to abortion has been somewhat curtailed, and a slender one vote majority prevents it from being declared illegal. As these examples suggest, the Supreme Court's power should not be underestimated. Presidents understand the power of the federal judges very well, and more than 90 percent of their appointments to the bench are from their own political parties. Thus in the twelve years of Reagan–Bush conservative administrations, they appointed 584 of the 846 judges. Their political philosophy is well represented on the bench. When Clinton arrived at the White House, there already were 102 vacancies for him to fill, and Bush arrived in 2000 with the strong likelihood that he will appoint several Supreme Court justices.

## 8. The Bill of Rights

When the Constitution was first proposed in the eighteenth century, many citizens refused to support its ratification because it was silent on many basic liberties they had won in the American Revolution. They only agreed to support it when guaranteed that certain fundamental rights would immediately be embodied in amendments to the original document. Thus one of the first actions of the first Congress was to pass ten amendments which collectively are called, "The Bill of Rights." (These are reproduced at the back of this book.) Many of the cases heard before the Supreme Court deal with these ten amendments. The most important is the **First** Amendment, which declares that the Congress cannot establish an official religion, that it cannot prohibit free speech or freedom of the press, and that it cannot pass laws preventing people from assembling peacefully or from petitioning the government. The first amendment in effect means that Americans have always had the right to march, to protest, and to petition, and it has encouraged a particular style of populist politics. It protects religious minorities and unpopular movements that want to exercise their rights of free speech and freedom of religion. Finally, this amendment ensures freedom for newspapers and other media, which cannot be censored, closed down, or muzzled by government. Americans can openly criticize any public official in the press. One organization, the American Civil Liberties Union (ACLU) devotes all its efforts to ensuring that these and other basic civil rights are preserved. ACLU lawyers have often gone to court to protect the rights of political minorities, including those on both the extreme left and right.

The **Second** Amendment guarantees to every citizen the right to bear arms. This provision was understandable at the time, for the British had tried to prevent the colonists from having weapons. In 1789 Americans were an agricultural people, most of whom occasionally hunted. Today, however, because this amendment is part of the Constitution it is extremely difficult to pass gun control legislation, despite the fact that more than 10,000 people were killed by handguns in 1990 alone, compared to less than 20 in Britain. Nevertheless, the conservative National Rifle Association (NRA) vigorously opposes any restrictions on firearms as a violation of the Constitution, and distributes bumper-stickers stating: "When guns are outlawed, only outlaws will have guns."

The **Third** Amendment also was a reaction against colonial British practices, as it forbade the government from quartering soldiers in private homes during peacetime without the consent of the owners.

The **Fourth** Amendment makes it illegal for police to search people's homes, persons, or papers unless they have a warrant that describes what is being sought. On television crime shows this amendment is routinely broken by private detectives, but in real life evidence gathered without a warrant (including recorded telephone conversations) cannot be used in a criminal case. Thus, for example, if police search a house without a warrant and find incriminating personal papers there, this evidence will not be recognized by a court of law.

The **Fifth** and **Sixth** Amendments deal with the arrest of suspects and the conduct of criminal trials, providing rules that already in 1790 gave greater legal protection to Americans than some Europeans enjoy today. The Fifth Amendment states that no one may be tried for a serious offense (such as murder) without previously being indicted by a Grand Jury, and that no one may be forced to be a witness against himself. During a trial the accused has the right to remain silent and cannot be forced to answer questions. The police may not torture a prisoner to extract a confession, nor may they hold a prisoner for more than two days without charging him or her with a crime. Prolonged imprisonment in isolation before a trial is absolutely illegal, and any confession elicited during such confinement would not be recognized by an American court of law. Indeed, following the Miranda decision of the Supreme Court (1966), an American prisoner who freely confesses to a crime may go free, unless the police have first told him that he has the right to remain silent, the right to consult a lawyer before making any statement, and the right to have a lawyer present during any questioning. The Sixth Amendment guarantees a speedy and public trial by jury and gives the accused the right to confront witnesses against him, the right to compel witnesses to appear on his behalf, and the right to a lawyer for his defense. The trial for the murder of the Swedish Prime Minister Olof Palme did not allow the accused to confront Palme's widow during her testimony, a procedure that would not be permitted in the United States. Finally, under this amendment, if a person is too poor to hire a lawyer, the court must appoint one to defend him.

The **Seventh** Amendment guarantees that facts established during a trial by jury cannot be re-examined during appeals to a higher court. The **Eighth** Amendment protects the guilty against excessive fines or "cruel and unusual punishments." Originally intended to prohibit such practices as torture, disfigurement, and excessive fines, today debate focuses on whether the amendment also prohibits the death penalty. The **Ninth** Amendment emphasizes that rights not defined or discussed in the Constitution are "retained by the people;" while the **Tenth** Amendment reads in full, "The powers not delegated to the United States by the Constitution, nor prohibited by it to the States, are reserved to the states respectively, or to the people."

Without the Bill of Rights the Civil Rights Movement would have had few legal protections, and the great public meeting where Martin Luther King gave his "I Have a Dream" speech could have been prevented as an illegal assembly. Likewise, the marches and draft card burnings that protested the Vietnam War were protected by the Bill of Rights, which also protects the right of newspapers and magazines to publish articles opposed to government policies, and the right of pacifists to refuse military service. In short, the Bill of Rights gives the individual or the small minority protection against the majority; it protects citizens against imprisonment without just cause, excessive fines, or other forms of oppression by big government.

In part because of these ten amendments to the Constitution, acts of intentional civil disobedience have long been a common feature of political life. First articulated by Henry David Thoreau in the 1840s, civil disobedience is a non-violent form of direct action in which individuals refuse to obey what they regard as an unjust law. By breaking that law they ask to be sent to prison, hoping to draw the attention of thoughtful citizens to an injustice. Throughout American history when the two major parties have been unwilling to confront a serious problem, such as human slavery or an undeclared war, there have always been individuals willing to employ civil disobedience. In 1846, Thoreau himself refused to pay taxes that would be used to help pay for what he regarded as an unjust war with Mexico. In later wars many also have refused to be drafted into the army. The most famous use of civil disobedience, however, took place in the early civil rights struggle, when Martin Luther King used it to raise the conscience of the nation against segregation and discrimination. More recently, civil disobedience has been employed by "right-to-life" groups in sit-ins and demonstrations against abortion clinics. Given the pragmatic nature of mainstream politics and the tendency of the two main parties to avoid controversy in order to control the center of the political spectrum, the tactic of civil disobedience is an absolutely necessary part of the American system, injecting it with a needed moral intensity.

# Foreign Affairs

## 1. The Conduct of Foreign Affairs

In the new millennium Americans confront a rapidly changing world. After the rigid stabilities of the Cold War, the 1990s were marked by violent ethnic rivalries between and within the nations formed out of the disintegration of the Soviet Union and Yugoslavia. As this instability becomes less acute, however, other conflicts and problems will take their place. Whatever the foreign policies of the United States may be in this new era, the institutional arrangements where they are formulated remain the same. Unlike European systems of government, foreign policy is not the prerogative of the President and cabinet alone. The foreign affairs of the United States are conducted in an uneasy partnership between the Congress and the executive branch. To the extent that diplomacy requires money, it is subject to the control of Congress, which can refuse to pay for policies it disapproves of. During the Reagan years, for example, Congress cut off funding for the "Contras", whom the President wished to support against the Sandinista government of Nicaragua. The discovery that Oliver North had organized an illegal secret sale of weapons to Iran, thereby raising money he used to aid the Contras, triggered months of Congressional investigations, leading to many resignations in the Reagan administration and talk of impeachment. The Constitution also limits Presidential action in another important way, by requiring that all treaties with foreign governments be approved by the Senate before they become binding. Thus a President can negotiate and sign an agreement only to find that he lacks the support needed to make it law. This happened to Jimmy Carter when he had to withdraw the Strategic Arms Limitation Treaty (SALT II) from an uncooperative Senate, despite the fact that it had been negotiated in good faith with the Soviet Union. Sales of weapons to foreign nations also come under the scrutiny and control of Congress, and a President at times finds it difficult to convince the legislators that a particular sale is wise, especially if it in any way involves nuclear technologies.

The involvement of Congress in foreign affairs automatically means that the public is also involved, particularly special interest groups and ethnic minorities. In practical terms, every administration finds certain aspects of foreign policy a hostage to powerful legislators who speak for Jewish Americans on Israel, Polish Americans on Poland, Irish Americans on Northern Ireland, and so forth. While the majority of the population cares little about what happens on much of the globe, these religious and ethnic groups complicate diplomacy by making special demands. For example, at the end of World War I Irish Americans demanded, and got, a clause in a piece of legislation calling for the emancipation of Ireland. Such pressure from ethnic groups is particularly intense in the area of foreign aid.

Large corporations and business associations also lobby in Congress for favorable legislation. Textile mills and automobile manufacturers complain about foreign competition and seek higher tariffs or quotas. Steel manufacturers complain that European mills operate with government subsidies and as a result can produce at an artificially low price. Many exporters also want Congress to solve their problems. For example, in recent years they have accused the Europeans of blocking agricultural exports and accused the Japanese of creating so many administrative barriers that foreigners cannot enter their market, even to sell American baseball bats. Since businesses are large contributors to political campaigns, Congress usually gives them a sympathetic ear.

Both the Senate and the executive branch expend a great deal of time and energy on foreign affairs. The Senate Committee on Foreign Relations has nine sub-committees, covering such areas as African Affairs, European Affairs, Asian Affairs, Multinational Corporations, Foreign Aid, and Oceans and the International Environment. Sub-committees monitor the actions of the executive branch and attempt to formulate policy in the form of laws. At the same time, the State Department seeks to control policy through its own internal bureaucracy. These parallel structures would seem to complicate matters enough, but in the past twenty years the National Security Council (NSC), which works directly with the President, has come to be the most powerful factor in foreign affairs, particularly in crisis situations where immediate action is necessary. When Henry Kissinger was Richard Nixon's security advisor in the early 1970s he increased the power of the NSC so much that the job of Secretary of State clearly became a secondary position. Thus the creation and administration of foreign policy today is a complex process that involves the Congress, lobbyists, the State Department, and the NSC, not to mention the President, the national press, multinational corporations, and the Defense Department. The many players in the policy game make secrecy difficult, and however frustrating this may be to some strategists, it ensures that most policy changes are intensively discussed. Just as important, policy discussions emerge from a distinctive historical context: the rise from a backwoods revolutionary colony in 1776 to the leading world power in 1945.

## 2. A Brief History of Foreign Affairs

International affairs were central to American life in the eighteenth century, when the thirteen colonies that would become the United States clung to the eastern edge of the continent. The Spanish colonies stretching from Argentina to Florida and Mexico were prosperous parts of a powerful world empire. The Spanish presence, together with the French colonies in Canada and Louisiana, seemed to promise that North America would become a perpetual battleground for the Great Powers. During the eighteenth century the colonists were drawn into each European war, at considerable expense and danger to themselves. Most of the officers who later led the American Revolution, including George Washington, gained their military experience in English wars against the French, who allied themselves with Indian tribes on the western frontier.

The Revolution itself could not have been won without skillful diplomacy. The Americans needed French support, and fortunately had a skilled diplomat, Benjamin Franklin, to send to Paris. He secured loans and naval support from the French fleet; both were essential to victory. Perhaps because Americans had so much experience in diplomacy by 1790, they chose to retreat as much as possible from the world stage. As President, Washington (1789-1797) adopted a policy of neutrality with regard to the French Revolution, to give the new nation a chance to consolidate itself. When Washington retired after eight years in office, he advised Americans in his Farewell Address to beware of the entanglements of foreign alliances. President Jefferson (1801-1809) also pursued a policy of neutrality in the Napoleonic wars, and only in 1812 did the Americans finally join in, on the French side. The unfortunate result was that the British attacked and burned Washington, D.C., and the Americans won no major battles before peace was concluded in 1814. However, most Americans have a complete loss of historical memory with regard to their alliance with Napoleon, and at least until 1970 it was common to hear politicians proclaim that the United States had never lost a war.

After this defeat, for virtually one hundred years Americans pursued a policy of neutrality toward Europe, a policy that was largely possible because the Atlantic Ocean formed such a formidable barrier to any attack, and because the British navy controlled the seas. Yet neutrality toward Europe did not mean inactivity. Rather, during the century from 1790 to 1890 the United States expanded from its original thirteen states across the continent. Indeed, British attempts to limit western expansion had angered the Americans in the Colonial period. When Thomas Jefferson purchased the Louisiana territory from Napoleon in 1803 – a transaction in which the Indians were not consulted – he almost doubled the site of the United States. Settlers poured westward, new states were added to the union, and soon Americans began to speak of "Manifest Destiny." This somewhat loosely formulated idea held that the existence of a vast, fertile continent ready for European exploitation was a part of a larger, divine plan. Americans seemed destined to rule a continent that would mediate between Asia and Europe. By mid-century, one writer contemplating the vast Mississippi Valley proclaimed that God "has planed down the whole valley, including Texas, and united every atom of the soil and every drop of the waters of the mighty whole. He has linked the waters with the Great Mississippi, and marked the united whole for the domination of one government and the residence of one people." Such ideas were used to justify the forced removal of Native Americans a thousand miles west of their woodland homes. Thousands died on this "trail of tears," which politicians justified as a journey to a new permanent home on the southern plains in an area where it was thought that whites would never settle. Yet even before the Indian removal, white ranchers were migrating into Texas when it was still a part of Mexico. They soon revolted and founded their own republic in 1836. The American government annexed Texas in 1845, provoking the Mexican–American War (1846-1848) in which the Mexicans lost almost half their territory. This war and Canadian boundary adjustments with the English in 1818 and 1846 defined the contours that would be filled by 48 states stretching from the Atlantic to the Pacific.

### Territoral Expansion, 1783-1853

**The West**

▤ Oregon Treaty with Great Britain, 1846

▥ Ceded by Mexico after War of 1848

▨ Gadsen Purchase, from Mexico, 1853

**The East**

▦ Louisiana Purchase, 1803

■ Treaty with Spain, 1819

▤ Ceded by Great Britain, 1818

▨ Annexation of Texas, 1845

At the same time that Manifest Destiny became a popular notion, the United States government adopted a policy of hegemony in its own hemisphere, first formalized in the Monroe Doctrine of 1823. Proclaimed by President Monroe at the moment when the South American countries were breaking free of Spanish rule, it stated that the two American continents were no longer open to colonization by European powers, and further claimed that the Americas had a political system different from that of Europe. The Western Hemisphere in fact was largely free from outside interference for the next century, because the British tacitly approved of the Monroe Doctrine for their own commercial reasons, and kept the other European powers out with their powerful fleet.

The American Civil War put this unofficial alliance to a severe test, however, creating a diplomatic crisis. Much of the English upper class sympathized with the South, and in addition huge cotton imports were necessary to keep British textile mills running. Had Britain recognized the Confederacy of southern states as a nation or used its Navy to break the North's blockade of southern ports, the United States would probably have broken apart. Only skillful Northern diplomacy and the English middle class's repugnance to slavery prevented British diplomatic recognition of the Confederacy.

As the United States expanded across the continent, a new attitude to the rest of the world had begun to emerge. With the invention of the telegraph, the steamship, and improved naval guns, the Atlantic and Pacific Oceans no longer seemed so impenetrable as protective barriers, nor were they any longer insurmountable obstructions to further American expansion. A popular clergyman, Josiah Strong, suggested in the late nineteenth century that the theory of Manifest Destiny ought to be applied not only to the American West but to the rest of the world, and he confidently predicted the global hegemony of Anglo-Saxon civilization. At the same time, many businessmen and farmers argued that overproduction lay behind the unstable economy from 1873 to 1896, and that the only solution was market expansion. A professor at the Naval War College, Alfred Thayer Mahan argued that control of the seas had always proved decisive in human affairs, and warned that without modern naval vessels the United States was vulnerable to foreign aggression. He advocated expanding the American fleet, the acquisition of coaling stations in outlying islands such as Hawaii, and the construction of a canal through Panama, to enable warships to pass rapidly from the east to the west coast. Thus popular philosophy, economic analysis, and military strategy all pointed to the same conclusion: the United States ought to expand into new foreign markets.

One of Mahan's avid readers, Theodore Roosevelt, became famous for his military exploits in the Spanish–American War of 1898, which vaulted him to national office. This "splendid little war" was justified to the public as a battle against colonialism. The Americans were only to help Cuban freedom fighters throw off the Spanish oppressors in what was to be a war against feudalism and tradition. In practical terms, the war pitted the modernized American fleet against Spanish ships whose firepower was so inferior that it could not reach the US vessels whose cannons were destroying them. The overmatched Spaniards lost Puerto Rico, Cuba, and the Philippines, while the Americans lost only 2,900 men, the vast majority to tropical fevers. Despite technological superiority, however, the Americans were unprepared, issuing winter uniforms for use in the tropics and evincing considerable disorganization in the Florida staging areas. In Cuba these logistical problems were not crucial because they had the support of local guerrillas, but in the Philippines a five-year period of bloody warfare was necessary to subdue the local inhabitants after the quick victory over the Spanish. In this way the United States was launched into overseas imperialism, after the European countries already had carved up much of the globe for themselves.

The old policy of avoiding foreign alliances had not yet been abandoned, however, and many rank-and-file Americans still retained an affection for neutrality and non-involvement. Thus the Spanish–American War spawned the Anti-Imperialist League, joined by many of the most prominent writers and intellectuals of the time, including Mark Twain and William Dean Howells. The League successfully lobbied against outright annexation of Cuba and pressed for a policy that would lead to independence for the Philippines after a period of preparation.

By 1900 the United States had the third largest navy in the world, and the Spanish–American War thrust the nation forward as one of the great powers. There shortly followed a convenient coup d'etat that proclaimed the Isthmus of Panama to be independent of Colombia, creating a new country whose only reason for existence was the construction of a canal linking the Atlantic and Pacific. Where the French had failed in their attempt to construct a canal, losing thousands of men in the process, Americans succeeded, opening it in 1914. Building the canal was a monumental undertaking that demonstrated determination, engineering skill, and the United States' new international ambitions. To further project American power in the region, President Roosevelt pursued a vigorous interventionist policy in the Caribbean. Most Americans saw these activities as incidental local affairs rather than as foreign involvement.

When World War I began, President Wilson kept the nation out of the conflict for more than two years, much to the satisfaction of the majority of the population. Wilson later led the country into the war on the side of France and Great Britain, and intervention was explained to the public as an effort to "make the world safe for democracy" by fighting "a war to end all wars." He intoned that "The force of America is the force of moral principle . . . there is nothing else that she loves, and . . . there is nothing else for which she will contend." Despite such rhetoric, thousands of conscientious objectors remained unconvinced and refused military service. In addition, the German, Austrian, and Irish ethnic minorities disliked aiding the Allies. The majority of the population, however, enthusiastically embraced intervention.

In little more than a year American troops decisively tipped the balance in the war, and Wilson brought his principles to the Treaty of Versailles, in which he convinced the Europeans to create a League of Nations. When he returned home, however, he found that most Americans had lost interest in European problems and disapproved of the long-term commitments that the League involved. They had been disillusioned by the war and wanted no entangling obligations in the peace. The Senate refused to ratify the Treaty of Versailles or membership in the League. Thus Americans tried to retreat from their status as a great power. In the 1920s and 1930s they encouraged world disarmament and returned to the traditional policy of neutrality. As late as March, 1941 a Gallup Poll found that an overwhelming 83 percent of the American people opposed entering World War II, much to President Franklin D. Roosevelt's frustration, as he was certain that US interests lay with Britain and France. Indeed, in June, 1940 Roosevelt had released surplus arms and aircraft to Great Britain, and at the time of the Gallup survey the Democrats had just passed the Lend-Lease Act, which gave the President the power to transfer or sell $7 billion in supplies to the Allies. Yet despite such aid, officially the United States remained neutral until the Japanese attacked Pearl Harbor on December 7, 1941.

## 3. America as a Global Power, 1941-

From the Napoleonic wars until World War II the United States refused to make foreign alliances and attempted to remain neutral in European wars, while proclaiming the right to exclude other nations from intervention in American affairs. During these years it regarded the Western Hemisphere north of the equator as its particular sphere of influence, and the Spanish–American War can be seen as a logical extension of this attitude. The post-1945 policies of establishing the United Nations in New York City, of building up the North Atlantic Treaty Organization (NATO), and of containing communism are thus, historically speaking, a major change that has often seemed confusing to the average American, who takes little interest in foreign affairs. However, the invention of atomic weapons at the end of World War II, the Soviet domination of Eastern Europe, the communist victory in the Chinese civil war, the development of intercontinental ballistic missiles, and the space race, all contributed to a new understanding that the United States could not avoid a central role in the world arena.

This role not only took the form of strategic alliances but also required extensive foreign aid to western European countries through the Marshall Plan in order to revive their war-torn economies. As articulated by Secretary of State George C. Marshall, his plan was an action taken "not against any country or doctrine but against hunger, poverty, desperation, and chaos. Its purpose should be the revival of a working economy in the world so as to permit the emergence of political and social conditions in which free institutions can exist." In 1948–1949 alone, $6.5 billion in non-military aid was given to European countries. (Western European nations did not mount as large a program to help Eastern Europe in the 1990s.)

Nor was the Marshall Plan all. In 1947 President Harry Truman gave extensive military aid to Greece and Turkey and announced that the United States would seek to oppose communist movements anywhere in Europe. This Truman Doctrine of "containing" the spread of communism soon led to actions to combat left-wing political groups around the world wherever they arose, even if they were nationalist movements in European colonies and dependencies. Thus the Americans assisted the French against Ho Chi Minh in Vietnam, the British against unrest in Iran, and Taiwan against mainland China. The most costly early commitment was to send troops into Korea, where thousands of Americans died in bloody fighting between 1950 and 1953. Later came the direct confrontations with the Soviet Union and its allies in the early 1960s, notably the construction of the Berlin Wall and the Cuban Missile Crisis. These two events came shortly after John F. Kennedy's inaugural address, which summarized the attitude behind the containment policy: "Let every nation know, whether it wishes us well or ill, that we shall pay any price, bear any burden, meet any hardship, support any friend, oppose any foe, in order to assure the survival and the success of liberty."

Kennedy's rhetoric apparently harked back to Wilson's idealism, but in fact from the late 1940s onwards academics and policy-makers strove to redefine the basis for foreign policy. The economic interests of the United States were not always the bedrock of policy, as the physical security of the country became an increasing concern after the perfection of intercontinental ballistic missiles. To deal with such threats, self-styled "realists" argued that policy had to be based on pragmatic analysis of power relations, and strategic alliances had to be based on national self-interest rather than moral pieties. One example of the new "realism" was the expansion of the Central Intelligence Agency (CIA), which did not limit itself to gathering information but engaged in covert actions and disinformation campaigns. Such activities were deemed expedient, and defended as necessary responses to communist agents who engaged in similar activities. Another new dimension of American foreign policy was an active military aid program, which distributed $100 billion around the world between 1946 and 1980, with much of the money being used to buy US arms. Many of the governments who received these weapons were not democratically elected, including dictators such as Franco in Spain and the Shah of Iran, or military juntas in Greece and Turkey. Critics attacked this "realism" as a debasement of the democratic values Americans had traditionally embraced at home, and which they believed were the only genuine basis for foreign policy. Certainly in retrospect the military aid of $1.4 billion given to Iran or the $16.4 billion sent to Vietnam ultimately failed to achieve its goal. And some have criticized the wisdom of simultaneous aid to traditional enemies, such as Turkey and Greece, Israel and Egypt, India and Pakistan.

## 4. The Popular Response

Beneath these official policy debates bubbled a cauldron of popular fears. The most famous manifestation of this fear was the spectacle later called "McCarthyism." It is misleading to consider Senator Joseph McCarthy apart from the context of the late 1940s and early 1950s. He did not create the Red Scare, but rather developed it for his own purposes. After World War II Americans found themselves in an entirely new political situation, which nothing in their past experience as a neutral nation had prepared them for. Nor was the world of 1948 a stable one that held still long enough for Americans to get a clear view of events and discuss them calmly. Several events shook American confidence, notably the conviction of a high government official, Alger Hiss, of being a communist spy, and the collapse of the Chinese nationalist regime. McCarthy charged that China had "gone Communist" because "left-wingers" had infiltrated the State Department. Many feared that the government itself was full of spies, and mandatory loyalty oaths became common. The fear of spies also contributed to the plausibility of the government's claim that the Soviets had only been able to build a nuclear weapon because the Rosenbergs, a radical couple, had given them top-secret scientific information. They were tried, convicted, and executed. Even today Americans debate whether they or Hiss were guilty.

McCarthy was only one of many who worried about "creeping communism," but he became well known through the newly available medium of television, which projected him into most living rooms. The hearings that McCarthy conducted in the United States Senate became one of the first great media events, as a parade of witnesses were questioned about their past activities. During the 1930s and 1940s some Americans had joined the Communist Party or its front organizations. This had been acceptable while Russia was an American ally during World War II. Those who had done so included prominent writers and intellectuals, and they were called to testify in Washington, including Lillian Hellman, Dashiell Hammett (who went to prison), and Arthur Miller. Yet despite these excesses, if one compares what happened in the United States during these years to the purges, mysterious disappearances, and other forms of repression that have occurred in other countries, including Russia, Pakistan, Iran, China, and Argentina, then the American "Red Scare" can hardly be called a purge. Its importance lay in the degree to which a democratic society for a time lost sight of some of its legal traditions, and undermined the guarantees of the Bill of Rights. In the end, however, the American legal system protected many of McCarthy's intended victims, and he was himself censured by Congress. The courts protected many of the accused who were brought to trial, and few actually went to jail. Unfortunately, most of the damage was done to reputations through accusations, and many people lost their jobs or suffered in their careers once their names had been linked with communism.

McCarthyism itself was fueled by deeper fears of nuclear destruction. At first the public celebrated the sudden victory over Japan that the bomb made possible, without fully realizing that a new era had begun. The government preserved this enthusiasm for atomic weapons, suggesting that only a few hours after one exploded it would be possible to leave a shelter and fight fires. The first bomb shelters were not incorporated into public buildings until the early 1950s. Yet while calming the public, the government was developing an even more powerful weapon, the H-bomb, because the USSR was also developing atomic weapons. Seeing this even more terrible weapon, the public was gripped by a fatalistic hysteria. College student debates centered on whether it was "Better to be Red than Dead." Many affluent families built private bomb shelters in their back yards, at considerable expense, and newspapers debated whether or not one should let the neighbors share such a shelter in the case of attack, if it was only stocked with enough food for one family. Two popular films caught the mood. *Fail Safe* (1964) depicted an American system failure that led to the nuclear destruction of Moscow. World War III was only avoided by an agreement to allow the Russians to destroy New York City in retaliation, and the final scenes of the film showed typical street scenes, made poignant by the realization that all these people were about to be blown up. *On the Beach* (1959) took place in Australia after a nuclear war had depopulated the rest of the planet. Radioactive winds slowly carried death southward, however, and the characters dealt with the end of the human race in every conceivable way, from excessive drinking, to suicide, to religion. The last shot shows an empty street, swept by the wind. Above hangs a banner from a religious revival, stating: "Repent, while there is still time." Despite this consciousness of impending doom, however, few joined the tiny ban-the-bomb movement, which only grew to a significant size along with the counter-culture of the 1960s. Then, in reaction to the psychology of fatalism, resignation, and fear, many joined the loosely related protest movements of the Beats, Blacks, feminists, the anti-war movement, and the ecology movement. By the 1960s dissent had developed into a rejection of nationalism as well. As Grace Slick of the rock group Jefferson Airplane put it, "I'd rather my country died for me."

## 5. Vietnam and After

The escalation of the Vietnam War in the late 1960s led to repeated mass marches on Washington, massive civil disobedience, and a wave of applications for conscientious objector status from young men who refused to be drafted into the army. Not only young people but the national press turned against the war, whose bloody consequences could be seen each evening on the television news. The war became the central campaign issue in the 1968 Democratic Presidential Primaries, where Senator Eugene McCarthy almost out-polled President Johnson, leading to Johnson's withdrawal from the race. The split in the Democratic party permitted Richard Nixon to lead the Republicans to a narrow victory in 1968. When he assumed office, troop levels in Vietnam had reached 535,000. While Nixon hoped to win the war, he began to pursue the policy of withdrawing American troops as fast as they could be replaced by newly trained South Vietnamese soldiers. At the same time, he stepped up the bombing of North Vietnam, in an effort to bring the North to the negotiating table. Ultimately, his "peace with honor" campaign meant the withdrawal of all American troops, leaving the South unable to defend itself for long, and the civil war came to an end in 1975, with the North victorious. By then, Nixon and Gerald Ford had defused the appearance of a communist threat by opening talks with the government of mainland China, which the United States had refused to recognize since the late 1940s. This diplomatic move exploited

*Soldier in Vietnam, 1971. – Wide World Photos.*

an already existing split between China and Russia, and marked the end of American attempts to see both nations as part of a unified global menace.

Few Americans found satisfaction in the way the Vietnam War ended. The student left could hardly feel that the withdrawal was a victory for pacifist or democratic principles, as it had created a North Vietnamese military machine that imposed a rigid rule on a shattered country. Conservatives claimed that the army had been forced to fight with one hand tied behind its back. The anguished experience of returning soldiers and their families created a mood of bitterness. There was no hero's welcome home and no feeling of patriotic satisfaction that their sacrifices had been appreciated. Novels such as Michael Herr's *Dispatches* and films such as *The Deer Hunter* and *Apocalypse Now* testify to the continuing American preoccupation with the war. Vietnam left ordinary Americans of both right and left suspicious of politicians and wary of overseas military entanglements. Only the far right objected when President Carter gave tacit approval to the Nicaraguan Revolution of the late 1970s and later refused to define the civil war in El Salvador as a major test of American resolve.

Instead, Carter made human rights the keystone of his foreign policy, much to the displeasure of the USSR, where many dissidents were imprisoned in psychiatric hospitals and Andrei Sakharov had long suffered under house arrest. Confrontational politics with the Soviets returned in the late 1970s, after Russia invaded Afghanistan and a popular religious revolt toppled the Shah of Iran. From the end of the Carter years that were scarred by the Iranian hostage crisis, through most of the Reagan Presidency, Americans once again heard the old Cold War rhetoric, but it made less impact. The invasion of tiny Grenada and the air attack on Colonel Gaddafi's headquarters in Libya boosted American morale after a decade of defeats, but most Europeans found these actions worrying in their recklessness. At home, Reagan declaimed against the Soviets as an "evil empire," but by the middle of his second term the Soviets began to tire of their own Vietnam-like experience in Afghanistan. Reagan began to accept friendly overtures from Gorbachev, whom he met several times, and this process of rapprochement continued during the Bush administration. In short, despite the apparent return to "containment" in the Reagan years, actual policy gradually was shifting toward a more accommodating stance. Then in the 1990s events outran policy, as the Soviet Union broke up into a loose federation of republics, riven by ethnic tensions.

With its old opponent dismembered, the American military maintained a confrontational posture in other areas, particularly in the Third World. However, the experience in Vietnam and the bloody stalemates in Lebanon and El Salvador together undermined popular support for prolonged overseas military activities and increased the desire for negotiated settlements rather than armed conflicts. In response to public distaste for extended operations involving large numbers of troops, the military developed the rationale and the capability for low intensity warfare. This term refers to a variety of military actions outside the United States to be undertaken by elite troops and advisors. They have been trained for rescue missions, anti-drug operations, punitive strikes, anti-terrorist actions, and assistance to anti-Communist groups in the Third World. When described by Pentagon planners, these actions are swift and surgically precise instruments of foreign policy. In practice, however, they are sometimes miscalculated and messy embarrassments. The air attack against Colonel Gaddafi of Libya killed many civilians while leaving its intended target unscathed; the mission to rescue the American hostages in Iran failed; support for the Contras did not topple the Sandinista government of Nicaragua, an election did; the early counterinsurgency action, Vietnam, ballooned into a disaster. Nevertheless, George Bush's support for military actions aimed at drug producers in Peru and Colombia and his invasion of Panama during Christmas 1989 showed that low intensity warfare remained a part of American foreign policy. If so, the old enemy of international communism will have to be replaced by something else, perhaps the international drug dealers.

# 6. The Post-Cold War Era

The break-up of the Warsaw Pact alliance that once bound Eastern Europe to the Soviets allowed Americans to withdraw some troops stationed in western Europe. At the same time, the old alliances that focused on containing communism were no longer adequate instruments of policy, as both Iraq's invasion of Kuwait and the crisis in the Balkans soon demonstrated.

In the brief period before these new problems emerged, Americans at home hoped to see a "peace divided." The Cold War had not been merely rhetoric but a costly reality. As Robert Sayre has noted, "the damage that the Cold War has inflicted on America and its people. The oxymoron cold war has somehow hindered us from seeing that 'cold' or not it has still done the economic, political, and social damage of a war. Americans have made wartime sacrifices – in diminished social programs, deferred up-keep of their public facilities and services, over-allocation of wealth and resources to weaponry, and many other ways too numerous to mention. . . . The rusting bridges and run-down railroads have not been bombed by enemy planes. They have been knocked out by Cold-War neglect." Little wonder that in 1991 many Americans wanted to redirect their resources to rebuilding their infrastructure.

Yet in the summer of 1990, even as Congress prepared to cut the military budget, Saddam Hussein sent his troops into Kuwait, and announced its annexation. The United Nations voted overwhelmingly in favor of economic sanctions against Iraq and demanded that it withdraw from Kuwait. Led by Great Britain and the United States, a multinational force of more than 600,000 was assembled in Saudi Arabia, and an unbelieving world watched as the crisis devolved into war in January of 1991. From its inception, many Americans analyzed this war in comparison with Vietnam. Yet the two conflicts could hardly have been more different, in their origins, aims, tactics, or final outcomes. Vietnam was an even less useful guide to the crisis of the Balkans, where Croatia and Slovenia broke away from Yugoslavia, fostering civil war and extreme instability, focused in Bosnia. Both the Bush and Clinton administrations hoped that the European Union would be able to solve this crisis on its own doorstep, but when it utterly failed to do anything constructive, Clinton got the main parties to negotiate an accord and sent in American troops as peacekeepers, alongside smaller detachments from NATO allies.

By 1995 it had become clear that not only would the Americans remain in Europe, they would encourage NATO to expand to the east. Despite several years of vocal Soviet opposition, by 1997 Poland, the Czech

Republic, and Hungary were poised to join NATO. The continued commitment to Europe was related to a growing awareness of China as the next superpower. With over one billion people and an economy growing by as much as 10 percent a year in the 1990s, it seemed more and more likely that American hegemony in the twentieth century might be followed by a century of Asian world hegemony.

## 7. Global Environmentalism

At the end of the twentieth century, foreign affairs are not just about conventional diplomacy and trade. Industrial civilization poses a serious threat to the environment. Los Angeles daily chokes on its own smog. Factory smoke carries across borders as acid rain. Over-farming that causes severe erosion in one area affects the environment elsewhere. The destruction of the Brazilian rain-forest potentially could undermine the global ecology. And what precisely is happening to the ozone layer? How can one stop companies from putting toxic waste in containers and dumping them in the ocean? How rapidly is air pollution creating a "greenhouse effect?" How should nuclear waste be handled? Does France have the right to explode nuclear bombs in the Pacific? Does Sweden have the right to operate a nuclear power plant across the sound from Copenhagen? Such questions,

*New York City under a blanket of smog. – Litton Industries.*

spurred by the major accident at Chernobyl, can be expected to become a major part of foreign affairs in years to come.

These challenges cannot be met by a military response; they will require scientific analysis, the redesign of production procedures and consumer products, and limits on growth. Americans began to face up to the problem in the late 1960s, when they realized that most of the fish in their great rivers had died or were inedible. One small river passing through Cleveland, Ohio contained so much industrial waste that it caught on fire. By 1970 the environmental question had intertwined with the American Indian Movement (AIM), the women's movement, and the anti-war movement; each saw the destruction of the landscape as an irrefutable illustration of its own critique of American society. Partly to defuse such criticism and partly as a reaction to the problem itself, Congress passed the Clean Air Act (1970), the Water Pollution Control Act (1972), and much other legislation. Use of the pesticide DDT was banned. Billboards along most American highways were pulled down. Catalytic converters and unleaded gas have been required on new cars for more than 20 years. Yet despite these advances, in 1988 each American on average used 1,125 liters of gasoline, 140,000 liters of water, threw away 84 kilos of plastic, and produced 590 kilos of garbage.

The United Nations Brundtland Report of 1987, *Our Common Future*, analyzed world environmental prospects. It advocated "sustainable development," but recognized, somewhat paradoxically, that to achieve it "the international economy must speed up world growth." People in developing nations will not be interested in preserving the environment unless they have a better standard of living, without poverty or ill-health. The World Energy Council estimates that if newly industrialized countries choose the most ecologically sound technologies available, the world's mean temperature will rise 1 degree Celsius in the next century, and if they continue to use their present high polluting technologies, the rise could be as much as four degrees. A rising level of $CO_2$ almost certainly will mean more air pollution, acid rain, global warming, desertification, and a rise in sea level. Nevertheless, US $CO_2$ emissions rose more than 10 percent between 1990 and 1997.

Environmental problems will require global cooperation, most probably through the United Nations, which has already done a good deal in this area. Nations will need to curb their use of energy. The United States has the highest per capita use of energy in the world, roughly 40 percent more than Denmark or Germany, double the level in Sweden, and almost three times as high as Japan. Americans represent 5 percent of the world's population, but they use 25 percent of the world's oil and release 22 percent of the world's carbon emissions. Alternative energies from sun and wind can help reduce pollution, but every country could also in a relatively short time achieve much greater energy efficiency. The Clinton administration promised to be more engaged in evironmental problems, but has not been a notable success so far.

Ultimately, pollution means not only destruction of the landscape but illness as well. The American Cancer Society made a historical study and found that a century ago one person in twenty-five had some form of cancer during their lifetime. In contrast, today the figure is one out of four. The World Health Organization has estimated that 80 percent of all cancers are related to environmental contamination, including not only pollution in air and water but also in the workplace, as well as chemical additives in foods. Rather than focus on finding a cure for the disease, which by implication would suggest that pollution would be rendered harmless, critics increasingly are focusing on the need for a clean environment to prevent cancer in the first place.

## 8. Americans Overseas

There are few cities anywhere without a few resident Americans, who despite whatever reservations they may have about United States foreign policy often find themselves cast in the role of unofficial ambassadors. Four million Americans live overseas, not counting members of the armed forces. One million of these are divided between Canada and Mexico. Another million plus are in Europe, particularly concentrated in Germany, Britain, and Italy, with the remainder spread around the globe. There are 60,000 in the Nordic countries. In addition to these permanent residents, every year 21 million Americans go abroad, half of them to Europe (10.3 million Europeans visit the United States.) Most are tourists on short holidays, but thousands are high school and college students who spend up to a year away from home. The results of these cross-cultural contacts have been incalculable, but almost certainly include a greater variety of food in American restaurants, greater interest in foreign language learning, a taste for foreign goods, and most importantly a greater understanding of other cultures. Perhaps the most famous institution in this area is the Fulbright–Hays Program for the international exchange of graduate students and professors. With commissions in most of the countries around the world, the Fulbright program relies on funding from both the host country's government and the United States. Many other programs also promote international exchanges with the goal of creating direct person-to-person contacts that lead to mutual understanding. Finally, of course, millions of recent immigrants in the United States maintain ties to their homeland. Overall, the majority of the American population has either traveled abroad or has a close relative with extensive overseas experience.

In addition to the flows of millions of Americans and immigrants across national borders, American corporations have established themselves around the world. Some have argued that American foreign policy is shaped by the needs of these corporations and of capitalism itself. Since more than one-third of the 130 largest corporations in the world are from the United States this argument obviously has some merit. However, note that multinational corporations often have interests that do not coincide with American foreign policy. Politically, the multinational corporation plays an ambiguous role, since on the one hand it may want to distance itself from the United States government as a way of being accepted in some foreign markets and yet on the other hand may turn to the government for assistance if overseas conditions become unstable. On the whole, as Alexis de Tocqueville observed, "I know of nothing more opposite to revolutionary attitudes than commercial ones. Commerce is naturally adverse to all the violent passions; it loves to temporize, takes delight in compromise, and studiously avoids irritation. It is patient, insinuating, flexible, and never has recourse to extreme measures until obliged by the utmost necessity." His observation is particularly apt to describe the situation before World War II, when the United States was officially neutral in world affairs, leaving each corporation relatively free to pursue its own interests. For example, Henry Ford provided assembly line technology to Russia during the 1920s at a time when the United States refused to recognize that country's government. Such independence was also evident during the Cold War, when Coca Cola was marketed to Communist countries, and when American exporters tried to remain neutral in the midst of Arab–Israeli confrontations in order to sell to both sides.

In general, a multinational corporation does not want to be so closely associated with Washington that it can lose a market because of unpopular government actions. Yet corporations trying to protect their foreign holdings, especially those who face possible expropriation of their overseas assets, do turn to Washington for help. Such has often been the case in Latin America, particularly in the small countries whose economies are not diversified. Yet if American corporations have exerted too much control over some economies, such examples are not representative of overseas operations as a whole. Most American trade is with the developed economies of Asia and Europe, and the vast majority of American businesses do not have a foreign monopoly. For sound economic reasons they try to remain free of political entanglements. Corporations often sell their goods in a nation where the United States government has poor or non-existent diplomatic relations, for example in the Eastern bloc during the 1960s, in Taiwan after the United States diplomatic recognition of mainland China, or in Third World countries during the Vietnam War. The most persistent ambassador for the United States, for good or ill, has often been American enterprise.

# The American Economy

## 1. Development of a Corporate Economy

In 1950 the United States had the highest standard of living in the world. How did it develop in 150 years from an eighteenth-century colonial backwater based on agriculture and the extraction of natural resources into the world's largest economy? The existence of abundant natural resources is part of the explanation, and yet such resources did not make Chile, Mexico, Brazil, or Argentina anywhere near as prosperous. Americans themselves have long stressed the importance of their stable political institutions in fostering prosperity, and certainly there is some truth in this argument. Just as important, few restrictions have impeded the establishment of new businesses. The national government has almost never granted monopoly rights to one company, as was long the custom in Europe. Anyone has the right to incorporate a new company, and most businesses can remain open as long as they wish. In all but a few areas prices are not controlled by any government authority. In short, in the United States, capitalism emerged with few of the restrictions imposed in older societies, where commerce was centrally controlled by the state and by producer unions, such as the guilds.

The German sociologist Max Weber explained the rapid growth of the United States as an instance of his theory of the Protestant Ethic. He noted that the Protestant religion, unlike Catholicism, did not permit a monastic retreat from the world, but rather stressed that an active business career could be an exemplary religious life. For Protestants, work became a form of prayer, and business success became a sign of God's favor. Profits were not to be used for personal amusement or luxury, but were given in trust to the believer, who as a good steward reinvested them for the good of the community. Weber found that sincere Protestants were driven to become honest, productive businessmen who practiced self-denial. Their ascetic form of capitalism lay at the heart of the United States' rapid development. Those who think there is nothing to this theory must explain why an American, regardless of whether he is a factory worker, administrator, or professional, averages less than 10 vacation days a year. (Europeans typically have four or five weeks off.)

Americans often explain their industrial development as a triumph of laissez-faire principles. Certainly, Americans are reluctant to grant a large role to the state, and outsiders are often struck by how many activities are private in the United States that are public elsewhere. Virtually all long-distance transportation is private – including the airlines, freight railways, and bus systems. The telephone system is private, and so is 80 percent of the electrical power service. In European countries, most television and radio is government owned and operated; in the United States, both are private. A great many American hospitals are private, and even the postal system must compete with private companies that deliver packages and important letters faster than they can. The Carter and Reagan administrations deregulated the American airlines, permitting new carriers to enter the market and creating a situation where ticket prices fell dramatically on heavily traveled routes. Reagan even proposed to sell off the National Weather Service. Nor are major artistic institutions paid for with public funds. The symphony orchestras, most major art museums, and almost all theaters are privately funded, as are all churches. Americans generally are suspicious of government, and often quote an old adage: "That government is best which governs least." Indeed, the average American would say that the economy developed through a policy of keeping government out of business.

Despite such popular wisdom, however, American growth was not a simple product of individualism. Throughout the nineteenth century the Federal Government protected American manufacturers from foreign competition with substantial tariffs, which were routinely kept at more than 20 percent and which occasionally soared to higher levels. Furthermore, the United States government used public funds or assets (especially land) to encourage private corporations. In the nineteenth century an elaborate canal, telegraph, and railway network quickly covered much of the nation, in large part because legislatures gave away both land and permission to operate to the private companies. In this way the American transportation network became the most extensive in the world. The policy stimulated the steel and lumber industries, which supplied the thousands of miles of telegraph lines and railway tracks, and it encouraged the metalworking industries which built the cars and locomotives. In part, because Americans gave away land in exchange for internal improvements, they rapidly created an industrial economy which in the 1850s could already challenge England in some areas of manufacturing.

The development of the new transportation network simultaneously transformed American agriculture. Today, slightly less than 3 percent of the population is engaged in agriculture, compared to 7 percent in France, 10 percent in Italy, or 6 percent in Denmark. In 1800 the United States was almost exclusively agricultural, with little industry and only a few small cities; 95 percent of the people then lived on the land. Starting in c. 1825 American farm life changed rapidly, as the new canals and railroads drew farmers into a national market, where they increasingly specialized in a few crops or in particular farm animals. Farmers adopted new technologies to improve productivity, including the steel plow, the mechanical reaper, the barbed wire fence, manufactured fertilizers, the wind mill, scientifically developed hybrid seeds, and better breeding stock. Together, these raised productivity so quickly that farmers chronically overproduced from 1880 on, and prices dropped almost continuously. Millions left the land for good, and by 1900 it was common to speak of the farms, where more than half of all Americans continued to live, as being in crisis. Poor, isolated, and squeezed by falling prices, at the century's end farmers had become dependent on the local banks for credit and on distant markets which determined the value of their crops. From 1900 until 1920 farmers enjoyed a prosperous period, because their own productivity barely kept up with rising urban demand.

Growth of the population and of the transportation network together created an integrated internal market with no trade restrictions, which in the nineteenth century was unmatched anywhere else in the world. The sheer size of this market made possible economies of production and distribution, spurring not only industrial development but making it feasible to create larger factories than ever before. In short, both the size and the integration of the American market were preconditions for the emergence of the great monopolies in the last two decades of the nineteenth century. This new national market was then energized by the coming of electricity and of the internal combustion engine between 1890 and 1920.

Surprisingly, this market emerged without the guidance of a national financial institution. The first national bank had been abolished by President Andrew Jackson, on the grounds that any such bank was a dangerous monopoly. Such attitudes prevented all attempts to regulate the American banking system from Washington until 1913, when Congress finally created the Federal Reserve System, an independent agency of the Federal Government that regulates interest rates and controls the size of the money supply. The chairman of the Federal Reserve is appointed by the President, and thereafter is relatively free from congressional or presidential control. The Federal Reserve Bank is usually able to dampen inflation or soften economic depression, although it can have no direct influence on many aspects of the economy, such as the balance of payments with foreign nations or the size of the national debt. Its chief functions are to ensure a steady supply of money to other banks and to provide a stable environment for corporate activity. In the 1930s, the first Roosevelt administration created an insurance system to protect the savings of individuals even if a bank went bankrupt.

Early corporations tried to control competition through cartels that controlled prices or by buying up the competition. They soon found, however, that price control agreements with their rivals invariably broke down and that buying out the competition was ruinously expensive. By 1900 corporations had learned that they could overwhelm competition by other means. The National Biscuit Company (Nabisco), for example, abandoned the policy of buying up competition, and instead focused on better internal management of its business. It saved through buying materials in huge quantities, it economized in manufacturing by focusing the work in a few large plants, it created a more systematic advertising program, and it improved the quality of its product. Within a few years its Uneeda Bisquit brands dominated the market. Likewise, the American Tobacco Company established a monopoly by first obtaining exclusive rights to the new Bonsack machine, a largely automatic device that could produce huge quantities of cigarettes. With the problem of production solved, marketing had become the key to monopoly control, and the company spent large sums on advertising. A similar combination of superior technology and extensive advertising underlay the rapid growth of the Swift meat-packing company, which adopted refrigerated railway cars that enabled it to reach a national market from centralized slaughter houses in the midwest.

Other large corporations came into being through mergers, including General Electric and United States Rubber, for example, which combined companies that had been major competitors. The new corporations were rigorously rationalized, giving them a competitive advantage not merely because they were larger but because they produced more cheaply and provided comprehensive service, in effect erecting barriers to the entry of new competitors. The largest corporations soon combined these advantages with well-funded research and development programs, which employed small armies of engineers and scientists to invent a stream of product improvements and new devices. The first American corporations were created not by financiers but by managers, and their companies grew because they controlled not only patents, but the whole product cycle from invention to production to marketing.

## 2. Twentieth-Century Developments

The corporation proved extremely flexible, adapting to new circumstances more rapidly than family companies and partnerships. By the 1920s financiers had a greater say in top-level decisions than managers, and vast corporate assets were bought and sold by men who had never seen the companies that changed hands. The creation of the new monopolies rested on an American willingness to abandon traditional forms of business – the family-run firm and the partnership – in favor of corporations run by managers. Where the traditional forms of business always faced problems of transition as their owners aged, corporations hired and fired their managers based on their performance, supplied them with large amounts of capital from the sale of stock, and orchestrated mergers with their competition.

In international perspective the United States was far ahead of Great Britain in abandoning family firms and in changing over to salaried managers who reduced the role of owners to that of outside overseers attending quarterly meetings. While in America this change was well underway by 1910 and substantially complete by 1930, as late as 1940 British companies were rarely under managerial control. The only important exceptions were the large international firms, but even after World War II these amounted to only 20 percent of the top 200 British companies. English holding companies in most cases were cartels of family businesses, which did not adopt managerial capitalism or rationalize their operations like the Americans. Consequently, Germans and Americans were even able to exploit the consumer market inside Britain. England's prolonged reliance on antiquated business organization during the first half of the twentieth century contributed to its loss of much of the international and home market to outsiders.

Just as the American corporate structure was at first unique, so too were its managers. To staff corporations some of the most prestigious American universities invented the modern business school, whose mission was not to turn out commercial lawyers and accountants but to train managers. The University of Pennsylvania, Harvard University, the University of Chicago, and New York University were among the early leaders, by World War I offering courses in such things as railroad operation, industrial organization, and marketing. By the 1920s a steady stream of university trained managers was entering large American corporations, bringing with them a new professionalism, expressed in management societies, business journals, and reliance on specialized consultancy firms.

Once American managers had learned how to run corporations that dominated a single product area, they began to create more diversified companies to spread the risk of their investments over several markets. The decentralization process appears to have started with the DuPont Chemical Corporation which had large war profits to reinvest at the end of World War I. The strategy of diversification quickly spread to other firms and became widespread during the 1920s. Producing and marketing several product lines had the attraction that, as one businessman put it, "Everything doesn't go to hell at once." But there were other good reasons as well.

A corporation with a research laboratory often develops valuable patents for new lines of business.

Both the formation and the diversification of corporations were abetted by mergers. Before the merger mania of the Reagan years, when more than 7,400 companies merged during 1985 and 1986 alone, there were three earlier waves of merger activity in the American economy. The first wave came between 1895 and 1900, leading to the formation of vertically integrated, functionally organized firms such as US Steel and US Rubber. About 1,200 mining and manufacturing companies were involved. The second wave came in the 1920s, particularly after 1924, and was based on the automotive revolution, which had brought with it the assembly line and the economies of large-scale production. In this wave 1,250 companies were involved, which had a somewhat greater net worth. The third wave of the 1960s was larger still. During 1968 alone, 4,400 companies were involved in mergers. To put the matter another way, just 11 firms acquired more than 500 others between 1961 and 1968, and these new acquisitions equalled 92 percent of their assets in 1968. These mergers and those of the Reagan years created diversified companies capable of competing in global markets.

## 3. Government Response to Big Business

The general public has generally opposed the growth of monopolies. In the late nineteenth century, politicians found that attacking the "Trusts" won elections. In 1890, Congress passed the Sherman Anti-Trust Act, which was intended to make monopolies illegal. However, until Theodore Roosevelt became President in 1901, its provisions were little enforced. Under Roosevelt, however, large corporations found themselves under attack. Rockefeller's Standard Oil was broken up into several corporations; Duke's American Tobacco Company was similarly split up. Such "Trust-busting" lawsuits checked the tendency toward absolute monopoly, but Roosevelt did not fundamentally change the movement toward large, consolidated firms. Rather, he established the federal government's role in dissolving absolute monopolies, favoring instead an oligopolistic model in which a few giant firms in each field competed with one another.

During the 1920s government contented itself with establishing industry-wide standards and specifications for many goods, but otherwise did not interfere much with business. The stock-market crash in 1929 and the Depression that followed, however, reawakened demands for more government controls in the marketplace. During the New Deal, President Roosevelt asserted new regulatory powers over the stock market through the Securities and Exchange Commission and over the electric utility in-

*Wall Street in New York City in October 1929, when the stock exchange crashed. – Nordfoto.*

dustry through the Federal Power Commission. Roosevelt also actively intervened in the economy, through deficit spending, job creation, and control of the money supply, with the aim of ending the Great Depression. Considerable government control of the economy necessarily continued during World War II. By 1952, when the Republicans returned to the White House for the first time in two decades, the Democrats had made the executive branch a far more active player in shaping the economy, and despite the laissez-faire rhetoric of some recent administrations, all Presidents since World War II have used their regulatory powers. Independently of the White House, the Federal Reserve Bank controls interest rates and the money supply with the aim of dampening inflation and encouraging moderate growth.

On the whole, business and government have not been on opposite sides. Building upon ties established during the New Deal and solidified during World War II, corporations learned to profit from big government, particularly in three inter-related areas: military contracts, research and development, and aerospace. Already by the end of the 1950s, President Eisenhower warned of the increasing power of what he termed the "military industrial complex." For the first time the United States had a large arms industry dependent upon government spending, which, as Eisenhower noted, amounted to more each year "than the net income of all United States corporations." Lobbyists and Pentagon planners soon learned to make common cause, sounding the alarm over any Soviet advance. When the Russians launched the first orbiting satellite in 1957, it justified a larger defense budget and a new space program, which the Kennedy administration pushed to land a man on the moon in order to "win" the "high ground" of outer space.

By the middle of the 1980s one million Americans worked in defense industries, almost half of them concentrated in New England and on the West Coast. During the Reagan years, when the number of men in the armed forces was far lower than during the Vietnam era, defense procurements rose to record levels. Yet to keep matters in perspective, note that even after the 1980s arms build-up the United States spent less of its Gross National Product on defense than did the Soviet Union (6.4 percent versus 10.7 percent). By 1993, United States' defense spending had declined to 4.7 percent of GNP, $60 billion less than its high point under Reagan. As part of this spending, the government remained the biggest single investor in research and development (R&D), supplying a little less than half of all R&D funds. Two-thirds of this public support still went to defense research, however. Although the United States devotes more resources to R&D than Germany or Japan and publishes 38 percent of the world's scientific literature, nevertheless it does not hold an advantage over either country in non-defense research. The Japanese in particular have developed a unique ability to coordinate private and public investments.

## 4. Corporate America Today

The American economy in the early 1990s was in a period of stagnation, with the result that George Bush found himself extremely unpopular. The weakness of the economy seemed to some merely a part of the business cycle, but it was also caused by the federal deficit and the collapse of hundreds of savings banks which had speculated carelessly or acted unlawfully in the under-regulated business environment of the 1980s. The end of the Cold War also had a serious short-term effect, as many military contracts were canceled. Some regions were particularly hard hit, as a good number of military bases closed down. Yet there were clear signs of underlying strength as well, particularly a surge in exports stimulated by a weaker dollar. By the time Clinton was elected the economy had begun to turn around, and he was able to take credit for eight years of uninterrupted growth when he stepped down.

One strength of the American economy is the relative ease of creating new companies. Not all of American business is concentrated in large corporations. Of course certain services, such as hair-styling, landscaping, or interior decoration, cannot easily be standardized, and, as in all other countries, these remain the province of small business. But more importantly, many small corporations are born each year, often created by a small group of scientists and engineers backed by entrepreneurial capital. Hence the paradox that although the United States apparently is dominated by big corporations, nevertheless there are millions of small businesses, most of them individual proprietorships, such as shops, but also many partnerships and corporations. Seventy-five percent of all corporations have a business volume of less than half a million dollars a year. If the remaining 25 percent control 90 percent of all the business, nevertheless there are successful small companies with niche markets, and some of these grow larger. Microsoft today is an enormous corporation, but 25 years ago it was just a few people writing software. Fueling the hopes of every small company are the examples of such little corporations that grew into giants – Xerox and America on Line to name but two.

Nevertheless, most of today's largest corporations already had emerged by 1920, including General Electric, Ford, General Motors, and United States Steel. While their names are the same, these companies are vastly different from those of 75 years ago. Not only are they much larger, but they have spread across many borders. There is nothing inherently nation-bound in the nature of the corporation, and many American companies today have placed manufacturing plants abroad. They may be inside the European Union, just over the border in Mexico, or in the rapidly developing Asian countries. The reasons for this diversification are many, including not only lower wages in Third World countries, but also avoidance of tariffs, access to new capital, and economies gained by manufacturing close to foreign markets. As a result, corporations are becoming multinational. Some automobiles are joint ventures of Japanese and American companies, which could be designed in California, engineered in Japan, manufactured as components in several countries, and assembled in plants inside each market. Not only is the "nationality" of the resulting car unclear, but the taxes on the profits reaped from its sale can be exceedingly complex. Not surprisingly, governments have an increasingly difficult time regulating the activities of multinationals, or tracking the flow of money by electronic transfers from one continent to another.

But even the man in the street can see that foreign investment in the United States has risen to record levels. Germans have bought a major publishing house, a Japanese corporation bought New York's Rockefeller

Center, and Sony purchased both Columbia Pictures and CBS Records. Indeed, in the early 1980s a historic shift took place, as foreign investment inside the United States became greater than United States investment abroad for the first time since World War I. Half of the investment came from Western Europe, while the Japanese represented only 12 percent of the total. Yet because the Japanese have a multi-billion dollar trade surplus with the United States, and because their automobiles compete so successfully with those made in Detroit, they are popularly perceived as the largest investors. In fact, both Japanese and American corporations are becoming more international, establishing many factories abroad.

Not only do multinational corporations straddle national borders, they engage in a wide variety of activities whose only logical relationship to one another is that they produce profits. For example, General Electric makes components for the aerospace industry, computers, electric railways, plastics, appliances, and nuclear reactors, and it engages in coal mining, to mention only a few of its activities. General Motors makes much more than cars. It produces robots, it is one of the nation's largest lenders, and it works in data-processing, financial services, and artificial intelligence. While these older corporations have diversified, some new corporate giants are conglomerates, such as Litton Industries, which builds ships, operates restaurants, sells packaged foods, makes office equipment, runs several service companies, and probably would happily engage in any other activity which turned a large enough profit. Such conglomerates are assembled from unrelated businesses and are usually run as a decentralized organization, leaving most administrative functions in acquired firms.

The diversification of the corporation was a logical part of the shift from an industrial to a service economy. Where in 1920 the majority of jobs were in the blue-collar sector, since World War II the majority have been white-collar jobs. To a small degree this change has come about because heavy industry has moved to sites beyond American borders, but for the most part the shift registers increasing efficiency in the factory. Factory output per man hour increased by more than 400 percent between 1900 and 1960; that is, on average one factory worker could produce what four had done before. It is inaccurate, therefore, to say that the United States has been de-industrializing. Manufacturing has remained almost exactly 20 percent of the gross national product since 1950. Rather, advanced manufacturing technology has permitted production to rise at the same time that the number of workers has declined. Between 1973 and 1985 five million blue-collar jobs disappeared, even though the total number of jobs increased by nearly 25 million. The trend continued into the next decade, as another 25 million jobs were created. Among the fastest declining jobs, disappearing at a rate of more than 25 percent a decade, are printers, long-distance operators, sewing machine operators, and packing and gluing machine tenders. The areas of rapid growth are all in the service industries or high-tech, notably computer engineers, physical therapists, teachers, legal secretaries, medical workers, and travel agents.

Changes in the workforce reflect changes in the corporation. The classical form of the corporation in 1910 was a functionally organized company in a capital-intensive industry. (In contrast, labor-intensive manufacturing, such as furniture-making, was far less susceptible to control by a few large corporations and remained decentralized.) As the majority of workers shifted from manufacturing to white-collar work, however, the character of the corporation was bound to change as well. The service economy that emerged rapidly after 1920 was manager-intensive. It required large capital combined with skilled teamwork. Individualism gradually became a secondary corporate virtue, of less importance than cooperation and flexibility.

This white-collar world grew and flourished from the 1920s until the last decades of the twentieth century. Its workforce was organized into a hierarchy in which managers held most of the power. Large corporations dominated the economy. During the 1980s and after this began to change, however. Less hierarchical, smaller companies that used computers and the Internet to the maximum grew rapidly, transforming established markets. In this so-called "new economy" electronic equipment, services, information, and software proved immensely profitable. Companies that few had heard of or which did not even exist in 1980 joined the 100 largest in the American economy by 2000, including Microsoft, Intel, and America Online. Technology stocks also drove up the value of the stock markets at an unheard of pace, so that the Dow Jones Industrial Average more than tripled during the 1990s. Since half of American families now own stocks, this surge also created strong consumer demand. By the end of the Clinton years a new kind of economy seemed to exist, one that combined low unemployment with little wage inflation and high growth.

## 5. Farmers and Workers

Agriculture has also been transformed by high technology. One half of all Americans still lived on farms in 1920. Between 1950 and 1993 the farm population declined from 23 million to 4.6 million, while the average farm doubled in size to 480 acres. This change affected regions unequally, as New England and the Middle Atlantic States lost almost 75 percent of their farmers, so that today but one person in 125 lives on a farm. Even in the midwest only 5 percent of the population works in agriculture. Tilling double the acreage with only a fraction of the previous manpower means that agricultural work is mechanized as never before, with each farm investing huge sums in machinery. In most cases, however, the industrialized farm of the midwest is still a family operation. So-called agribusiness, or farming by corporations, is not well suited to all kinds of agriculture. Indeed, businessmen are often wary of investments in farming because of its high degree of unpredictability. For example, farmland nearly doubled in value between 1970 and 1980, due to world food shortages and predictions of global famine, but it dropped in value just as rapidly during the early 1980s. Farmers, who had been urged to borrow and expand up to the limit, suddenly found themselves uncomfortably close to bankruptcy.

Agribusiness focuses on predictable agriculture, which in practice often means farming based on irrigation. The Tejon Ranch Corporation near Los Angeles, for example, is listed on the American Stock Exchange. Made possible by new irrigation water that came into a dry farming area in the 1970s, it required more than $50 million for development, including a computer-controlled piping system. Tejon Ranch specializes in grapes, citrus fruits, nuts, figs, and expensive vegetables. Some of these plants are genetically transformed. It requires 66 tractors, 50 jeeps and trucks, and a private airplane to farm land in this way. A journalist who studied the ranch closely concluded that it was not as efficient as individual farmers, but gained a good deal from tax laws favorable to such investments and from the privilege of getting irrigation water. He concluded, "It seemed as if the corporation could buy workers' time, managers' time, planners' time, and even all of their skills, but that to buy a human's sense of responsibility is beyond the reach of big business." Farming remains for most not a corporate investment, but a way of life.

Slightly less than 20 percent of American workers are members of trade unions, however, in contrast to most of the European nations where well over half of all workers are. One result of this situation in the United States is that the minimum wage is only about half that of the Scandinavian countries, although the average wage is comparable. White-collar jobs in banks, offices, schools, or retail stores usually are not unionized, nor are the newer industrial jobs such as computer manufacturing. Unionized workers are concentrated in older manufacturing industries and the construction trades; on average they make 33 percent more than non-union workers.

In most industrial countries workers made a united response to industrialization and the growth of monopolies. By the early twentieth century strong union movements and labor parties were among the greatest polit-

*Union Organizer addressing longshore workers in the 1930s. – UPI.*

ical forces in Germany, England, or France. Yet in the United States unions never organized a majority of the workers, nor did they create a national political party that could displace either the Republicans or the Democrats. The high-water mark for the Socialist Party came in the decade before World War I, when it polled nearly one million votes in a presidential election and elected mayors in a number of industrial cities, such as Schenectady and Milwaukee. In the same years the International Workers of the World (IWW) also became influential among many workers, as they led a series of strikes in coalfields, western mines, and textile mills. Owners and local governments often met militancy with violence, most dramatically perhaps in the Colorado strike of 1903-1904, in which troops occupied towns and violated the Bill of Rights with impunity, but ultimately failed to intimidate the miners, led by Big Bill Haywood, who won the strike. Such gains were short-lived, however, and unions were weak during the 1920s. Despite (or perhaps because of) the rapid rise to an advanced form of capitalism, workers did not create a political alternative to liberalism.

The reasons for American exceptionalism in this case must be traced back at least to the middle of the previous century. By the 1880s it was clear that in a country with great internal mobility and a constant stream of new immigrant workers unions would have difficulties uniting industry-wide. Instead, under the guidance of the American Federation of Labor, craft unions organized skilled workers by trade. Such craft unions succeeded because they monopolized a scarce commodity: skill. As a result, American workers were soon divided into a large number of separate unions, whose members were more loyal to those with the same skill than to those who worked in the same plant. This condition itself did not favor creation of a large labor party, but a more severe political difficulty was the heterogeneity of immigrant backgrounds. In the late nineteenth century, European enmities reappeared in America. How could a labor organizer expect immigrants from Ireland and England to get along? Or those from Germany and Poland, Russia and Austria, Yugoslavia and Greece? Old World hatreds did not die out easily. Immigrants tended to live in distinctive neighborhoods, from Chinatown to Little Italy, and to organize along ethnic lines.

*Workers striking against the J.P. Stevens textile plant, seeking the right to unionize, 1976. – AP.*

Italians joined the Knights of Columbus, and Norwegians joined the Sons of Norway.

In asking why socialism remained weak in America, then, part of the answer is ethnic diversity, another part is the split between the skilled and the unskilled, as well as the divisions between the different craft unions. Moreover, during the late nineteenth and early twentieth centuries, American workers had weaker incentives to become socialists than European workers, since they enjoyed a higher standard of living. The average American worker in 1900 dressed better and ate better than his European counterpart, and was more likely to own his home. Radical leadership was also a problem. After 1920 communist leaders constantly shifted tactics under the direction of the Soviets, who had little understanding of United States politics. Furthermore, the American press was long overwhelmingly conservative, encouraging American workers to hold fast to the ideology of individualism.

Despite all these impediments, during the hard times of the 1930s unions grew in strength, successfully organizing most workers in heavy industries such as automobiles and steel manufacturing. While a minority joined radical groups, the majority of union members largely remained within the Democratic party, as Roosevelt's New Deal programs satisfied many of their most pressing demands. After World War II union strength remained concentrated in the heavy industries that had been organized before 1940. In 1948 the United Auto Workers won an important victory: automatic wage increases to keep pace with increases in the cost of living. But while the old unions prospered, conservative post-war legislation made it difficult to create new ones. The Taft–Hartley Act of 1947 forbade the creation of "closed shops" or workplaces restricted to union members only, and state legislatures added other laws that hindered union organizers. During the 1950s union membership remained stable at about 16 million, and failed to keep pace with the growth of the labor force. By 1990, even though the actual number of union members had increased slightly, only one worker in five had joined. The newer white-collar jobs remained largely non-union, with the significant exception of government workers. Gradually, much of the public lost sympathy with unions. Indeed, President Reagan enjoyed the support of the majority of the population when he virtually destroyed the air traffic controllers' union by firing most of its membership after they went on strike.

Perhaps the most serious problems faced by unions were in manufacturing, where corporations continually adopted new technologies, transforming their modes of production and reducing the number of employees to a minimum. As unions weakened, there were human costs. In 1989 American newspapers ran a story on hazards in the workplace, noting that as the number of production workers decreases, due to automation and cost-cutting, the dangers to workers in some industries increase. As assembly line speed goes up in the name of efficiency, so do the number of workers who are injured. In the meat packing industry, for example, the number of employees dropped by 10,000 in the last five years of the 1980s, while production increased by almost 20 percent. The human cost has been repetitive trauma disorder for meat packers, who must continuously cut and chop. This is a sometimes disabling ailment of the hand, arm or wrist, in which the tendons swell painfully and the worker loses most of the strength in the hands. Some computer operators have had similar problems. Overall, the industrial accident death rate in the United States is significantly higher than in European countries. Thirty-six out of every one million employees die in accidents each year in the United States, compared with ten out of every million in France, eight in Germany, four in England, and one in Sweden. These differences can in part be explained by the greater danger of some work in the United States, which has large extractive industries such as coal mining and lumbering. But the figures are also another testimony to the weakness of American unions, who often are unable to control the dangers posed by the implementation of new technologies and find themselves limited to discussions of wages and benefits.

## 6. Looking Ahead

The twentieth century has often been called "The American Century," a phrase that accurately suggests the rise to dominance of the United States between 1900 and the 1990s. It is unlikely that this dominance can long continue into the new century, however. There are two sets of arguments to support this prediction, those that have to do with foreign affairs and those which are domestic.

The United States is the world's greatest military power at the dawn of the new millennium and the predominance of English as the global language of science, the Internet, and business, ensures a central place to the United States in the coming century. Yet its economy no longer produces one third of the world's goods, as it did in c. 1920. The greatest opportunities for growth lie in Asia, where China and India each have populations four times as large as the United States. There, too, the "tiger" economies of nations such as South Korea, Taiwan, and Malaysia have already shown that Japan is by no means the only Asian nation capable of mastering advanced technologies and competing in the global marketplace. At the same time, the launch of the Euro currency and the expansion of the European Union to include new members has created a counter-weight to the North

American free trade zone of the US, Mexico, and Canada. If in terms of sheer size, the US economy continues to grow, as a percentage of the world economy it is becoming smaller.

Not only is the US economy becoming a diminishing part of the world's economy, but also the globalization of business is eroding the centrality of the American market. In one sense, this globalization represents the triumph of American business values, but in another sense, globalization erodes the importance of nations, merging them into larger markets and into international organizations. Environmental problems such as global warming and energy shortages will almost certainly increase the pressure to think internationally, rather than in more narrow, national terms. Smaller countries have learned this lesson already, but it appears to be difficult for larger countries to recognize their interdependence, and hardest of all for the United States, as the last remaining superpower, to do so. Regrettably, Washington has not been a leader in reducing global air pollution, for example, and the 2000 election campaign did not result in an environmentally sensitive administration. Quite the contrary, President Bush, as a former (failed) oil entrepreneur, wants to drill for more oil on public lands and nature reserves. His Cabinet has many ties to the oil industry, and as a whole is full of experts from the "old economy" with ties to the automobile industry and pharmaceuticals, but no one from a firm such as Microsoft or Intel.

Which brings us to some domestic reasons why the United States may slip from its current position of global hegemony. While the economy remains dynamic, the objects selected for development may not be those best suited for the long-term. The huge American investments in private automobiles and highways have created a rigid infrastructure that sprawls across a large landscape, in contrast to other nations that have invested in high-speed trains and public transportation that concentrate the population and give them more flexibility of movement. In much of the United States, consumers have no choice but to use their automobiles even to make the smallest purchase. When energy shortages return, Americans will be unable easily to alter their consumption patterns to respond to the crisis. In the marketplaces for housing, transportation and conveniences, the majority of American consumers have ignored long-term environmental problems such as global warming, and thought too little about the energy needs of the rest of the world, while insisting on their consumption (and pollution) practices. The central institution involved in these patterns of consumption remains the American family.

# 7. A Typical Family Economy

The median American family annual income in 1997 was $44,568 a year. To satisfy its most basic needs, it spent $13,700 on housing, including heating, utilities, and telephone, and $4,800 for food. The father worked full time, while the mother worked in another occupation and received 78 percent as much per hour. After deductions for children and interest payments on the house, they pay income tax, but at rates that seem impossibly low to Europeans. American tax rates in the 1950s ranged from 20–90 percent, but the Tax Reduction Act of 1964 lowered them to from 14–70 percent. Further reductions followed, most dramatically the Tax Reform Act of 1986. Additional reductions in federal income taxes were expected in 2001.

If taxes are low, however, Americans face four large expenses, which most Europeans pay for through one comprehensive income tax. Indeed, at the level of the family budget, one can clearly see the American emphasis on private rather than public funding for health, education, and welfare. Most conspicuous perhaps is the American pension system. Social security payments toward an old age pension are obligatory on most jobs, and cost up to 7.15 percent of wages. Yet these payments are inadequate to ensure a comfortable retirement, and the median family of 1997 also paid $3,223 into pension schemes and life insurance. A second large expense is the town property tax that pays for local schools, and which is indexed to the value of the family home. Third, there is a state income tax, which varies between 0 percent (New Hampshire) and 14 percent (New York), but which on average is 4 or 5 percent. Fourth, the government only provides medical care to the destitute, the elderly, and war veterans. To protect itself, the typical family spent $2,400 for health care and doctor's bills, plus medical insurance and the often considerable expense of dental care. When a pension, local property tax, state income tax, and medical costs are added to federal income taxes, the difference in expenses paid by European and American families is considerably reduced. Note that the American rejects comprehensive state funded programs, and retains the right to select his or her expenses, to live in a state or town with lower taxes, to buy more or less medical insurance, to save for a child's university education or not.

Furthermore, in contrast to Europeans whose taxes help support comprehensive public transportation, Americans cannot realistically expect to have sufficient mobility to shop, work, and live in their society without at least one automobile for the family. Indeed, by 1985 there were two cars for every three adult Americans. The typical family of four might start out with only one car, but if both parents work – as is increasingly the case – both will likely have automobiles. Teen-aged children often manage to buy an older car by the time they leave high school. In Los Angeles, there is one automobile for every adult. Insurance on all these vehicles is often more expensive than in European countries (particularly those which have free public health care), because American automobile owners must cover the hospital expenses of anyone injured in an accident, not to mention the possibility of a million dollar law suit. Finally, parking the car is often expensive, particularly in the larger cities, where a private space may cost hundreds of dollars a month. Taken all around, owning and operating automobiles demands $6,500 from the median American family, which spends more for transportation than for food. Finally, if there are children, and on average there will be two, the cost of bringing them up will be great. There is no free day care, only minimal free dental or medical care through the schools, and perhaps most important of all in a nation where education is considered vital to success, no free university. In short, while Americans enjoy a lower tax rate than citizens of most other industrial nations, in exchange they must pay for many large expenses as they arise

Finally, there is the expense of moving. When the parents are between ages 20 and 30, chances are the family will move every three years, often to a nearby place within the same county. After age 30 there will be two more moves before the parents reach age 45. With each change, the likelihood is greater that they no longer rent an apartment but have bought a house in a metropolitan region, somewhere in the suburbs where two-thirds of all Americans prefer to live. The average house has six rooms and two bathrooms and it costs $152,000 if new, $128,000 if used. To buy one requires a down payment of 25 percent of the purchase price. Put another way, the typical 1997 family used about one third of its disposable income to pay the mortgage, and housing prices are rising much faster than incomes. As recently as 1980 home ownership required only one-sixth of household income. Despite the apparent boom of the late 1990s, both wages and costs were rising and many citizens did not enjoy higher real incomes than they did two decades earlier. Thus the rapid growth of the 1990s did not alter the American class structure, to which we now turn.

# Class, Race, and Gender

## 1. Class

In April of 1992 televised images of the Los Angeles riots showed crowds looting and burning shops, a powerful reminder that wealth is divided unevenly in the United States today. No industrial nation has entirely abolished poverty, but for generations Americans have hoped to attain this egalitarian goal. During the prosperous 1960s, the nation had even waged a "war on poverty," determined to "wipe it out." The *Declaration of Independence* decrees that all men are created equal and that they have the right to life, liberty, and the pursuit of happiness. Americans do believe that every person is as good as the next, and that they are equal before the law. But given this initial equality, they see themselves in a race for success, which can be measured in terms of wealth. They do not favor high taxes to redistribute income.

### Distribution of total income

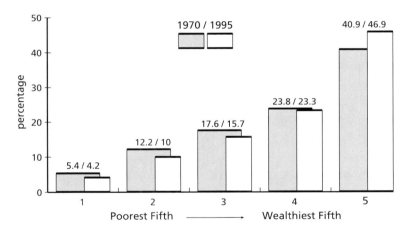

The gap between rich and poor is substantial, and it has grown larger in the last quarter century. In 1995 the top fifth of the population received over 46 percent of the income, while the poorest fifth had to make do with only 4.2 percent. This distribution has not changed a great deal during the twentieth century, though it has become less egalitarian in the last twenty-five years. During World War II, industries offered full employment, and the working class became relatively richer. Likewise, the social programs intro-

*John D. Rockefeller, just before his 96th birthday in 1935. – Wide World.*

duced in the 1960s tended to increase the income of the poor. During the 1980s and 1990s, however, the wealthy increased their share of the total income.

Given this unequal distribution of income in the United States, it would seem plausible to assume that Americans must have a sharp awareness of social class. In fact, they do not. There are no hereditary titles. No one at birth is a duke or a count, and Americans believe that anyone may rise to great wealth. Social class in the United States is not simply a matter of wealth, of course. Old money has more prestige than new. Education is also important, and not just anywhere. Older universities, especially those with the most rigorous admission standards, are more highly valued than others. With inherited wealth and a good education come a set of manners. While the newly rich tend to flaunt their money through conspicuous consumption, old money is quiet, hidden, unobtrusive. One analyst concluded that the highest classes were those who were almost literally out of sight. Their houses are not visible from the road, their social functions are not described in the newspapers, and their clothing or behavior usually does not draw much attention. By comparison, the professional athletes, movie stars and TV personalities who are so visible in the media are, despite their wealth, literally not in the same class.

Since those with inherited wealth are largely invisible, they do not provide role models for most people, who see themselves as being members of the middle class. This group is defined less by income than by having attended college (even if only for a few years), holding a white-collar job, and living in the suburbs. People are acutely aware of the relative costs of housing in different suburbs, but this does not translate into a sense that new social classes arise with each increment in income. The middle 60 percent (or the middle three fifths) of the population shares a style of life defined by commuting, television, suburbia, children, support for local sports teams, and so on. The fact that some people drive newer or more expensive cars or have larger houses in somewhat better suburban areas does not define a class line. These gradations mark the ladder of success which each hopes to climb.

If Americans wish to identify with the working class, this can prove difficult. The constant mobility of the American population prevents the formation of strong community ties. Furthermore, the blue-collar workforce has not only declined in numbers but it has a wide variation of incomes within it. "Blue-collar aristocrats" such as crane operators, machine builders, electricians, plumbers, or computer technicians are far better paid than most white-collar workers. In contrast, non-union industries may offer a salary that is just above the poverty line.

The vast majority of Americans readily claim to be part of the middle class. However, a lack of class identification is a part of American ideology, which makes each individual responsible for his own fate. A person who fails to find a job habitually blames himself, not the state or the economy. An American who is poor usually does not hate the rich, but rather expects that he or his children will emulate them. One of Theodore Dreiser's characters goes out for a drive to see "the fine houses of the millionaires, which were then nearly all on Prairie Avenue. Money to him was a wonderful thing. The application of the term millionaire was as grand as the possession of a title. Like all Americans, he confessed a certain amount of scorn for the latter, but accepted its equivalent, with almost pathetic admiration." Americans recognize class distinctions, but they do so only in order to create a standard they can measure up to. They expect to rise to a higher social position.

Yet are Americans upwardly mobile? In terms of what they own, they are. During the twentieth century most people have experienced a distinct improvement in their material life, because their buying power and wealth has improved. When Americans compare themselves to their grandparents, they usually see two obvious improvements. First, they see that two generations ago most jobs were in the blue-collar sector or agriculture. Today most jobs are in the white-collar sector. Second, Americans can also see a measurable advance in terms of property ownership. Immigrants almost invariably arrived with little, and their descendants can see a marked improvement, particularly in terms of home ownership. Likewise, between 1940 and 1970 most Americans experienced a real gain in their per capita disposable income. On average they had more money available each year after meeting fixed expenses such as mortgages and taxes. Coupled with this increase in discretionary income, the prices of some consumer goods have actually declined while their quality has improved, including such items as radios, stereos, cameras, and washing machines. During the twentieth century the average family has experienced material progress, which is often understood to be a kind of social mobility. They have more and better things than their grandparents. Yet when the population is viewed as a whole, these material improvements occurred without markedly changing the distribution of wealth or the families that hold that wealth. Hence the paradox: most Americans believe that their families have been upwardly mobile, even though most of them remain in roughly the same class position vis-à-vis the rest of the population.

During the 1970s, however, median family incomes ceased to advance. Peaking in 1973, total income (and hence discretionary income) stagnated or declined for a decade, regardless of whether one was Black, White, or Hispanic. Yet if income stagnated in the 1970s, this did not lead to a general recognition of class stratification, but rather to an intensification of the struggle to get ahead. During the Reagan years family income again began to rise, but the gains were unequally distributed, as Whites made larger gains than Blacks or Hispanics. These inequities were felt all the more during the economic stagnation of the early 1990s, and they were not overcome when the economy began to improve.

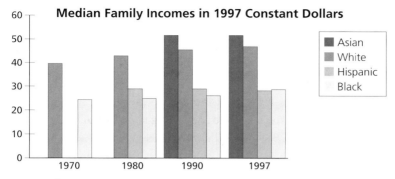

**Median Family Incomes in 1997 Constant Dollars**

- Asian
- White
- Hispanic
- Black

Separate figures on Hispanics were not compiled before 1973.
Source:*Statistical Abstract of the United States 2000.*

What was making class differences greater? Productivity gains were not being translated into higher wages. Only the top fifth of all wage-earners benefited. The real wages of the other 80 percent of the work force fell 18 percent between 1973 and 1995. Yet output per person was going up by 25 percent in the same years. Management used computers and automation to eliminate many semi-skilled jobs and to weaken union power. Factory computerization made possible "lean production." Highly-paid but only semi-skilled workers in the automobile industry were particularly vulnerable. In 1991 General Motors laid off 74,000 workers, 18 percent of their labor force. A parallel process occurred in the white-collar world, and was usually called "re-engineering." Some routine decision-making and form-processing could be incorporated in computer software, reducing the time required and the number of employees needed. Companies that computerized often adopted a "flat structure," which eliminated layers of middle management, leading to lay-offs and job insecurity among those who remained. In light of these changes, ordinary Americans have begun to discuss class differences more in the late 1990s than they have since the 1930s.

## 2. Race

In the United States almost every issue ultimately has a racial dimension, whether housing, schools, work, military service, or crime, to take some of the most obvious examples. Housing discrimination against African Americans has been an endemic problem, and, while now illegal, no law can prevent Whites from moving out of a neighborhood if Blacks move in. Once some Whites depart, housing values fall, and the rest soon follow. The phenomenon is called "White flight." In a society where people move frequently anyway, an entire neighborhood can become predominantly Black in only one decade. Harlem is a good example. It shifted from being a White to a Black area of New York during World War I and just after. Changes in housing immediately affect the schools, not only in the obvious sense of who goes to the school, but also in its financing, which depends on local property taxes. If housing values fall, the school has less money. The neighborhood is no longer attractive to families with young children, and middle-class Black families also try to leave it.

Jobs are another area of racial tension, especially during periods of high unemployment. Black and Hispanic Americans are often the last hired and the first fired, and they have higher rates of joblessness. A generally poorer level of education for inner-city youth contributes to this unemployment. Since work is hard to find, many minorities join the military, which promises regular pay, training, and veterans benefits. The American all volunteer army is more than 25 percent African-American. These are the success stories. The poor who stay in the inner-city live in a world with few opportunities and a good deal of crime. In 1994, 46 percent of all American prison inmates were African-American, most of them males. It costs about as much to put a man in prison for one year as it would cost to send him to the university.

While there is also a growing African-American middle class, its members still face discrimination. They are less likely to identify themselves with Whites who have a similar income than with other Black people. Class identification in the United States thus is undercut by ethnic and racial di-

*During the Los Angeles riots of 1992 1,800 Korean-owned businesses were destroyed. – Black Star/Ifot.*

visions. An Italian American who works in a factory may identify more with an Italian in management than with a fellow African-American worker.

In the last two decades, the racial tension between Whites and Blacks has been complicated by the influx of Hispanic and Asian immigrants. Hispanics have achieved much political and economic success in a single generation, and will be the largest minority group by 2010. Some African Americans feel that they have been passed over once again, while a new immigrant group is being welcomed into the mainstream. This is not an abstract argument, but a question of who is preferred by employers. But Black-Latino relations are comfortable compared to their relation to Asians. African Americans have been around for almost four centuries; Asians little more than a century. When Koreans or Vietnamese set up small businesses and make a tidy living from them, or when their children graduate from the best American universities, Blacks somewhat understandably feel that something must be wrong. During the Los Angeles riots of 1992 1,800 Korean-owned businesses were destroyed. Korean Americans used small arms to defend their businesses against looters and arsonists, many of whom were Black. The *Los Angeles Times* editorialized: "The popular notion that Los Angeles was transforming itself into a harmonious, multi-ethnic model city seemed to waft away in the smoke billowing over the city. Each new televised image – Black, Latin and white looters rampaging through ruined stores, mostly White police officers and National Guard soldiers, dazed motorists beaten by angry Black assailants, frightened Korean merchants guarding their shuttered markets with guns – threatened to reinforce fears and prejudices." Likewise, racial incidents have increased on American university campuses in the 1990s, often polarizing students into racially-based interest groups.

Racial problems have a long history. Even before the Mayflower landed in New England in 1620, the first African slaves were imported into Virginia. By the time slavery was abolished more than 200 years later during the Civil War, Blacks had lost many of their African customs and all but traces of their original languages, in contrast to the slaves in Haiti and Brazil who kept more of their language and culture. In the United States it had been illegal to educate a slave, and after emancipation virtually none were able to read and write. Since most of them lived in the agricultural South, at first they continued to live and work as farmers and share-croppers. A much smaller number of educated free Blacks existed in the North at the end of the Civil War. They were concentrated in cities, where they lived in ghettos. Indeed, the ghetto was a Northern invention that was completely inappropriate in the South, where slaves lived among and served White people and had intimate daily contact with them. Only the North had developed an aversive form of racism, granting Blacks some rights but isolating them in separate communities. In contrast, after 1865 Southerners did not avoid Black people, but gradually imposed a complex set of laws and customs, designed to "keep them in their place." These so-called "Jim Crow laws" created separate schools, separate drinking fountains, separate restaurants, and even separate entrances to public buildings, as a constant reminder to Blacks that they were socially inferior. Faced with this systematic racism, which denied them political power, between 1865 and 1965 almost half of the Black population of the South left for the North. Much of this migration is comparatively recent. Detroit was 9 percent Black in 1940, but it is two-thirds Black today. Those who stayed behind relied on a tightly knit local community focused on the church, with clergy taking the leadership roles.

In the 1950s southern ministers such as Martin Luther King organized Black protest movements, which pushed for the desegregation of public institutions, Black voter registration, and increased political power. Nevertheless, today, African Americans are mostly in the bottom half of the population, trapped there because they lack the education and specialized skills needed in the better jobs of a high-tech economy. For a time this seemed to be a temporary problem that would be overcome as a result of the successes of the Civil Rights Movement. After the Supreme Court declared school segregation illegal in its landmark *Brown v. Board of Education* decision in 1954, Blacks at least in theory had access to the same education as Whites. Likewise, the passage of the *Civil Rights Act* and the *Voting Rights Act* in the 1960s seemed to ensure fuller Black participation in American political life.

Yet at that very moment the American ghettos erupted in violence, fuelled by frustration. During the summer of 1965 the Watts area of Los Angeles was virtually destroyed. There were more disturbances the next year, and in 1967 terrible riots took place in Newark and Detroit, where 43 people died, hundreds were injured, and the damage was in the millions. Accompanying these violent protests was a new rhetoric of Black power. Many African Americans declared that they did not want to integrate into White society. The Student Non-Violent Coordinating Committee renounced the non-violence tactics that it had used in sit-ins and marches, and called for militant resistance to oppression. Its leader, H. Rap Brown, quoted Chairman Mao: power came from the barrel of a gun. While Martin Luther King was assassinated in April, 1968, riots broke out in over 100 cities, including Washington, where buildings were on fire only a few blocks from the White House.

During the 1970s, the Black community gained more political control over its own destiny. They elected Black mayors, including Los Angeles, Cleveland, Detroit, Chicago, Atlanta, and, in 1989, New York. Today there are over 7,000 African-American elected officials, including 300 mayors. At first, Black economic and educational gains seemed to mirror these changes in politics. During the 1960s American universities began actively to recruit Blacks, spurred by a guilty conscience that soon was reinforced by Federal laws. Within the academy some African Americans refused to assimilate White values, but rather demanded the creation of Black Studies programs and the inclusion of their culture in literature, art, and history. In the same years African Americans improved their income relative to Whites, but this trend was reversed in the more stagnant economy of the 1970s, when only the small Black middle class continued to make real gains, while the majority of Black people did not.

The continuing failure to integrate the majority of African Americans into the economy is reflected both in their lower pay and in their higher rate of unemployment, which usually is twice as high as the rate for Whites. A variety of explanations have been offered for this divergence, which is made all the more striking by the more successful assimilation of Asians into the economy. Inevitably, racists claim that Blacks simply are inferior. Radicals blame institutional racism and the system of capitalism itself. Liberals often argue that Blacks are caught in a "culture of poverty," meaning that they grow up in surroundings that undermine self-confidence and discipline. A variant of this explanation blames Black family organization.

Whatever the truth of such theories, none can deny that for centuries Blacks were simply denied both education and the better jobs. To end such discrimination, the federal government passed laws requiring that minorities be given preference in hiring. This form of affirmative discrimination is called "Affirmative Action," and in theory it means African Americans will be hired more readily than Whites. In practice, however, the policy has had less effect than anticipated. Studies have found that Black males on average had a better chance of getting a white-collar job before Affirmative Action went into effect in 1970 than they did eight years later in 1978. In education the picture is less gloomy, as the Black rates of high school graduation and college attendance have approached those of Whites. Nevertheless, though better qualified than before, African Americans are still discriminated against. In 1998, their unemployment rate was 8.9 percent, more than twice that of Whites, and somewhat worse than the Hispanic rate of 7.2 percent.

Black poverty and unemployment in turn have an effect on family structure. Only half of all African-American families have both parents present, compared with 85 percent of White families. Some blame the structure of the American welfare system for the absence of Black men from so many families. Single mothers were once eligible for larger welfare payments than families with both parents present. But extensive studies have found that the organization of welfare payments does not encourage women to live alone or to have more children. A large number of Black families have long been headed by women, but this fact only became obvious as programs of aid to dependent children expanded. Whether the Black family has been weakened by economic hardship or not, African Americans utilize a more extended family structure than Whites, perhaps because they have greater need for a system of mutual support.

## 3. Gender

Divisions based on class and on race are further complicated by the gender gap, which grew wider as the United States became an urban, industrial nation. When most men and women were farmers, they shared many tasks and worked together in the same space. By the 1830s, however, society had become urbanized and class distinctions had increased to the point that some men worked outside the home while their wives ostentatiously did not need to work. These ladies defined a middle-class ideal of leisure, in contrast to both farmers' wives and the mill girls in the new factories. At this time, virtually no women received an advanced education or worked in the professions.

Historically, the two problems of racial and gender discrimination have intertwined. Many women were active in the anti-slavery campaigns. In the process of fighting against the slave system they became aware of parallels between the oppression of Blacks and their own situation. Two southern women wrote: "The female slaves are our countrywomen, they are our sisters, and to us as women, they have a right to look for sympathy with their sorrows. . . . Women ought to feel a peculiar sympathy in the colored man's wrong, for like him, she has been accused of mental inferiority, and denied the privileges of a liberal education." Women could not vote, they could not attend the university, and their rights were subordinated to those of fathers, brothers, and husbands. When lecturing against slavery, women faced harassment for appearing in public as speakers. They were told it was undignified and unladylike to engage in such activities. Nor were such attitudes presented as mere opinion, as women confronted "scientific" biological theories which denied that they were men's intellectual equals, and which declared that too much mental development in a woman could damage her reproductive organs.

In the nineteenth century women were told to stay at home, which was to be their sole sphere of influence. New brides were warned that bad housekeeping could ruin a marriage, and they were urged to make the home a nurturing, peaceful environment animated by religious values. Women were to be passive, pure, and polite. Men were to engage in the demanding strife of business, while their wives remained untainted repositories of virtue, maintaining the home as a "haven in a heartless world." They were subject to their husband or father in ways that were milder than slavery, but nevertheless placed them in a legally inferior position. Little wonder that in 1848 a group of women met at Seneca Falls, New York to formulate a *Declaration of the Rights of Women*, which was to be the basic feminist document of the nineteenth century. In it, using language that echoed the *Declaration of Independence*, they called for equality with men, including the right to vote. Indeed, but two decades later in 1869 the western territory of Wyoming granted women the vote, followed in the 1890s by Colorado, Utah, and Idaho. For the remainder of the nineteenth century, winning female suffrage became the central women's issue, but not the only one. Women fought to gain admission to professional schools, so they could become doctors, dentists, and lawyers. They also played a central role in successful campaigns to ban child labor, to abolish the sale of alcohol, to bring home economics into school curriculums, and to create new public parks. During the same period women's universities were established, to give them access to the same education that men enjoyed. Other campaigns were less successful. For example, both abortion and the sale of birth control devices remained illegal in much of the United States well into the twentieth century.

Most leaders of the suffrage movement came from the middle and upper classes. But women were also active in the formation of labor unions, particularly in the garment industry and textile mills. They focused on different issues: pay, safety, and working conditions. If nineteenth-century middle-class women were not expected to work, working-class women often had little choice. Canneries and textile mills at times hired entire families, including children. For such working women, the central struggle was that of getting equal pay for equal work.

While women won the right to vote in time for the presidential election of 1920, after that victory their political status did not dramatically change. Women did not form their own party or become powerful within the existing parties, and only a few women ran for office in the following decades. There were other changes in social mores, however. Divorce, which had been rare in the nineteenth century, became more common. In the 1920s women learned to drive automobiles, and they asserted their right to smoke cigarettes and drink in public. Young women adopted the boyish flapper-look, and many moved into white-collar jobs. As a host of new labor-saving appliances came on the market, such as electric vacuum cleaners, washing machines, and irons, it seemed that women were being emancipated from the home. In fact, the time devoted to housework remained the same, over 50 hours a week for a married woman with children.

During World War II millions of women were drawn into the workforce for the first time and became accustomed to the independence that came with a regular pay check. While many lost their jobs when factories retooled for post-war production, they soon were back in the workforce, where female participation increased throughout the 1950s. Like Blacks, women found that they had their "place" in the job market, with less authority and lower pay than White men. They seldom were promoted to managerial positions. While there has been some progress in getting women into the professions, gender segregation of work remains widespread. In 1994, women were still 98 percent of the secretaries, 94 percent of the nurses, 88 percent of the waiters and waitresses, 86 percent of the elementary school teachers, and 82 percent of the librarians. Meanwhile, men held more than 80 percent of the jobs as engineers, architects, and doctors.

Reacting against such discrimination and against the little-valued role of being a housewife, during the 1960s a second wave of feminism began. Again it emerged in tandem with a Black struggle for equality. Women involved in the Civil Rights movement realized that discrimination in the workplace based on gender was not so different from discrimination based on race. Thus it is fitting that both women and African Americans are covered by laws on Affirmative Action, which have gradually reshaped many corporate board rooms and university faculties. The law requires that women and Blacks be actively sought to fill vacant positions and that written reports be filed to explain what actions were taken. Companies and schools are required to interview minority candidates or they face certain loss of Federal grants and subsidies. Those failing to hire women and minorities in sufficient numbers over time also risk losing all Federal money. Similar guidelines govern all institutions and corporations that receive government contracts.

In the universities women not only have taken many more positions, but they have challenged the traditional curriculum. In literature they have attacked the largely male canon of American literature, arguing that Edith Wharton must be included with Henry James, Willa Cather with Ernest Hemingway. In traditional male bastions such as economics and political science they have questioned fundamental assumptions about the existence of "political man" and "economic man," and persuasively argued that contrary to previous theorizing, men and women cannot be treated identically. Within the field of history they have created an impressive body of scholarship, reclaiming the past so that it includes women as well as men. In history departments today the interest in African Americans, women, workers, and minorities has to a considerable extent displaced interest in social, intellectual, and economic elites.

Success inside the academy does not always translate into gains outside it, however. Pregnancy-leaves are generally short. Child-care facilities are inadequate, and millions of working single mothers have to rely on the private sector. Even legal protections for women are still lacking. In 1972 Congress sent to the states an Equal Rights Amendment (ERA) to the *Constitution*, which stated: "Equality of rights under the law shall not be denied or abridged by the United States or any state on account of sex." Between 1972 and 1979 the ERA's supporters worked for its ratification in at least 75 percent of the states, as is required for any amendment to the *Constitution*. They failed, not least because many working-class women feared that it would overturn their hard-won gains to special considerations in the workplace. Women also failed to get legislators to legalize abortion. Instead, a liberal Supreme Court, in *Roe vs. Wade* (1973) declared abortion to be a legal right. (This decision is opposed, however, by most of the conservative judges whom Ronald Reagan later appointed to the Court.) Abortion remains a hotly contested issue, with many conservative Christian groups militantly opposed to the very existence of abortion clinics. In a few cases, individuals have attacked these clinics with bombs or bomb threats, and occasionally the violence escalates even further. Several physicians have been killed because they worked for such clinics. Since 1988 the platform of the Republican Party has been "pro-life," while the Democrats have been "pro-choice." In short, American women have by no means secured equality, nor can they be sure to get a hearing for even modest feminist proposals.

Leaving aside public controversies, at home American men and women have found it difficult to adjust their gender roles to changing circumstances. In 1987 *Woman's Day* magazine conducted a survey of 60,000 married women and found that 39 percent felt like their husband's housekeeper and 27 percent felt like his mother. To escape these contradictions many women turned to Harlequin Romances, which first appeared in the 1960s and proved so popular that many publishers quickly entered the market. Romances now constitute 35 percent of the entire mass market in paperbacks. One reader pointedly stated that, when reading, her body was in the room but she herself was not. Asked why she read romances, another suburban housewife replied:

As a mother, I have to run 'em to the orthodontist. I have to run 'em to the swimming pool, I have to run 'em to baton twirling lessons. I have to run up to school because they forgot their lunch. You know, I mean really, and you do it. And it isn't that you begrudge it. That isn't it. Then my husband would walk in the door and he'd say "Well, what did you do today?" You know, it was like "well, tell me how you spent the last eight hours, because I've been out working." And I finally got to the point where I would say, "Well, I read four books, and I did the wash and got the meal on the table and the beds are all made and the house is tidy." And I would get defensive like, "so what do you call all this? Why should I have to tell you because I certainly don't ask you what you did for eight hours, step by step." But their husbands do that. We've compared notes. They hit the house and it's like, "Well all right, I've been out earning a living. Now what have you been doin' with your time?" And you begin to be feeling, "now really, why is he questioning me?"

Such complaints do not mean, however, that marriage as an institution is less popular. The divorce rate has remained almost unchanged at about 45 percent since 1975, and when marriages fail people often remarry.

African Americans are only half as likely to remarry, however. Millions of single mothers, Black and White, have a median income half that of single fathers. Many today speak of "the feminization of poverty" because a disproportionate number of the poor are women, especially those with young children. They may not be chronically poor, however. Half the recipients of welfare leave the rolls after one or two years. Yet at any given time there are almost twice as many women as men below the poverty line. While Blacks and Hispanics are over-represented, the majority of these poor women are White. One major cause is the popularity of "no fault" divorces, in which a single mother receives no alimony. Furthermore, women still make only 75 percent of male salaries.

In the past two centuries women have made many gains, but they have by no means achieved equality. Two women now sit on the Supreme Court, and one out of every four lawyers under 35 is female. Yet less than 5 percent of corporate officers are women, and most professionals are still men. Nor is the public united in trying to undo these inequities. Quite the contrary. In the 1990s a backlash against affirmative action spread across the country. In 1996 Californians passed Proposition 298, which prohibited preferential treatment based on race, sex, ethnicity or national origin. Aimed at ending affirmative action in education and the job market, it became law in the most populous state.

Considering class, race, and gender together, the 1990s were a period of limited progress. The nation was becoming more divided along class lines, it was sending more Black men to prison than ever before, and it had begun to turn away from the policy of affirmative action, without putting any other instrument in its place. On the positive side, more women and African Americans are at universities than ever before. The Black middle class continues to grow. Two of the most popular political figures in the nation are African-American Colin Powell, formerly the highest ranking general in the United States military, and Bush's Secretary of State and Madeleine Albright, the former Secretary of State.

*Former United Nations Ambassador Madeleine Albright became the first female Secretary of State of United States in January 1997. – AP/Nordfoto.*

And yet the racial divide remained enormous. In 1995 and 1996 the nation was polarized by the O. J. Simpson trial. Simpson, one of the best football running backs of the last thirty years, had seemed to exemplify the success of racial integration. He was rich, popular, and married to a beautiful, blond, White woman. Advertisers often employed him to endorse their products, and most Americans knew his name, face, and voice from television. Most of them did not know that Simpson was estranged from his wife, Nicole, and that their separation had been stormy. When Nicole and a White man were found murdered outside the Simpson home in one of the most fashionable neighborhoods of Los Angeles, much of the circumstantial evidence seemed to point to the former footballer. The murder trial that followed became the biggest news story of the 1990s. As the case unfolded, the evidence against Simpson was not always clear, but the investigation did reveal undeniable, virulent racism in the Los Angeles police force. Most White Americans became convinced that Simpson was guilty, while most African Americans believed he was innocent. The jury in the murder trial found him not guilty, but a subsequent civil suit against Simpson uncovered further evidence that convinced another jury of his guilt. He was ordered to pay millions of dollars to the families of the murder victims, leaving him bankrupt but on the street. Few Americans, Black or White, felt that justice had been done. A trial should be an impartial investigation that leads to consensus in society. The two trials of O. J. Simpson revealed the failures of integration on many different levels: the failed interracial marriage between Simpson and Nicole, the overt racism of the police, the polarization of public opinion, and the two contradictory legal decisions.

The Simpson trial also revealed the central place of the media in American life, discussed in the next chapter.

# The Media

## 1. Newspapers

The mass media have long both reflected and shaped American society. This is not a recent phenomenon. The development of newspapers and the creation of an independent United States occurred at the same time. Both reflected the emergence of a public sphere. Newspapers were widely distributed before the American Revolution, and they carried much of the news and debate that fostered the spirit of rebellion. Since then newspapers have been understood as an essential political institution – the so-called "fourth estate." Thomas Jefferson declared that if he had to give up either the free press or the state he would keep the newspapers. The Bill of Rights (reprinted in the appendix) guarantees freedom of the press, and American journalists have generally had fewer formal legal restrictions than most others. Today, newspapers and other forms of media are less overtly political organs than they were in Jefferson's day. Instead, they have become independent institutions which wield political influence, while generating large profits and creating multiple connections between the media and the consumer society. The Watergate Scandal would never have come to light had it not been for investigative reporting of a kind that seldom is seen in many countries.

Conventional wisdom twenty years ago held that newspapers would inevitably diminish in number and circulation, victims of radio and television which could bring news more quickly into the home. On the whole this shift in media has only been the case in cities of over 1 million inhabitants, where both evening and morning editions have done badly. Overall, since 1970 the paid circulation for all dailies has remained about the same (60 million subscribers), but circulation of morning newspapers has shot up in smaller cities. It has doubled in communities of less than 100,000. In other words, television and radio have penetrated most successfully in the large urban markets, but they cannot cover the local and the rural communities as well. Advertisers have also continued to invest more money in newspapers than television, suggesting that predictions of the newspaper's demise are premature. In 1995 there were 1,586 morning and evening papers in the United States, plus 886 Sunday papers. A typical daily has a circulation of about 40,000.

The press as a whole is dominated by a few large newspapers and the national wire services, Associated Press (AP) and United Press International

(UPI). There is no single dominant American newspaper, however, which is not surprising given the size of the country. Rather, in each region there is one serious paper with a large circulation, notably: *The New York Times, Los Angeles Times, Washington Post, San Francisco Chronicle*, and *Boston Globe*. In addition, there are several newspaper chains, whose owners supply each paper in the chain with comic strips, feature stories, and syndicated columns.

While in some instances newspapers have taken strong political stands, in general American journalists are trained to draw a firm line between the factual article that tries to be objective, restricted to the "who, what, and when," and the editorial, which expresses a political opinion. This practice first came into common use in the middle of the nineteenth century, as newspapers tried to reach the largest possible number of readers. Before then most newspapers had been openly partisan, because they were directly connected to political parties or causes. Today, American newspapers want to appear objective. However difficult this may prove in practice, they are assisted by some of the general circumstances of journalism in the United States. As in Europe, large advertisers can exert pressures that compromise a newspaper's objectivity. But unlike many European countries, in America there is no official secrets act and no government news service. There are no censors, and courts do not have the authority to prevent the printing or distribution of newspapers. In addition, under the Freedom of Information Act any citizen can demand access to government records.

American journalists do not necessarily receive their training in schools of journalism. Many of them work for university newspapers while majoring in English or another discipline in the humanities. Journalism itself is not a long course of study, but typically is a one-year or two-year graduate program whose students come from many different backgrounds. Newspapers are not required to hire people with degrees in journalism, however, and they often prefer those with experience in particular fields. As a result, American newspapers and magazines have very good reporting on developments in the sciences, engineering, art, music, and architecture. Those trained in journalism usually handle the routine stories of accidents, deaths, taxes, politics, and crimes. No matter what area they cover, American journalists aspire to write feature stories, or long articles that synthesize a wide range of material. On Sundays, in particular, American newspapers carry a good many long articles, at times gathered together in a magazine section of the paper, as is the case with the *New York Times*, for example. The typical Sunday newspaper is a cornucopia of information, and literally cannot be read in one day. Americans are often surprised to see how thin European newspapers are by comparison.

## 2. Publishing

While books were once precious hand-made objects, today they are a central part of the mass media. Novels become films and then television shows, and vice-versa. Corporate conglomerates may own both a major studio and a publishing house. Beyond direct ownership, interlocking networks of people connect newspapers, magazines, and the other mass media, and the site where this "networking" takes place is New York City. Here most of the major publishers have their offices, here the *New York Times* publishes its list of best-sellers, here the *New Yorker* determines the limits of genteel literary concern, and here also is published *The New York Review of Books*, which disdains to review most of the best-sellers, capturing the high-brow and general academic market instead. Just as importantly, many of the nation's largest circulation magazines are edited in New York, and these often pick up their articles and fiction from the small army of freelance writers living in or near the city. There are also significant publishers in Chicago, Boston, San Francisco, and a few other cities. Indeed, hundreds of publishers are scattered across the country, but most of these are small, and New York remains the undisputed center of the commercial book world.

About 65,000 books are published each year in the United States, far more than anyone could hope to read, and many more than any newspaper will ever review. The author of a new novel cannot assume that a few days after its appearance it will be reviewed and discussed in the press. Even to stay abreast of the 3,000 or more new novels would require a newspaper to review ten a day. In addition, during any given year there are roughly 14,000 books published in the social sciences and history, 8,000 in science and medicine, 1,400 in art, and 3,000 biographies. The profusion of titles explains why book reviews and marketing are central to getting any book noticed by the public, and it also explains why bookstores cannot begin to carry more than a small percentage of the works in print. A new more comprehensive kind of bookstore has emerged on the internet, however, offering to ship virtually any book in print within a few days.

Too often outsiders judge American intellectual life by the best-seller list, unaware that there is a vibrant alternative publishing culture, centered in small magazines and publishers such as New Directions. This imaginative company published much of the fiction of Henry Miller and John Hawkes, and the poetry of William Carlos Williams, Lawrence Ferlinghetti, Denise Levertov, and Kenneth Rexroth. Countless other small presses support experimental writing and new authors. Equally important are the university presses, which publish most of the serious research and also some fiction. Large university presses, such as those at Princeton, Yale, Harvard, Berkeley, and MIT can literally fill a campus bookstore with their own publications. Such university presses have a large full-time staff and produce more than 100 new titles each year, most of which are not by members of the school's faculty. While they typically sell only a few thousand copies of a book, they keep titles in stock for as much as a decade, unlike commercial presses which keep a book in print only during the rush of initial sales and then "remainder it" after one or two years. University presses also publish most of the serious journals, covering every academic topic from art to zoology. All university publications are subjected to intensive scrutiny and anonymous review by two or more specialists before being accepted. Well over half of all scholarly manuscripts submitted are turned down, and even those which are published often receive considerable criticism in the journals.

## 3. Radio and Television

Radio was first developed at the end of the nineteenth century, under the misconception that it would serve primarily as a wireless form of telegraphy. The government, particularly the military, and the telephone and telegraph interests were naturally those most interested. Until the end of World War I radio was not a broadcast medium. Rather it was used for point-to-point communication. But in the 1920s local amateurs began to broadcast what today would be called general programming, just for fun, reaching only a few fellow enthusiasts with crystal sets in their immediate neighborhoods. These local experiments proved so popular that the large electrical interests began regular stations, still without knowing how the service would be paid for. Then advertisers discovered radio, and by the early 1930s corporations had created national networks out of local stations and they broadcast regular shows and entertainment. By the end of that decade radio was a fixture in every home and a central medium through which Americans heard national sports, listened to President Roosevelt's "Fireside Chats," and danced to the latest popular music.

By the early 1980s more than 500 of the 9,000 American radio stations were owned by newspapers and magazines, who in effect had merged with their competition. Recent laws have prohibited this practice, however, and today no newspaper can own a radio or television station. As this example suggests, the government plays the role of a regulator. It assigns broadcast bands, monitors programs to make sure they are not obscene, and determines the minimum qualifications of radio announcers, who must pass an examination before being allowed on the air. No government, state or local,

*Jesse Jackson (left) and Michael Dukakis at a live television debate in New York City, during the race for nomination as Democratic presidential candidate 1988. – USIA.*

demands that listeners pay for a TV or radio license. Federal regulations also lay down a Fairness Doctrine, which states that when radio stations broadcast editorials they must be willing to give an equal amount of time free of charge to any group that wishes to argue a different point of view. Americans do not want the media to be used to concentrate government power. Therefore both national and local governments are prohibited from owning or operating radio stations, except within the armed forces.

This minimal government role and the primacy of the three major radio networks served as the model for television. Broadcasting images and sound together was technically possible in the 1930s, but only became the basis of a new industry after 1946. Television inherited its three major networks from radio; it borrowed some shows and entertainers from radio; and it developed a new visual vocabulary out of film. While producers soon found that the small television screen made different demands than the silver screen, the original shows were clearly linked to earlier forms of popular culture. For roughly three decades (1950–1980) television served as a powerful force integrating the local and the ethnic into one national culture. Both the number of TVs and the viewing time increased dramatically during the 1950s, so that, by 1960, 87 percent of all households had sets, making television the major form of mass culture.

Over the years, programming stretched longer and longer over the day and night, until now it runs continuously. However, most people see television only in the evening. Serious programming starts with the news, divided into two half-hour segments: local news created by a nearby station, and the national and international news, which comes live from the networks. In the middle 1960s television news began to play a more important role in American culture, partly because new satellite and cable connections made it possible to cover world events virtually as they happened, giving television a crucial time advantage over newspapers. Politicians also have made increasing use of television, gradually adapting the older oratorical style of the platform and meeting hall to the quieter, more nuanced style that the intimacies of the new medium require. The 12 second "sound bite" that could be used on the evening news began to be a measure of political success.

After the news comes "prime time" programming, so-called because the largest viewing audience exists between eight and eleven each night. To evaluate this programming, stations soon adopted the ratings system, which in effect made popularity into the measure of program quality. The more households that watched a program, the longer it would remain on the air, and the more the advertisers would be willing to pay to sponsor it. This policy, coupled with the frequent commercial interruptions in programming, created a distinctive American television style. Slowly building a long dramatic scene was seldom possible, as shows were broken up into distinct segments, each of which had to end in an exciting way, so that viewers would "stay tuned" during the advertising to see what would happen next. Soon critics began to charge that television was a cultural and political wasteland. It was banal. It was endlessly repetitious. It appealed to the lowest common cultural denominator, and demanded little of its audience.

To some extent these charges were true, but perhaps too much was expected of a new medium in its first two decades. (Compare the inadequacies of early television with the early history of film between 1895 and 1915.) In the first years the camera was merely pointed at actors who performed as though they were still on the stage; today, television acting is shaped to the medium's intimacy and immediacy, combined with a stunning technical virtuosity. Likewise, news programming, which was once little more than someone sitting at a desk reading a text, today presents images from all over the world transmitted by satellite. Thus programs have increased a great deal in visual complexity and technical skill during the past forty years. Many of the innovations were pioneered in advertisements, which had to develop ways of packing a great deal of visual material into as short a time as thirty seconds. Today, the audience takes for granted both such techniques and nearly instant coverage of events almost as they happen. Indeed, many political events are crafted for television, most notably the national party conventions, but also the space launches, and the inauguration of the President.

Such "media events" are quite distinct from ordinary television viewing. The media event interrupts routine and monopolizes the airwaves on all major channels. They are broadcast live and are somewhat unpredictable, although organizers usually cooperate with television channels out of mutual interest. Usually media events are consciously organized and pre-planned. Examples are the Olympic Games, the Watergate hearings, and ceremonial occasions such as the visit of Anwar Sadat to Jerusalem or the royal wedding of Prince Charles and Lady Diana. Some media events are unexpected, however, like the fall of the Berlin Wall or O. J. Simpson's flight and police pursuit. Media events are not numerous, and when they occur they are understood to be historic. Such moments draw enormous audiences. In the culture as a whole they unite the population in a common experience.

Aside from these extraordinary events, however, daily television tends to become self-referential. The talk show host interviews an actor whose new show is about to begin, and together they make jokes based on advertising slogans. A dramatic program is about a television journalist. A children's show is sponsored by a company selling dolls that are copies of the characters in the show. In these and many other ways television tends to create an endless tapestry of images and counter-images. Some critics worry that viewers, especially children, may not always be able to draw the line between television and the rest of the world. Yet recent research into how people watch television suggests that children do recognize the difference between image and reality, and that by age fourteen they have a sophisticated understanding of how programs are put together. Studies have also found that the number of hours a television is on in a home should not be confused with viewing time. Often a TV set operates as a kind of background noise in a room where people are coming and going. Furthermore, while a set may be on for seven hours in a day, both children and adult family members are included in this total, which does not represent the viewing time of a single person. Some recent researchers argue that television viewers are not passively soaking up television messages, but rather are engaged in an active process of decoding and interpreting.

Whatever their viewing habits, however, by the 1960s many well-educated Americans had found network television too limited. Following a 1966 study commissioned by the Carnegie Endowment, Congress passed the Public Broadcasting Act of 1967. Unfortunately, this act did not ensure stations a steady source of revenue (as is the case in Britain or the Nordic countries, for example) in the form of a tax or fee. As a result, the Public Broadcast System (PBS) was much less centralized than the private networks. It was built up from a few local stations into a loosely organized network, with 300 stations that blanket the entire country. The typical public station broadcasts four hours of teaching and nine hours of general programming each day. The PBS created Sesame Street, the widely imitated children's program, and it has produced thousands of documentary programs and dramatic series based on literary works. In more recent years cable television, satellite receivers, and home video have further increased the options available, to the point where Americans often can choose between thirty or more simultaneous programs, twenty-four hours a day. The dominance of the three traditional networks has weakened as a result. New cable stations often focus on particular segments of the audience, such as children, sports fans, or movie buffs. New networks cover one area exclusively: news, history, science, cartoons, sports, and so on. Such "narrow casting" may largely replace "broadcasting" as it has in radio.

In this light, PBS can be understood as programming for the well-educated, which some corporations are eager to sponsor. While much of the funding for public television comes from government, during the Reagan years both federal and local support was cut back. Individuals, who voluntarily pay a membership fee each year, doubled their contributions in response. Corporate sponsors also play a role in public television. While they are not permitted to insert commercials, sponsors are mentioned at the beginning and ending of each show, and they gain prestige from association with it. Mobil Oil long underwrote the popular Masterpiece Theater series, whose programs were purchased from the BBC. A pharmaceutical company paid for the broadcast of The Boston Symphony, and Exxon donated half a million dollars for a year's support to the MacNeill-Lehrer Report, a news analysis program watched by businessmen and government leaders. While $500,000 may seem a considerable sum, in fact it would not buy a one-minute advertisement during a major sporting event such as football's Superbowl. Corporate sponsors of serious programs acquire prestige and the patina of social responsibility comparatively cheaply.

### Public Broadcasting System, Sources of Income [%]

|                                  | 1975 | 1984 | 1997 |
|----------------------------------|------|------|------|
| Federal government               | 25.3 | 17.2 | 17   |
| State and local government       | 42.9 | 34.1 | 28   |
| Subscribers, auctions, marathons | 11.6 | 22.1 | 25   |
| Business and industry            | 6.9  | 14.7 | 14   |
| Foundation                       | 7.9  | 2.8  | 6    |
| Other                            | 5.4  | 9.1  | 10   |

In recent years it has become fashionable to attribute many profound cultural changes to American television. Some charge that it has cheapened politics, transforming a system of rational debate into nothing more than the manipulation of slogans and images. Those making such claims ignore much of American political history, which generally has not been characterized by European-style ideological parties. As early as the 1830s critics complained that Americans ran for office by creating a false image, usually that of a man born in a log cabin rising to success by his own personal drive and merit, and politicians campaigned with banners, parades, posters, picnics and barbecues for voters. Television has not debased a once noble, rational process so much as exposed traditional politics to view. American parties have always tried to avoid taking strong ideological stands, and they have always sought to find candidates who could appeal to the broad majority of the population. Another false claim is that television has made it mandatory for candidates to be handsome figures possessed of acting ability and a persuasive manner. While such arguments seem plausible when considering Reagan's Presidency or Perot's successful exploitation of the medium, they do not explain how two men who were not very handsome and who lacked charisma – George Bush and Mike Dukakis – became the candidates in 1988. Bob Dole, hardly a master of medium, became the Republican candidate in 1996, and Al Gore, despite a stiff demeanor and speaking style ill-adapted to television, won for the Democratic candidacy and the popular vote in 2000.

## 4. Advertising and Social Class

Both radio and television are financed through advertisements whose length, content, and audience appeal were first created on radio and in cinema. Already in the early twentieth century advertising permeated popular culture, projecting images of male–female relations, how to dress, how long hair "ought" to be, what to drink, what to smoke, where to go, and how to get there. Copywriters often wrote in an intimate style, as though talking to a friend with a problem such as body odor or pimples. The strategy was designed to make readers feel insecure unless they made a good first impression, and had smooth skin, sweet breath, new cars, and clean sinks. By the 1920s all Americans were subjected to thousands of such appeals.

Given the complexities of the American social system, with its many ethnic groups and minority interests, how have American advertisers divided up the public? In fact, they have seldom regarded race or ethnicity as a controlling factor in designing advertising campaigns. In the 1920s and 1930s they saw the public as consisting of three groups, conceived strictly in terms of income. At the bottom were those whose income was so small that they were unable to make many consumer choices. At that time this group included almost half the population, as 40 percent of the people still lived on farms, to whom could be added the majority of Blacks and the urban poor. Advertisers did not see these people as part of "mass" society, which they defined as being above all the urban middle class. Finally, there was the "class" market, i.e., the richest 5 percent of the population. For decades this basic conception of the American population served advertisers well enough, leading them to focus almost all their efforts on broad campaigns directed at the "mass" audience in the middle. This crude analysis worked in part because poorer people in America have long identified themselves with the middle class, and the white-collar sector of society was growing rapidly during these years. The traditional idea that a class system should look like a pyramid, with the largest and poorest group at the bottom, no longer bore any relation to reality.

What then were the supposed characteristics of this "mass" society? Advertising executives, who were overwhelmingly male, well-educated, and upper-class, assumed their audience was female, impressionable, and middle class. They saw this audience as being vulgar and intellectually inferior, and they developed characteristic dramatic tableaux to capture their interest. In these tableaux, by definition, men were businessmen and women housewives. Older people, particularly women, were almost always seated, usually in rustic settings; children were charming but not distinct as personalities. Ethnic minorities seldom appeared, except as skilled workers, and African Americans could not be found at all in advertisements of these years, except for very limited roles as cooks and maids. Advertisers assumed that the average life was so drab that many products were best sold as parts of fantasy worlds of wealth, leisure, and power.

The advertising of the 1920s and 1930s helped to create a massive middle-class audience that held a core of common attitudes and ideas. The content of individual advertisements helped establish the image of a shared culture, and the fact that these advertisements underwrote the existence of the national media of radio and magazines further established the "reality" of mass culture. For years advertising dollars paid half the cost of producing national magazines and even more of the cost of radio and television network programs. Today, in contrast, most of the national weekly magazines that once tried to reach the entire public have gone bankrupt. Radio stations are no longer as tightly linked to national networks as before, and they emphasize local programs. These changes occurred in part because advertisers shifted money away from these media to television. Today, television is undergoing a similar process, as national networks are gradually losing their dominance to a multi-channel system made possible by cable and satellite. The ways available to reach the public have multiplied, prompting advertisers to use their money in new ways that have accelerated a process of market segmentation. Rather than broadcast messages to the entire population, advertisers have become more selective, buying space in the magazines that reach a particular group, or making commercials for a particular kind of radio station (country-western, soft-rock, classical) that reaches those with a specific lifestyle.

At the same time as the media used by advertising have changed, sociologists have found the traditional notions of class increasingly irrelevant in sorting out the "mass" audience. In the 1950s, sociologist David Riesman in *The Lonely Crowd* proposed that there were two basic types of Americans, the other-directed and the inner-directed. Later Herbert Gans persuasively argued that Americans were divided into four distinct taste cultures, each with its own preferred types of music and literature, each with its own media, creators, and critics. Furthermore, Gans argued, "the major issues in the politics of culture are different in America and Europe. In Europe, where high culture has considerable power and prestige, the question of how much high and popular culture are to be distributed by the mass media is a major issue. In America, high culture is politically too weak to appear in the mass media, and the major cultural-political struggles take place within popular culture." American network television almost never contains ballet, opera, poetry readings, or lectures, and consequently those with "high taste culture" pay little attention to it. Television, like Hollywood films, best-sellers, and Broadway musicals, is directed at the lowest common denominator: those in semi-professional and white-collar jobs and the working class.

The work of Riesman, Gans, and other sociologists has become the basis for models used by advertisers, which divide the population into groups, based on lifestyles. In contrast to the older idea of *social class*, which was fundamentally based on one's place in the productive system, the notion of *lifestyle* concerns the choices one makes in the system of consumption. "Class" assumes that consciousness is forged through work; a "lifestyle" suggests a self-created identity that exists largely outside work. This is not merely a change of terminology, because the thousands of advertising messages that each American sees in a typical week are an important source of identity formation. Thus, the advertiser's "description" of the class system, to the extent that consumers believe in it, can become a self-fulfilling prophecy. An increasing amount of advertising appears on the Internet, which makes it possible to vary the messages sent to each individual, depending upon tastes, interests, and spending habits.

# 5. Computers

The latest addition to the twentieth-century media explosion, the computer, has penetrated into all areas of American life with startling rapidity, and has given rise to quite divergent theories about its social meaning. Like radio, it was first designed as an instrument for government and large corporations. For thirty years the computer was large, expensive, and so complex that only people with special training could hope to operate one. IBM dominated the market, along with a few smaller competitors. Between the late 1940s and 1977 less than 500,000 machines had been sold in the United States. In the late 1970s, however, small entrepreneurs began to manufacture personal computers, which can now be seen virtually anywhere and operated by anyone with a minimum of typing skills. By 1990 fifty million computers were in use in the United States, and the industry had grown to be one of the largest sectors in the economy. In 1997 almost half the total workforce dealt directly with computers on the job. This was possible because the price of computer power and memory had fallen drastically, and so many new competitors had successfully entered the field that by 1991 once dominant IBM was fighting hard to stay profitable.

If the previous 150 years of growth had been spurred in turn by the railroad, the electrical industry, and the automobile, growth since 1980 was in large part due to the computer. For computers do far more than merely store and transmit information. They have become central parts of the production process in factories, newspapers, and virtually every form of white-collar work. CAD-CAM, or computer aided design and computer aided manufacturing, have become standard in most large factories. Typically, a new product's design, manufacture, advertising, and marketing are all computer-assisted, a process that will become even more common as the new technology of virtual reality matures, since it will permit architects and designers to "see" and experience an idea as a three-dimensional object.

Computer chips are commonly embedded in new machines and appliances. Hundreds of American companies are now experimenting with allowing employees to work at home at terminals connected to the office, suggesting a future where instead of having people commute to work, the work will be transmitted to them. Other companies whose employees are linked by cellular phones and computers have reduced overhead costs by eliminating most individual offices and substituting lounges, meeting rooms and shared offices for temporary use. As these examples suggest, the computer is such a fundamental innovation that it is difficult to classify. It is clearly far more than a way of storing information or solving complex mathematical problems. At bottom, it is an enabling device which makes it possible to process information so much faster that this quantitative change becomes a qualitative difference. A machine can do in seconds calculations that a trained mathematician once needed a month to do. Of course, few companies ever had the resources to pay hundreds of mathematicians, even if they might have been persuaded to do such routine work. If the computer eliminates some labor, it also encourages us to conceive of new forms of social organization and new tasks that could not have been done before.

The long-term effects of computers are still unclear, but, because they reach into so many areas, they are likely to have many different consequences. Just as television has at times been depicted as a centralized form of political manipulation, it was once common to fear that computers would become instruments of domination and social control, creating an Orwellian world of constant surveillance. Such worries have diminished somewhat as the machines have proliferated. Unlike the old mainframes, personal computers and networking systems have democratized access to information. Because the personal computer makes it possible for individuals to store and transmit large amounts of information and to engage in desktop publishing, its use was virtually forbidden in Eastern Bloc countries until 1989, when their governments were overthrown by popular pressure. (Indeed, until 1989, Romania strictly controlled and required registration of typewriters.) Yet if computers at present seem inimical to totalitarianism, it is well to remember that two decades ago they appeared ideally suited to centralized control. They still can be used by any group to mount a sophisticated advertising or public relations campaign, to keep extensive records on other people, to break into banking systems, to monitor each worker individually, or to steal secrets.

In the last ten years the growth of the Internet has radically increased the flow and the amount of information available to anyone with access to a desktop machine. One specialist in communication history has predicted that, "Networked computers will be the printing presses of the twenty-first century." These new "presses" reach the reader with their messages much faster than those which Jefferson valued so highly, but they are not public and available in the same way. Already some journals are published electronically, and a wide array of databases is available on compact disk or through cable hookups, but it requires a greater capital investment and more expertise to find this information than it does to read a newspaper. Instant global communication by electronic mail is possible for many, and routine activities, such as paying bills or parking fines, may be done by computer as well, but it remains to be seen if these new benefits will be well distributed to all citizens. Will the computer usher in an age of greater prosperity, productivity, and equality, or a society divided between a wealthy "digerati," or knowledge elite, and an unwired underclass condemned to welfare and low wages? At the end of the twentieth century the answer is not yet clear.

Overall, the media in America are the most developed in the world, with the result that they have a disproportionate influence outside the United States. For example, many foreign newspapers use the Associated Press and United Press International for their news, because they cannot afford to send out their own correspondents world-wide. Likewise, American television shows are widely shown abroad because it is far cheaper to buy them than to make alternative programs of the same quality. Because Americans early dominated the computer industry, English became the language of most computer research, teaching manuals, software programs, and the Internet.

American dominance in the news, entertainment, and computer industry, combined with increasing sales of records, films, textbooks, bestsellers, and information services, has raised fears abroad of American cultural hegemony. Just as Europeans in the eighteenth century blamed America for its colonial wars, depopulation, and epidemics, today they worry that mass culture from the United States will overwhelm them. Furthermore, the media in general and television in particular are often accused of fostering a postmodern sensibility which values replication over authenticity, and this new sensibility at times is considered to be peculiarly American. But Europeans in fact produce the majority of their own mass culture, and what they do take from the United States receives its own distinctive inflection from the way they select and interpret it. Changes that seem to emanate from the United States to a considerable extent measure the general shift to a service economy, in which the mass media and computers play a central role. The issues raised are best understood in a comparative, international perspective, rather than falling back on clichés that insist that the United States provides the model for an inevitable European future. It does not, as can perhaps most readily be seen by turning to a central area of cultural difference: religion.

# Religion, Social Services, Education

## 1. Religious Pluralism: Protestant, Catholic, Jew

The United States is the most religious of all the advanced industrial nations. It has confounded the expectations of social scientists, who once confidently predicted that society would become more and more secular as it became industrialized and as education became universal. American churches receive no state support and their income comes entirely from private donations, but the social climate is so agreeable to all forms of the Christian and Jewish religions that in 1995 they owned buildings worth $3.6 billion. Six out of every ten Americans belong to a church or synagogue – the figure has fluctuated little from 1960 to the present – but typically they attend only 40% of the services. Catholics are the most regular, averaging 50 percent. Roman Catholics form the largest single church in the United States, with 59 million members, while there are more than 90 million Protestants divided into many denominations, 5.9 million Jews, 4.1 million of the Eastern Orthodox faith, and many others, including 100,000 Buddhists.

In any American city Sunday morning is a quiet time. A few drug stores and pancake houses open, dispensing swollen Sunday newspapers and fattening breakfasts, usually consumed together. The shopping malls remain closed until the afternoon, and until then the chief attraction for half the population is going to church. Families arrive in their best "Sunday go-to-meeting clothes," the men in ties and jackets, the women in fine dresses and hats. Black, White, or Hispanic, North or South, the basic impulse is the same, though the churches are not. The architecture of each church usually announces its members' background. The Congregationalists often have a white building with a tall steeple. While they prefer the traditional eighteenth-century look, Unitarians often have a modern design, with an open floor plan. Episcopalians [Church of England] usually build a grey Gothic stone church, and Catholics almost always preserve the traditional cross shape in the floor plan, although Italians, Poles, and Irish each tend to build churches that recall the styles of their homelands.

An average congregation, including children, numbers between 300 and 500 members. This size permits each member to know the others reasonably well, and also makes it possible to pay the salary of one minister and keep the church in good repair. Clergy are not subject to most taxes, and churches pay no property tax. Yet despite these advantages, running a church is expensive. The members alone must pay for the construction and maintenance of the church, the minister's salary, the choir robes, the flowers, and every other cost, and they do so voluntarily. Since churches by law cannot receive funds from the government, regular contributions are essential to their survival. Americans give more money to religion – $39 billion in 1991 – than to any other charity. This was an average of $300 per church-goer. This average hides huge differences. The Evangelical Mennonite Brethren each give over $1000, while those in the Lutheran Church in America averaged only about $200. Generally, the more fundamentalist churches elicit the largest contributions. Immigrant groups usually make their church a center of cultural life, and they also raise large sums. The intensity of belief and the church's cultural function are more important than the average income of the membership in determining how much money is raised. Episcopalians have an above average income level, but they give $340 per member, or only half as much as the Baptist General Conference. The Catholic Church is more disciplined and centralized than the Protestant churches. Its 59 million members are divided into large congregations of about 2,000, served by several priests and often accompanied by a school.

The church remains a very important social institution in the United States. Its coffee hours not only last longer than worship services, but they often elicit more enthusiastic participation. They provide a kind of instant community available to anyone who wishes to join, and indeed when Americans move to a new place they commonly "shop" for a new church where they will feel at home. This practice is by no means limited to Protestants, who may change from one denomination to another when they move, basing their choice on factors ranging from the location, the preacher's manner, the social class of the membership, the quality of the Sunday school, and the taste of the food at the coffee hour. Catholics choose between a variety of ethnic congregations in the inner city and more assimilationist churches in the suburbs, and Jewish people must decide whether they want to join a strictly orthodox synagogue or a more liberal one that does not require them to wear certain clothing or eat kosher food. Whatever their choice, the church becomes a community center, sponsoring a wide variety of activities beyond the worship services on Sunday, including bake sales, trips, sports, dances, psychological counselling, retreats, lecture series, concerts, and much more. They serve to keep ethnic and religious communities alive, often enough by introducing marriageable men and women to one another, helping the group to sustain itself from one generation to the next. Church-

*Flotilla of Lanterns Float Out to Sea. Buddhist Rite in Hawaii.*
*– Robert Goodman.*

es also organize charity for the poor, provide emergency shelter for the homeless, engage in missionary work both inside the United States and abroad, and often provide spokesmen for the underprivileged.

The social importance of the church extends particularly to the African-American community, which for hundreds of years was denied political power. For the most part, Blacks are Protestants, which means that the power of Black preachers is not controlled through an extensive hierarchy, but rather remains local. In terms of doctrine, it is all but impossible to generalize about Black religious beliefs, which run the gamut from fundamentalism to liberal interpretations of the Bible. Yet one can generalize that Black churches provided slaves with a way to understand their plight in terms of community, shared suffering, and redemption that entered into their folklore and songs. Preachers became the spokesmen for Black people, explaining their needs to the White community, and later, during the Civil Rights period, voicing their demands. The Black church has also long provided a wide range of social services, often acting as a funnel for funds given by outside groups. Black churches commonly run shelters for the poor, distribute used clothing and furniture, and feed the hungry in soup kitchens. None of this is unique to Black churches, as virtually all American churches perform the same functions in times of crisis or hardship. What makes the Black church distinctive is the long period of political disenfranchisement, which meant that the preacher controlled many charitable functions while acting as a central spokesman for the community. He was simultaneously administrator, politician, and spiritual leader.

## 2. Denominations and Fundamentalists

Why does the United States have so many different religious denominations? Colonial history provides the answer to this question, and the contrast with Mexico and South America is instructive. The Spanish and Portuguese conquered these areas in the early sixteenth century and ruled for three hundred years, imposing religious uniformity. The Catholic Church is still the predominant religion south of the Rio Grande, and a person is either for it or against it. In contrast, the British and the French could only begin to settle in North America after 1585, when the defeat of the Spanish Armada made it safe for them to establish colonies across the Atlantic. The century delay meant that the United States and Canada were settled during the upheaval of the Reformation, and many immigrants fled to the New World to escape religious persecution. For example, the Puritans arrived in Boston in 1630 in order to practice their form of Calvinism. In a sense, they did not so much want to be in America; they wanted not to be in England. They were determined to create a new society, better and purer than the old one they had left behind. They hoped to create an admirable "city upon a hill" which other societies would imitate. While this dream of a religious Utopia failed, today there are several million Congregationalists descended from the Puritans. Similarly, the English Quakers came to Pennsylvania to create a pacifist society of believers, free from persecution, and for most of the eighteenth century they dominated Pennsylvanian Colonial politics. Like the Pilgrims and the Quakers, other groups came to North America with the goal of creating ideal communities. The Mennonites, including the Amish sect, arrived in Pennsylvania from central Europe in 1683, and created village communities based on traditional agriculture. As part of their refusal to accept industrial technologies or modern social arrangements, they make enormous financial contributions to maintain 1,200 churches, more than 2,000 clergy, and an extensive system of charities.

Perhaps the most remarkable sect of all was the Shakers, who came from England in 1774. They believed that God had first come as a man,

Jesus, and later as a woman, their founder, Ann Lee. As the second incarnation of God, she signalled that the end of history was near. In the early nineteenth century the Shakers converted thousands, and built up a series of communities whose members gave up all property and all sexual relations. The membership poured its energies into creating a distinctive plain style of architecture and furniture, and became famous for its excellent seeds, clothing, and practical inventions, such as the flat broom, circular saw, improved clothes pin, and washing machine. Since the Shakers had no children, they survived as a sect only by converting new members, and yet at one time numbered more than 20,000.

While religious communities and sects based on ethnicity have often survived for a considerable time, secular Utopian experiments generally have not lasted as long. For example, the English industrialist Robert Owen came to the United States in the 1820s and attempted to create an ideal community at New Harmony, Indiana. The enterprise quickly failed, however, largely because the enthusiastic volunteers came from too many different backgrounds. They quarrelled about Utopian theories, while overlooking practical matters. A similar fate awaited the group of New Englanders, including novelist Nathaniel Hawthorne, who tried to establish a communal life in the 1840s at Brook Farm outside Boston. American conditions favored the survival of many religious sects, while most imported political ideologies soon died out.

Today there are hundreds of churches in the United States, with new movements arising almost every year. Many of these are short-lived, based on the charismatic leadership of single preachers, some of whom have developed into television evangelists. A few sects seek to combine elements of Christianity and Eastern religion, as compounded by a spiritual leader, who often as not comes from Asia. In the 1970s many Americans visited an ashram in India to hear Rajneesh lecture. He had adopted a "personal eclectic style, telling Zen parables, jokes, stories from the life of Buddha or the Sufi sages, and citing for example, Gurdjieff, Socrates, and Bob Hope all in a single lecture." Rajneesh came to the United States in the early 1980s and set up a short-lived communal society in rural Oregon, much to the displeasure of local conservative Christian residents. If a growing minority of Americans remains interested in finding a common system linking Buddhism, Christian mysticism, western philosophy, and psychology, the majority are religious in more conventional ways.

American religion on the whole is active rather than meditative. It expresses dissatisfaction with the world as it is. It encourages reform movements, restlessness, and desire for change. More ominously, it implies new endings. Many American Protestant sects fervently believe in the apocalypse, or the end of the world, as prophesied in the Bible. Two religions invented in the United States, the Mormons and the Seventh Day Adventists, stress that the apocalypse will come soon. Indeed, the religious purpose of building a "city on a hill" or joining a sect like the Shakers was to prepare for the coming end of the world. In the last days of the world, as prophesied in the Book of Revelation, a great battle will take place between the forces of good and evil. While far less than half of all Americans take this idea literally, a few take it very seriously. Millions of Americans have seen Christian films, such as those of Donald Thomson, whose *A Thief in the Night* (1973) depicts Christ's return to earth and the last judgement. It long circulated in more than 600 prints. Ronald Reagan's Secretary of the Interior, James Watt, when asked by reporters if American natural resources might not be depleted under his policies, remarked that, "I do not know how many future generations we can count on before the Lord returns." Reagan himself used the image of America as a "city on a hill" in his speech accepting the nomination for President. He once called the Soviet Union an "evil empire" and on another occasion said that he expected to see the climax of the struggle between the forces of light and darkness "in our generation." Jerry Falwell, popular television preacher and Reagan supporter, predicted in 1980 that the apocalypse would begin in the Middle East.

Yet Falwell and other television evangelists have lost a good deal of their popularity in recent years, reminding us that American religious life has passed through waves of revivalism ever since the middle of the eighteenth century, when the Great Awakening occurred. Since then, roughly every half century another revival of conservative religion has taken place. Scholars who expected religion to diminish in importance as the United States industrialized and urbanized have been confounded. If anything, the dislocations of modernization and the fears caused by nuclear technology have kept fundamentalist religion alive.

Officially, religion in America is relegated entirely to private life, and it cannot be involved in politics. Yet Presidents Carter and Reagan both felt it necessary to declare in public that they were "born again Christians," meaning that they had experienced a powerful religious conversion. In practice, it is impossible to keep the public and private entirely separate, because some political issues touch directly on church doctrines. The most obvious example is the abortion issue, but churches are also concerned with such questions as whether evolution could be taught in the schools, or whether each school day should begin with prayer or not. While these examples suggest that churches are conservative institutions, ministers have also been leaders of protests against the Vietnam War, the war in El Salvador, and nuclear weapons. Nor can one forget the religious background of the Reverend

Martin Luther King and the Reverend Jesse Jackson. American churches are by definition not a part of the state, and at times they mobilize against it.

## 3. Philanthropy

Not all charity work involves money. Five million people annually give blood to the Red Cross, and millions of days' work are freely given to non-profit organizations. The powerful American impulse to religious good works is suggested by the money given to charity each year. In 1997 America's approximately 44,000 private foundations together held more than $330 billion in trust, gave away $15 billion, and received $15.8 billion in new donations. Foundations are hardly on the wane: their assets quadrupled between 1970 and 1984, and have quadrupled again. Most of these funds accumulated as bequests from wealthy men and women who chose not to leave their money to family members, or who wished to avoid inheritance taxes. Instead, they created foundations to give the money away. Many donors believe in the Christian idea of stewardship; they feel that their wealth is not a private possession but a public trust. At the turn of the century Andrew Carnegie was one of the most famous of these philanthropists. After accumulating a fortune in the steel industry, he spent the last years of his life giving it away for a wide variety of projects, including the creation of more than 2,800 public libraries. Carnegie believed that free libraries would give every person an equal access to knowledge, and therefore an equal chance to become a success. His largesse was not motivated by income tax laws, which were insignificant at the time, but by the feeling that a man had no right to die rich. However, many of the large foundations created in later years, such as the Ford Foundation and the Rockefeller Foundation, were set up in part to avoid paying inheritance taxes to the government.

What do these foundations support? Half of all their giving is to health and welfare, as they help keep alive more than 50,000 non-profit social service establishments, which do everything from feeding old people and making cassettes for the blind to offering psychiatric counselling and birth control. Almost a fifth of the funds go to education. Money is often given for university faculty research or retraining, for student scholarships, and for experiments in new curricular designs. Foundations are also a major source of support for American theaters and symphony orchestras, which receive no guaranteed support from the state. A few are devoted almost exclusively to the arts, offering scholarships to writers and artists, sending poets on tours of the public schools, or underwriting the expense of major exhibitions. In addition, corporations annually give away almost $6 billion, with the lion's share for health and education. Corporations also gave $245 million to museums and the arts, and General Electric even sponsors a poetry contest.

Foundations and corporations do not give the most, however. Individuals do. The Robert Frost Library at Amherst College was the gift of one anonymous donor, for example. Universities frequently name professorial chairs or buildings for donors, who give more than $1 million in exchange for the honor. Massachusetts Institute of Technology received as a single gift both a laboratory building and funds to hire an entire biomedical research staff. On an even larger scale, the prestigious Duke University was created almost entirely from the gift of one family that had made a fortune in the tobacco industry. As these examples suggest, giving by foundations and corporations is a small fraction of individual philanthropy, which amounted to $109 billion in 1997 – more than the gross national product of Denmark or Norway in the same year. The largest share of this private charity went to churches and religious organizations. To put this giving in perspective, in a single year it would be enough to retire all of the public debt of Russia, Poland, and Bulgaria.

Charitable giving is not limited to the very wealthy, as the government permits every citizen an income tax write-off for contributions to nonprofit organizations. Three out of every four households gave an average of $1,017 to charity in 1997. One of the best known conduits for giving is the United Way, a federation of many charities which makes a united appeal for funds, primarily at the workplace, where employee giving is often matched by the employer. Much charity money is also secured through auctions, church rummage sales, bingo games, lotteries, or unusual special events, such as Meadow Muffin Megabucks, which connects money and excrement in a way that Sigmund Freud never thought of.

### Meadow Muffin Megabucks

F.A.S.T. (Funding Activities for Students Today) is a committee comprised of community citizens dedicated to raising money for the 1990–1991 school year. Our first event is Meadow Muffin Megabucks, which is a very unique fund-raising event for the autumn. It will be held at Oxford High School at 11.00 a.m. on Saturday, October 28. The high school football field will be marked off in one square yards. The cow will be placed inside the football field. Wherever the cow muffin lands in one square is declared the winner. 1 Square Yard purchase is $10.00 – Sale of deeds will be limited. Buy Now for the Big Event.

# 4. Social Services

Just as Americans have an eighteenth-century *Constitution*, they have inherited a system of social services defined two hundred years ago. At that time, 95 percent of all Americans were farmers, and even the cities were small. Life expectancy was much lower than today, and relatively few people lived to the present retirement age. In 1800 no Western nation had a social security system, socialized medicine, or free education. Such services were only partially provided by the state. Instead, wealthy individuals, churches, and local governments built the hospitals, alms houses, schools, and universities. With few exceptions, private businesses displayed only minimal interest in their employees' welfare. Tocqueville contrasted their sense of social obligation with that felt by a feudal aristocracy. "The territorial aristocracy of former ages was either bound by law, or thought itself bound by usage, to come to the relief of its serving-men and to relieve their distresses. But the manufacturing aristocracy of our age [the 1830s] first impoverishes and debases the men who serve it and then abandons them to be supported by the charity of the public." In the United States that public was local, as state and town governments were long responsible for welfare, with the result that no unified policy evolved. The patchwork that resulted was further reinforced by the division of the population into many ethnic groups, the penchant for self-reliance, and the many different religious sects. The result today is a hybrid system that combines local, private, and federal institutions. Thus, there are university hospitals, religious hospitals (particularly Jewish and Roman Catholic), city hospitals, and military hospitals for the veterans of foreign wars. Likewise, there are both private and public old people's homes, schools, charities, and pension plans. The system is not comprehensive, nor is it meant to be, for here, as in most things, Americans believe in self-reliance and expect a market system to regulate the flow of services.

Work gives an American a meaningful existence. One of the first questions asked of any stranger is "What do you do?" Occupations not only provide status and ensure a livelihood, they give Americans their social identity. Those without work often feel lost, and rather than admit to being unemployed, they often prefer to use circumlocutions, such as "I'm between jobs." "I'm retraining." or, "I'm doing some freelancing right now." Such answers not only deny the fact of unemployment, but they imply that one is in control. So great is the shame attached to receiving unemployment benefits that many at first refuse to claim them.

As the identification with the job implies, the social welfare system is founded on the individualistic belief that every person is responsible for his or her own life. Americans do have reasonably comprehensive programs to help those who cannot take care of themselves – such as the blind, children, or old people – but they have long rejected the idea that the government has an obligation to give healthy adults any more than the barest essentials. Until the 1930s most Americans rejected the very idea of a welfare state that could provide a comprehensive security net of programs to feed, clothe, and house every citizen and provide medical care. They did not see such protection as a birthright, like free education, free libraries, or freedom of speech and religion.

The problem with such a system of self-reliance, of course, is that it cannot deal with widespread unemployment, which makes the population as a whole vulnerable. Thus the private, individualistic, and voluntary nature of American social welfare simply could not meet the challenge of the Great Depression that began after the stock market crashed in 1929. With almost a quarter of the workforce idle, and those who had work often on part time, the sheer scale of the problems overwhelmed private charities and local governments. Roosevelt's New Deal responded by making the traditional distinction between the deserving poor and the undeserving poor. Those who had worked hard all their lives deserved to have a pension, hence a social security program was enacted into law in 1935, which tied benefits directly to working. Likewise, in the New Deal those who were willing to work but could not find a position in the private sector deserved a job, and were offered one by the government. Roosevelt created the Civilian Conservation Corps to work in the national forests and parks, and the Works Progress Administration, to repair roads, build parks, run community theaters, and do other jobs in the cities. The premises behind such programs were clear: work was better than welfare; those who would accept work deserved to have it, and those who would not deserved nothing.

At the end of World War II veterans lobbied for special benefits, based on the argument that those who had risked their lives for the country deserved medical care, subsidies for education, inexpensive loans to buy houses, and other benefits. The resulting set of state and federal programs has been called the G.I. Bill of Rights, creating a near welfare state for veterans. From such beginnings the Federal Government gradually became more and more deeply involved in providing social services. For example, the Hospital Survey and Construction Act of 1946 was intended to help returning soldiers, but by 1961 it had led to the construction of facilities with 239,000 hospital beds, far more than the veterans needed. Such expansion often built upon changes that at first went unnoticed. Thus the Aid for Dependent Children Act, assuring a minimum income to poor families, was amended in 1950 to include single parent families, and over time it became one of the most costly government programs. Expansion of welfare also came about as a by-product of other programs. For example, the Work Incentive Program (WIN) required that welfare recipients take vocational training courses, giving them new skills that would improve their chances of finding a job. To create this program the government not only had to set up training courses, but it was forced to create day-care centers for the students' children.

Once such programs are established, they have an inexorable tendency to spread their coverage to more and more people. Indeed, an international comparison of welfare programs found that "the single most powerful predictor of [the extent of] coverage is the age of the program under study." Between 1960 and 1981 the proportion of the gross domestic product devoted to social expenditures doubled in the United States to 20 percent. (By comparison, European countries in 1981 used more: France, 29 percent; Germany 31 percent; and Sweden 33 percent.) Lyndon Johnson implemented many new programs as part of his War on Poverty, including Medicare, that gave healthcare to the elderly; Medicaid, that gave healthcare to the poor; and the Food Stamp program, that provided the poor with coupons that could be exchanged for food in supermarkets. He also introduced a wide range of other programs designed to "break the cycle of poverty" through education, job training, and regional economic development. The thrust of these programs was not toward creating a guaranteed income, but rather toward opening doors for the poor, so that they could become self-sufficient members of the middle class. As one popular slogan put it, they were to get a hand up rather than a handout.

To protect the legal rights of the poor, the Office of Economic Opportunity created an extensive legal services program, with 1,800 lawyers working in 850 offices. As a result of their determined work, the Supreme Court struck down many local statutes and regulations. For example, states had been able to deny some poor people welfare benefits because they had not lived in the state for a year. Such residency requirements in effect had prevented poor people from moving to a new place. Because of such legal assistance, the number of poor families receiving welfare payments shot up from about 33 percent in 1960 to more than 90 percent in 1971. An important change had taken place. Poor Americans were no longer afraid or ashamed to apply for aid. Welfare was considered less a stigma than a right. As a result of the War on Poverty and the other programs introduced in the post-war years, American welfare spending, measured in constant dollars, increased by 400 percent between 1950 and 1977 when Jimmy Carter assumed the Presidency. Carter advocated a guaranteed minimum income of $4,200 per year for a family of four. This idea, let alone the spending involved, never passed through the Congress. By 1980, welfare had reached a stalemate where few new programs could be introduced.

Nevertheless, Johnson's programs initiated changes that have forced a shift in the federal budget away from military spending to social services, a shift that largely took place between 1968 and 1988 during Republican administrations despite their attempts to prevent it. Thus, in 1981, President Reagan announced his intention to roll back the cost of welfare, repeating the old distinction between the deserving and the undeserving poor. "Those who, through no fault of their own, must depend on the rest of us – the poverty-stricken, the disabled, the elderly – can rest assured that the social safety net of programs they depend on are exempt from any cuts ... [but] Government will not continue to subsidize individuals or particular business interests where real need cannot be demonstrated." He proposed, and Congress soon enacted, legislation that eliminated 400,000 single working mothers from the welfare roles. Previously, they had received supplementary payments that together with their wages brought them over the poverty line. Likewise, by 1984 Reagan had reduced funding to the mentally ill by 25 percent and cut funding for public housing by slightly more, while making deeper cuts in job training programs. Despite such cuts and despite Reagan's drive to privatize health services, however, by his last year in office the cost of social security, unemployment, and aid to unmarried mothers had increased so much that it was greater than the combined cost of the military, the State Department, and the Space Program. When Medicaid, Medicare, Food Stamps, and other social programs were added in, paying for the welfare state in 1988 required 46 percent of the Federal Budget. This amounted to more than half the funds available after 13 percent was used to service the national debt.

Because welfare programs grew so rapidly at a time when the government refused to raise taxes, funds for other needed programs were cut back. In 1960, 6 percent of the federal budget was used to protect the environment or to build highways, water projects, and recreation facilities. By 1988, only 1 percent of the budget could be devoted to these activities, despite increasing public awareness of acid rain, deteriorating highways and bridges, and airports stretched beyond their capacity.

The rising cost of social programs was rooted in demographic change. There were three million more poor children in 1982 than in 1968, and their numbers continued to grow in the 1990s. An increasing number were born to single mothers, who were entitled to welfare payments for housing and Food Stamps. Federal funding only partially paid these benefits, however, and each state decided how much additional money poor families should receive. Conservatives attacked this system, claiming that it fostered the poverty it was supposed to eliminate. In 1996 the combination of the most conservative Congress in decades and a strong economy with generally low unemployment led to a radical restructuring of the welfare system. A sign posted in a national park suggests the attitude of a majority of Americans toward welfare programs: "Please do not feed the squirrels. If you feed the squirrels, they'll become overweight and prone to disease. Their population will grow, and they'll lose their ability to forage for food on their own. They will expect you to feed them and will attack you if you don't. They'll become like little welfare recipients, and you wouldn't want to do that to them."

With the aim of ending "welfare dependency," Congress abolished the expensive Aid to Families with Dependent Children (AFDC) program, and replaced it with Temporary Assistance to Needy Families (TANF). The new law established an absolute time limit for benefits, and no adult was to receive more than five years of support during his or her lifetime. Thus if an unmarried mother uses up four years of assistance by the time she is 25, she can only receive one more year of welfare, even if she lives to be 100. Furthermore, welfare payments are by no means automatic even during these five years. Instead, re-training and education have been made mandatory. TANF is administered at the state level, partially funded by block grants from Washington. Time limits, retraining, and local controls together have dramatically reduced the number of people on welfare. To some extent, this change stems from a strong economy with low unemployment. The next economic downturn will test how effectively TANF helps the poor.

In contrast to the radical changes in welfare, the Social Security pension program was not touched by these 1996 reforms. Taxpayers have contributed to this pension system throughout their working lives, and if there is one program that cannot be touched, this is it. Yet its costs are rising by more than $20 billion a year. Because life expectancy is increasing, every year more retired people are entitled both to payment of social security and to medical care, under the Medicare program. Already old people account for 40 percent of the use of short-stay hospitals, and expenditures for Medicare are increasing more than $30 billion annually. Thus the two programs together threaten in the long run to overwhelm the federal budget. Yet any attempt to cut back on these programs for the elderly immediately results in powerful opposition, because old people are politically active, with a higher voting percentage than young people. As a result, the poverty rate among the elderly has dropped decisively. One of every three lived below the poverty line in 1960; a generation later only one in seven did.

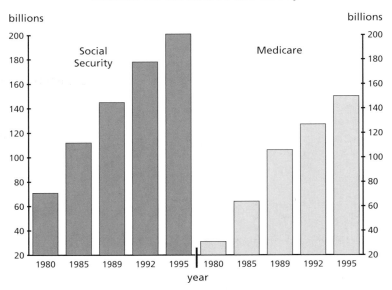

**Benefits for the Retired and Elderly**

Although care for the elderly has improved, the patchwork of individual investments, government programs, and private charities does not cover the rest of the population very systematically. No comprehensive medical program protects each citizen, as is the case in some European nations, and 98 percent of all working Americans get medical insurance through their employer, who usually pays about half the cost. As a people, Americans use 12 percent of the gross national product to pay for medical care, and yet 37 million people are not covered by an insurance program. In 1992 the high cost of this incomplete health coverage became an issue in the presidential campaign, when both Perot and Clinton pledged to introduce cost controls and comprehensive coverage, following European and Canadian models. However, Clinton's plan failed to muster sufficient political support in Congress.

The need for a new healthcare system remains obvious. A detailed study of inequalities in healthcare in Chicago concluded:

> What is it like to be sick and poor in the United States? It depends on how sick, how poor and how old you are. It depends on where you live. It depends on the color of your skin. It depends on your sex. If you are either very poor, blind, disabled, over 65, male, white or live in a middle- or upper-class neighborhood in a large urban center, you belong to a privileged class of healthcare recipients, and your chances of survival are good. But, if you are none of these, if you are only average poor, under 65, female, Black, or live in a low-income urban neighborhood, small town, or rural area, you are a disenfranchised citizen as far as health rights go, and your chances of survival are not good.

These faults in the American medical system are particularly evident in its attempts to deal with AIDS. As many as one million Americans are estimated to be infected with the virus, and many will fall ill in the next decade. Worse, it appears to have spread in the sectors of the population with little health insurance. Those who suffer from the disease will not have the money they need to pay for constant medical care. They cannot be neglected because of the threat AIDS poses to the public health of the population as a whole.

As with medical care, American welfare benefits are not designed to be comprehensive. They give people a bare subsistence for only a short period. For example, the poor receive food stamps, which they can use in supermarkets like money, but as their income rises, food stamps are correspondingly cut back. Likewise, unemployment payments last for six to nine months and usually amount to only about one quarter of a worker's previous wage. To maintain the same quality of life an unemployed person must find another job quickly, and it is expected that people will move if they cannot find work where they live. It is the job, not citizenship, that entitles Americans to medical care, a living wage, and a pension. And to get a job, one needs a good education.

## 5. Public Schools

Starting in Colonial times Americans had many primary schools, and although only a small proportion of the population had more than basic schooling, the country could nevertheless pride itself on being one of the most literate nations. Only in the 1830s did pressure build up for compulsory free education, and an extensive system of primary schools existed in all the states by 1850. The reasons for this commitment to basic education

## Organization of Education

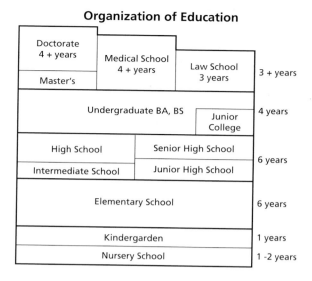

| | Years |
|---|---|
| Doctorate 4 + years / Master's; Medical School 4 + years; Law School 3 years | 3 + years |
| Undergraduate BA, BS; Junior College | 4 years |
| High School / Intermediate School; Senior High School / Junior High School | 6 years |
| Elementary School | 6 years |
| Kindergarden | 1 years |
| Nursery School | 1 -2 years |

are not hard to find. Thomas Jefferson and the other founding fathers believed that only an educated citizenry could ensure the survival of a democracy. Protestant clergy were equally sure that to maintain the hold of Christianity on the people they ought to be able to read the Bible. In the nineteenth century industrialists became particularly eager to improve the schools, because they required workers who were able to read, write, and calculate. Each of these left their mark on the school system, which did not resemble that in Britain, as it was more democratic in organization and aimed at more practical education. In the 1830s Tocqueville noted, "I do not believe that there is a country in the world where, in proportion to the population, there are so few ignorant and at the same time so few learned individuals. Primary instruction is within the reach of everybody; superior instruction is scarcely to be obtained by any."

Until the end of the nineteenth century most left school by age sixteen, while few completed high school and fewer still ever reached college. After 1900, however, high school gradually became a requirement. First grade begins at age six, junior high school begins at thirteen, and three years later students begin senior high school. Throughout these years students are graded and tested, and in junior high school they are put into classes of students of the same ability level. This "tracking" of students makes it possible to set up special, accelerated classes for the best students, but it also means that the rest of the students fall further and further behind them. A survey of all 18-year-olds showed that 80 percent finished high school, compared with only 50 percent in the 1950s. About six out of every ten students prepare for university. This has long-term implications, as hourly wages rise with the level of education. A high school drop-out earns on average $7.62 an hour, a high school graduate $9.43, a college graduate $14.77, and those with post-graduate degrees, $19.24.

The most obvious consequence of having a mixed system of education and social services, based on both public and private sources, is that quality varies a great deal. A wealthy town generally is willing to tax itself sufficiently to pay for an excellent school system, a good hospital, a fine library, and so forth. These services in turn attract new residents, and make real estate in the town more valuable. In contrast, a poor community often finds itself caught in a downward spiral, as it lacks the capital to pay for a fine school system, which in turn makes living in the town less attractive, driving away parents with young children, making the town poorer still.

One of the most controversial problems that each school board must face is adopting textbooks acceptable to their children's parents. Fundamentalist groups, for example, insist that the Biblical story of the creation be included in biology books alongside the Darwinian theory of evolution. Ethnic minorities object to history texts that put their homelands in a bad light. Catholics protest against sex education that includes birth control and abortion. The lively texts that teachers and students often prefer can raise controversy. To avoid offending any group, some publishers offer texts that will satisfy the most conservative states, such as Texas. But these cautious books are boring, taking all the life out of important issues, creating a dilemma for teachers who want to bring debate into the classroom.

The educational goal for the high school years and the first two years at university is to give students a broad knowledge of the sciences, humanities, and social sciences. While in Europe specialization begins already in gymnasium, Americans believe that early specialization is not in the interests of good citizenship. They believe that with no idea of biology the citizen cannot understand ecological problems, that with no grasp of physics developments in astronomy and nuclear weapons will remain too mysterious for a voter to make an informed judgement, and that without some knowledge of history and literature a citizen can easily fall prey to political slogans or specious analysis of social problems.

Unfortunately, many signs suggest that most high schools fail to achieve these goals. A series of private and public reports in the 1980s attacked the quality of American education. While the United States is lavish in spending on its universities, pre-college education has been unevenly supported. According to a report from the Economic Policy Institute, the country ranks only fourteenth when the sixteen major industrial countries are compared to see how much of their gross national product they spend on schools. In suburban communities the quality is often quite high, but rural areas and large cities have problems. A judge who examined the New York City public schools in 2000 concluded, "The majority of the city's public school students leave high school unprepared for more than low-paying work, unprepared for college, and unprepared for the duties placed upon them by a democratic society. The schools have broken a covenant with students, and with society." Other cities such as Boston, Minneapolis, and Seattle, were coping better, however, and one cannot generalize from New

York City to the nation as a whole. President Bush came into office determined to change the funding of public education, by giving parents the right to select their children's school. If adopted, parents would receive *vouchers*, or funding guarantees for each child, that would be transferable. The intention is to create competition between schools for pupils, by treating education as a marketplace.

However, it is easy to exaggerate the extent of the problem. Articles appeared in the European press a few years ago claiming that up to one fifth of all Americans are illiterate. This is patently untrue. According to the United Nations, the United States literacy rate is 99 percent. There is another problem, however, called "functional illiteracy," whose precise meaning is still a matter of debate. The basic idea is clear enough, however: some people read and write so poorly that they cannot interpret the brochures explaining their income tax, and they are unable to write a decent letter of application for a job. Undoubtedly, some of these functional illiterates represent failures of the school system. In addition, many of the immigrants who enter the United States each year cannot speak or write English adequately.

Because the quality of public schools varies, and because many families want a special education for their children, there are also many private schools in the United States. These receive no money from the state or federal government. Most notable are the religious schools. The Catholic parochial schools alone educate two million students, with many of the teachers members of religious orders. The Protestant churches also maintain a good many schools, in some cases in order to ensure that their students get a Christian education, but also in some cases to create *de facto* segregated schools. The quality of the education received varies a great deal, in some cases being considerably better than the standard of the public schools, not least because private schools can simply expel unruly students, while public schools cannot. However, the high cost of science education gives the public schools an advantage, as they almost always have more funds available. They can also afford to pay higher salaries, particularly in the richer suburban areas. The very best schools, however, are private boarding schools, which charge as much as $15,000-20,000 a year in tuition. These elite schools serve less than 1 percent of the population, and are one of the most important ways for the upper class to reproduce itself, giving students a set of manners, an intense discipline, and a more rigorous education than they can get elsewhere. The better, private boarding schools are extremely difficult to enter, despite this high cost, as they prepare students for the finest universities. Former President Bush, for example, attended a private boarding school before entering Yale.

## 6. Universities

The inspiration for the American university community undoubtedly comes from Oxford, Cambridge, and other university towns, such as Göttingen, Heidelberg, or Leiden. Like them, American universities are created as distinct realms of life, and they are expensive, privileged cultural enclaves where most students live full time and where all the facilities are organized to help maintain an intellectual way of life. Thus Harvard – or any of the other top two hundred universities in the United States – has a daily student newspaper, a radio station, a good art museum, a playhouse, a professional concert series, a round of weekly sporting contests, and a calendar of social events that runs day and night the year round. By comparison, most European universities have no radio stations or art museums. Their newspapers come out infrequently, they are short, and they are often not published by the students. The campus is open only during the day, and by five in the evening the telephone switchboard is closed, the cafeteria has stopped serving meals, the library is locked, and the buildings are deserted. Perhaps the most striking contrast between European and American universities, however, is their libraries. Harvard University has one of the largest and best libraries in the world, which is inaccessible to the general

*Snow Sculpture at the Dartmouth College Annual Winter Carnival. – Adrian Bouchard.*

public, though its open stacks are available to students and professors. In contrast, despite their antiquity, most European universities have much smaller libraries, which often consist of scattered collections in individual departments, but no central library worthy of the name. Instead, along with the general public, European academics often use their national library and other public libraries, which fortunately are not bad, though hardly as good as those of the major American universities, which not only have larger collections but remain open most evenings and weekends.

American universities are far more than teaching institutions. They are centers of research where roughly half of the world's Nobel Prize winners lead research teams. As one character in a Saul Bellow novel deftly summarized:

> Vast powers stream from the universities into government – the Defense Department, the State Department, the Treasury, the Fed [Federal Reserve Board], the intelligence services, the White House. Your modern university also is a power base in biotechnology, energy production, electronics. Academics polarize light for copying machines, they get venture capital from Honeywell, General Mills, GT&E, they are corporate entrepreneurs on the grand scale-consultants, big-time pundits, technical witnesses before congressional committees on arms control or foreign policy.

This description holds true whether one speaks of the public universities, which have an enrolment of 11.5 million, or the private universities with 3.3 million students. Most of the latter began as religious institutions, and many are today elite schools that accept only students from the very top of their high school class. Amherst College, for example, is one of the most selective colleges in the country. Although the applicants for admission come from the top of their high school class and have scored high on national tests, the majority will be rejected. The selection process requires a large full-time staff at each university.

Virtually all high school students who plan to go on to the university take the same examination, the Scholastic Aptitude Test (SAT). This examination is given on the same day at the same time all over the United States. It lasts several hours, and consists of hundreds of multiple-choice questions, which are divided into two groups: verbal skills and mathematical skills. The test score for each group ranges from 200 (no questions answered correctly) to 800 (a perfect score). In recent years the national average has hovered between 450 and 500, with few students managing more than a 600 on either examination. Taking such a test is a traumatic experience, and students wait anxiously to hear the results. Colleges naturally prefer to admit students with high scores, and although high school grades are important, good SATs can open the door to many a good university, as well as ensure scholarship money. Students usually wait to decide what colleges they will apply to until they see how well they have done on the tests.

Since there are more than 3,700 universities and colleges, choosing the "right" one is a time-consuming process, requiring correspondence, a good deal of reading, and advice from professional counsellors who often must convince parents that their child has no chance of getting into Harvard. Actually, Harvard and Yale are by no means the most selective universities in the United States, as smaller elite colleges such as Williams, Amherst, Wesleyan, or Reed turn down a larger percentage of their applicants, and have a higher average SAT score among those they select. Indeed, the most elite schools pay less attention to such scores than other schools, and insist that in addition to being a good student each admitted candidate ought to have some special quality, such as writing ability, athletic prowess, musical talent, or a gift for acting.

It costs as much as $100 in application fees for every school, and students typically apply to at least three or four. Moreover, before colleges make their final selection, they not only want to see grades, SAT scores, letters of recommendation from teachers, and an essay written by the student; they also like to meet the candidate for a half-hour personal interview, followed by a tour of the campus. Very good candidates are given special treatment, but no one willing to pay the application fee is denied an interview. The fierce competition for admission occurs despite an enormous financial burden on parents. Tuition at a prestigious private college like Amherst is more than $25,000 a year, or almost $100,000 over a period of four years. These figures do not include the cost of travel to the university, books, a personal computer, entertainment, or clothing, so the total cost is much higher. Private colleges know that their tuition is high, but point out that a student's education costs much more, up to $40,000 per year. Because Amherst has an endowment of over $150 million, every student in effect receives a subsidy. To send one child to such a university, parents must start saving for tuition soon after the child is born, and in most cases they will also borrow money from the government at low interest rates. For students from poor families, many scholarships are available. At Amherst, for example, 40 percent of the students receive scholarships, which average $10,000 a year.

Colleges such as Amherst and the Ivy League universities were founded in the early years in order to train Protestant clergy, and long were the only schools of higher education. When the Midwest was being settled in the nineteenth century, however, it became government practice to create a public university in each new state, paid for from the sale of unoccupied lands. These so-called "land grant" institutions today include such internationally recognized universities as Michigan, Minnesota, and Wisconsin. The University of Vermont, a better than average public institution, offers a typical example of what public higher education cost in 1997. State universities' tuition and fees are lower than those of private colleges, varying according to the prosperity of the state and the willingness of its citizens to invest in education. Nevertheless, by European standards the cost is high. At Vermont, state residents paid $6,468 and non-residents $22,289 for one year. Students received some medical care through the university health service for $185, but they also needed accident and sickness insurance, which the university sold for $542 a year to those who were not covered by their parents' insurance policies. To these expenses must be added the cost of travel to the university, textbooks, entertainment, laundry, and other expenses, including a personal computer. The total for a resident comes to at least $15,000 per year, while students from other states need $25,000. (One curiosity of recent years: in some states, retired persons, who do not need an education to make a living, can attend public university courses for free or for a nominal fee, in contrast to young people who must pay.)

**Cost of Studying, University of Vermont, 1996-1997.**

|  | Vermont Residents ($) | Out of State ($) |
| --- | --- | --- |
| Tuition | 6,468 | 16,164 |
| Dormitory room (Double) | 3,242 | 3,242 |
| Meals (minimal plan) | 1,390 | 1,390 |
| Books and supplies (estimated) | 510 | 510 |
| Library and athletic bond fee | 92 | 92 |
| Health service fee | 185 | 185 |
| Accident and sickness insurance (optional) | 542 | 542 |
| Student association fee | 80 | 80 |
| Student center fee | 22 | 22 |
| Transportation fee | 46 | 46 |
| Inter-residence association fee | 16 | 16 |
| Minimum cost per year | 12,593 | 22,289 |

Both public and private universities organize their curriculums in a way that is unfamiliar to most Europeans. While an English, Danish, or German student expects to concentrate on one or two subjects at the university, American students often enter without having chosen a major field, and select one only later. In the first year they take a broad range of courses, in part to fulfil distribution requirements, and in part to decide what subject they will pursue. Students frequently change their minds several times about their major field, but unlike Europe where such changes would mean a great inconvenience and loss of time as the student shifted from one faculty to another, in the United States this causes only minimal problems, because each course followed is considered an individual unit. Once completed, it will "count" toward graduation in most majors. In marked contrast to European universities, individual courses usually can be transferred from one university to another with relative ease, facilitating exchanges and ensuring that a student need not repeat a course merely because he or she has transferred from one school to another.

Most American university students stop living at home when they begin their studies, but because their parents pay much of the high cost of tuition, they remain financially dependent on them until they get their first job. In contrast, Scandinavian students pay no university tuition at all and receive a monthly stipend from the government. Their parents pay taxes to the state, which in turn finances their education. This difference may also account for why American universities send a steady stream of information home to the parents, including not only grades but also invitations to sporting events, plays, and concerts. In addition, one day each year is designated "Parents Day," when fathers and mothers are invited to visit the campus, meet the faculty, and participate in a full program of activities. Keep in mind that American students start university at age 18, a few years before their European counterparts. This imposes an additional role on the university, which works with the parents in preparing young people for adulthood. In contrast, European students are usually older. Their universities are often administered as bureaucratic extensions of the state, and therefore make few overtures to parents. For related reasons, American universities periodically conduct fund-raising campaigns, to enlarge their endowments, to increase scholarship aid, and to construct new buildings. The alumni of even a small college may give more than $1 million a year in response to such appeals. Europeans just pay taxes.

The American system results in students who are free to explore a wide range of fields, who enjoy a close relationship with some of their teachers, and who devote themselves full-time to a university life in a separate community. It has the drawback that undergraduate students are less mature and remain financially dependent upon their parents for a long period. This can delay emergence into independent adulthood, as the American undergraduate is pressed to study with a single-minded intensity, in a highly competitive environment for four years. Only one student in ten goes on to the graduate level to obtain a professional degree: such as law (three years), medicine (four years plus an internship), dentistry (three years), business (two years), and the Ph.D. (four to six years, depending upon field.)

Competition for grades and for admission to graduate school can create pressures and anxieties, particularly at the end of each term. Racial differences may increase the tension, which can be unleashed by external events. For example, in April of 1992 at the University of Massachusetts in Amherst, hundreds of students demonstrated in support of the Los Angeles rioters. This action polarized the campus. Less dramatic, but every bit as important, are individual racial incidents that continue to occur on American campuses, and which have been on the increase in recent years.

To bind the students together, most universities have long emphasized athletics. They usually have excellent facilities and require students to take some form of light exercise in their first year. The facilities are also available free to faculty. The most notable spectator events vary by school, as some emphasize basketball or hockey, but usually the most important are the fall football games, which often draw more than 50,000 spectators, as well as a national television audience for a few selected games each Saturday. As Allen Guttmann has noted, "the football weekend is the closest American equivalent to a Roman holiday." Surrounding the actual contests are parades, pep rallies, dinners, and formal dances, promoting an atmosphere of revelry and drinking sharply at odds with the seriousness maintained during the week. "The most remarkable aspect of this situation is that American academics, apart from a bemused or embittered minority, accept this curious state of affairs as if it were part of the unalterable order of nature." Indeed, while not a formal part of the curriculum, sports embody many of the most important American values.

# American Values

"In the United States a man builds a house in which to spend his old age, and he sells it before the roof is on; he plants a garden and lets [rents] it just as the trees are coming into bearing; he brings a field into tillage and leaves other men to gather the crops; he embraces a profession and gives it up; he settles in a place, which he soon afterwards leaves to carry his changeable longings elsewhere. If his private affairs leave him any leisure, he instantly plunges into the vortex of politics; and if at the end of a year of unrelenting labor he finds he has a few days' vacation, his eager curiosity whirls him over the vast extent of the United States, and he will travel fifteen hundred miles in a few days to shake off his happiness. Death at length overtakes him, but it is before he is weary of his bootless chase of that complete felicity which forever escapes him." – Alexis de Tocqueville

## I  Individualism

The restlessness Tocqueville described is still very much alive. Americans have idealized people who do not settle in one place, starting with Davy Crockett and other frontier heroes, including the families in covered wagons who have "pulled up stakes" and moved on. Many works of American literature express the fascination with movement, and the hunger for new experience. In 1855 Walt Whitman expressed this restlessness near the end of his "Song of Myself."

> I tramp a perpetual journey, (come listen all)
> My signs are a rain-proof coat, good shoes,
>    and a staff cut from the woods,
> No friend of mine takes his ease in my chair,
> I have no chair, no church, no philosophy,
> I lead no man to a dinner-table, library, exchange,
> But each man and each woman of you I lead upon a knoll,
> My left hand hooking you round the waist,
> My right hand points to landscapes of continents
>    and the public road.

*Vida Blue pitching in the World Series, 1972. – Wide World.*

Likewise, Mark Twain's Huckleberry Finn refuses to settle in one place or to adopt a fixed identity, and the Hemingway hero is by definition permanently away from home. John Dos Passos evoked the same theme in the first pages of his trilogy, *U.S.A.*, in which a young man walks through the streets, "Fast, but not fast enough (faces slide out of sight, talk trails into tattered scraps, footsteps tap fainter in alleys); he must catch the last subway, the streetcar, the bus, run up the gangplanks of all the steamboats, register at all the hotels, work in the cities, answer the wantads, learn the trades, take up the jobs, live in all the boardinghouses, sleep in all the beds. One bed is not enough, one job is not enough, one life is not enough." Thus the Dos Passos hero in Tocqueville's expression, "leaves to carry his changeable longings elsewhere." The film *Easy Rider* depicted two young men on motor cycles dedicated to the ideal of continual wandering that Whitman and Dos Passos describe. The extreme form of this rootlessness is the life of the trailer park. For every ten families that own homes, an eleventh family has a mobile home up to ten meters long, designed to be towed from place to place. Some of these are vacation vehicles, but several million Americans have chosen the nomadic life, carrying all their possessions with them like the homesteaders of the nineteenth century. They no longer seek land but work or escape, moving restlessly with no final destination. Finally, there is the darker side of this individualism, the several million homeless in America who live from day to day. They wander from soup kitchen to park bench to railway station, and sleep in abandoned buildings or on hot air grates beside large buildings. For them, the dream of mobility and the freedom of the road has become a nightmare.

*Michael Jordan (left), the most celebrated American athlete in the nineties, during the finals in 1997. – PolFoto.*

The national restlessness is based in part on an American belief in the perpetual possibility of new beginnings, a belief based on more than three centuries of experience. While the geographical size of European countries has not changed a great deal in the past two centuries, the United States has tripled in land area. While European population has grown slowly in recent decades, the population of the United States has more than doubled since 1930, and the population of 1930 was double that of 1890. To translate this growth into something more concrete, consider that the annual birth of more than 4 million children and the arrival of 800,000 new immigrants means that a large new city of houses, schools, jobs, stores, hospitals, and every other facility must be added every single year. Because this growth has been combined with general prosperity, one American historian has characterized Americans as a "people of plenty," whose life expectations are shaped by the general availability of material goods. Even during the depression of the 1930s the population grew by nine million, and Americans experienced not a shortage of goods but a lack of money to buy them. Because material things are so generally available to most Americans, they often cease to be the most important thing in life. Instead, Americans restlessly search for self-fulfilment and hunger for new experience.

## 2. Values Expressed in Everyday Life

Beyond restlessness, individualism, and the effects of material well-being, Americans themselves often feel it is difficult to list other national traits. Because of the many ethnic groups, regional variations, and religious denominations, American academics also are reluctant to define a set of values shared by all citizens. Yet the European can spot an American tourist immediately, noting any number of small signs: the use of knife and fork, an intentional carelessness and practicality in dress, a slouching relaxed walk, and in speech, broad vowels and a distinctive "R" sound. The outside observer feels that these shared characteristics hint at a common culture and a common mentality, however diverse the surface of American society.

Each culture has its rituals, routines, and unconscious assumptions, and these are embodied in such concrete events of daily life as eating. In Scandinavia, for example, eating is far more ritualized than in the United States. A Dane presented with a smorgasbord selection of herring, salmon, cold turkey, warm beef, and cheese will eat the items in the order listed, and will finish each item before taking the next one. But an American who has just arrived in Denmark cannot know the local rules for eating these foods, and will eat them in random order, often starting a second item before the first is fully consumed. Just as important, Americans as a group would not be likely to develop a set of rules prescribing how to eat these dishes. Such differences in eating habits are not trivial. They reflect the pluralism and individualism of American culture and the rejection of the European idea of the formalities of the table. When Americans do sit down to a formal meal, it seldom lasts more than an hour. More often, they eat on the run, and so have invented many kinds of fast food, including the ice

*Child eating fast food. – Byron Schumaker.*

cream cone, hot dog, hamburger, and pizza. They want portable food, to be eaten quickly, in any order. Americans snack often during the day, and family members frequently do not eat together, especially now that the micro-wave oven is in three out of four homes. It has made food preparation so rapid and easy that even young children can make a passable meal in less than ten minutes.

Just as there is little sense that there is a proper place to eat, so too Americans will eat at almost any time. Every city has its all-night restaurants and cafés, its supermarkets open until midnight. Because meal time is not regarded as an activity securely located in time or taking place in private space, Americans often combine eating and business. They do not merely go out to dinner with business associates; they combine breakfast with formal meetings held before eight in the morning. American university teachers commonly hold "luncheon meetings," combining a department meeting with a bag lunch. The American day is not firmly segmented into distinct units, and often a meal has to be squeezed in as an afterthought in the midst of a busy schedule, or occasionally there is no time to eat. Fast food is also standardized food, produced through mechanization and the use of assembly line methods, to deliver it quickly, to keep its price low, and to minimize the time required. Habituated to a fast tempo of eating, Americans are irritated by a leisurely meal, while Europeans are disconcerted by how little time Americans remain at the table and how they behave while there. A recent survey found that only one-third of the time do adult Americans eat at a table with other people without distractions. At any given mealtime 64 percent watch television, read, work, or do something else while eating. Fast-food restaurants have found that customers kept waiting more than a few minutes are impatient. To make fast food even faster, some shops have eliminated seats for customers who no longer have time to sit, and they have installed computer stations that permit customers to punch in an order that goes directly to the food preparation area, saving valuable seconds. In their meals Americans blur the distinction between public and private life. They prefer to save time rather than eat well, and they give more importance to work than to food.

Lord Bryce, the great British observer of American society in the nineteenth century, suggested that the foreigner ought to study baseball in order to understand the United States. The national game unites members of every social class, ethnic background, and political disposition in a common passion. Apparently a value-free leisure activity, baseball is quite unlike European football, which is played on a rigidly defined field for a specified time. In contrast, baseball at least in theory has no spatial or temporal limits. A batter is encouraged to hit the ball as far as possible, and two perfectly matched teams could play forever. Even the confrontation between a batter and a pitcher has no set time limit. The play in soccer is continuous and regulated by the clock, baseball is a game of discreet actions, each quite distinct, followed by a pause. Every one of these actions has its winner and loser, as each gives an advantage to one team or the other. Between these plays nothing seems to happen, but each side is planning its next move. Where soccer requires continuous effort and stresses improvisation, baseball alternates between extremely rapid, planned plays and still moments of strategy. It requires from the players both physical agility and the mental habits of a chess master. And where every player in soccer is in constant motion, acting as part of a team, usually the baseball player must act alone or with one or two others. Each baseball player has a distinct location on the field where his play can be scrutinized, with the result that the responsibility for almost every event in a baseball game can be quantified. Player performance can thus be compared statistically according to an apparently objective scale. In contrast, beyond counting the goals, quantification is not important in soccer. Finally, baseball is a spring and summer game, associated with good weather, natural grass, and pastoral views. It suggests an escape from time-bound routines in a potentially limitless absorbing entertainment. Analysis of baseball thus provides a list of traits that Americans accept as natural: freedom from spatial restraints, timelessness, pastoralism, and individualism, and it consists of quantifiable actions bracketed by continual strategic planning.

Yet American values cannot be read from baseball alone, for there is another distinctive American sport, football, which has become more popular since World War II, and which is well-suited to television. While individualistic baseball was once by far the most popular American game, football has steadily gained in appeal during the past four decades. In these years, when corporate work also became dominant, football's values of teamwork, violent competition, and the submersion of the self in group effort became increasingly appealing. American football retains baseball's bursts of action organized by strategic planning, but it is more of a team sport, in which twenty-two players all move at once. So much happens in the 10 to 15 seconds of the average play that the actions of only a few players are distinct to the fan. Each football play is so complex that it requires a whole staff of coaches to observe what is happening on the field, plus extensive videos that can be analyzed in slow motion later. Football reflects the modern bureaucratic life of the large corporation: it has hierarchy, planning, technology, teamwork, intense competition, and the pressure of meeting inexorable deadlines. In addition, where baseball fans are largely spontaneous in their cheering, football has cheerleaders (rows of young women in short skirts) and brass bands, who march with rhythmic military precision. Together, baseball and football, which are equally popular, express a tension between two different ethics, which can be described in paired oppositions such as: individualism versus teamwork and hierarchy; or timelessness versus time pressures.

# 3. Contradictory Values

The study of sports and eating habits suggests a set of national characteristics. They express an American mentality shared by all social classes and ethnic groups, which is neither a matter of conscious moral principle nor a subject of debate. Nevertheless, something is lost if the analysis stops here. As the comparison of baseball and football suggests, every pronounced national characteristic is in tension with another, opposite trait, forming a series of contradictory pairs. Not surprisingly, foreigners often see only one half of the pair, and draw over-simplified conclusions. Thus Americans are often described as "individualistic," in the sense that they dislike authority and take responsibility for their own fate. Hereditary titles are illegal, and distinction in the world must arise through individual effort. In the eighteenth century, Benjamin Franklin personified this trait, running away from home, breaking off his apprenticeship, starting his own printing business, and becoming a wealthy man, famous inventor, and national politician. Franklin's image of himself as being "self-made" has appealed to Americans ever since, and is embodied in many popular songs, such as Frank Sinatra's "My Way." Put more broadly, American individualism means a limited role for the state and freedom from binding obligations, whether to the church, the military, or another centralized authority.

Yet this well-known individualism is partly balanced by attraction to many forms of communalism, found not only in the churches, but in social experiments. Both the Pilgrims at Plymouth in 1620 and the settlers at Jamestown in 1607 experimented with sharing all their material goods. The United States was also the stage for an astonishing number of socialist experiments during the first half of the nineteenth century, a few of which still survive to this day. Likewise, in the 1960s social critics were surprised to see how quickly many middle-class Americans joined the communal experiments and religious communities that blossomed in the counter-culture. If individualism is a dominant American trait, there is also a weaker, but persistent impulse toward simple communism, toward escape from being the only one responsible for success to being part of a group where personal success is no longer a value. Indeed, the existence of this attraction may help explain why Americans found communism frightening. It called out to their own shadow side.

Americans are often accused of being materialistic, yet how can this be so if they are also so religious? This contradiction can be resolved if one understands that possessions are highly symbolic to Americans. Lacking a precise sense of class or a strong sense of region, the American uses property to define himself, to say who he is. More than Europeans, Americans announce who they are through the car they drive, the clothing they wear, and the house they live in. Their possessions are not highly valued as objects, and indeed quickly lose their use value. Hence the tremendous circulation of used goods in American society, where every weekend is marked by innumerable yard sales or garage sales, where a great range of small furniture, books, magazines, glassware, half-broken appliances, and "collectibles" are advertised in the newspapers. Indeed, churches themselves are quite involved in this circulation of used goods, holding rummage sales in their basements, and thus uniting in one event religious-based social contact, philanthropic ends, and the recycling of consumer goods.

There are many other ways in which Americans are contradictory. If they are fanatically egalitarian and would never permit the establishment of royalty or hereditary titles, they nevertheless love visits from royalty, especially from England. If they are anarchic and suspicious of discipline, they are also fascinated with order. The assembly line was a popular tourist attraction when it was first in operation, both at the Ford plants and at world's fairs. Yet if the Americans have the world's most advanced computers, they refuse to use them to create a "personal number" system like that in the Nordic countries, because they fear the government will abuse such a system.

Americans are individualistic and yet they are "other-directed." This term was coined by David Riesman, but in fact Americans have been other-directed at least since the 1830s when Tocqueville observed them and found that they were far more concerned to know what other people thought of them than Europeans. Americans want to be accepted by others, even as they pursue their individual path. Americans love new machines, and they take up each new device, from the cordless telephone to the personal computer to the microwave oven to virtual reality with an almost childish delight in its novelty. Yet even as they embrace technology, they also identify with nature. They want a pastoral retreat from civilization, supplied with a new computer. Indeed, Americans often blur the line between nature and culture, as is the case with Disneyland. There, trees are made of plastic, wild animals turn out to be machines that threaten visitors on cue, and one can visit simulations of the African jungles and outer space in the same day. As one European commented, "Disneyland tells us that technology gives us more reality than Nature can."

## 4. The American Sense of History

As their love of technology suggests, Americans are notoriously future-oriented, focusing on where they are going rather than where they have been.

*Future oriented*

*Sources of future orientation*

*Pragmatism*

In political terms, this means that there is no political conservatism in America, in the sense of traditionalism. Virtually no one wants to keep things the way they are or return to an earlier historical era, and presidential politicians have been successful with slogans calling for a "new freedom," a "new deal", a "new frontier," and, in 1992, Clinton's "new covenant." For the American, change itself is a good thing, and a person's life or the worth of a society is measured not by its past but by its potential. When Americans long for the past, they adopt a nostalgic mood, looking over their shoulders at earlier times which they feel have been irretrievably lost.

Every culture has its own sense of history, its sense of the larger rhythm that incorporates immediate events. Some societies see the present as an imperfect copy of an earlier golden age. Others see the present as a slightly improved repetition of the past. Americans have long tended to see the present as only a faint outline of the future. Even during the 1930s the populace doggedly held on to visions of a better tomorrow. In the middle of that decade of depression, sociologists investigating a typical American community found that it "teaches its members to live at the future rather than in the present or past." The sources of this future orientation included Christian eschatology, capitalism, the frontier tradition of building "tomorrow out of a crude present," and the theory of evolution. But equally important was "the hypnotizing promise of more and more things tomorrow which . . . machine technologies and [a] rising standard of living offer."

Given their orientation toward the future, Americans tend to be philosophical pragmatists. They adopt an idea as a kind of technique, good for today only. Its truth value is not an absolute but it is determined by its utility. What works is what matters. Thus, informally educated inventors such as Thomas Edison and Henry Ford are folk heroes, while few citizens can name a single American scientist from the nineteenth century. This lack of interest in metaphysics or formal theorizing in the general population is not so characteristic of the academy. Yet even there, in the 1890s William James formalized the American habit of mind into his philosophy of pragmatism.

*anti-intellectualism*

The hidden side to this pragmatic thrust toward the future is a fascination with the past, which represents an exotic, lost world that appeals to the American hunger for new experience. Because their own history begins only after 1492 and takes no definite shape until the seventeenth century, because the country itself came into existence only a little over two hundred years ago, Americans have long been awed by the antiquity of Asian and European civilizations, which stretch back through thousands of years of written records and architectural monuments. Most European museums pay little attention to collecting art from the United States, with the exception of Native American artefacts and avant-garde work produced since 1945. In contrast, when the great American museums were created in the last years of the nineteenth century, huge sums of money were expended on antiquities from Greece, Rome, and Egypt, and enormous collections of European fine art were assembled. By building these museums Americans paid tribute to their European background, but at the same time they were calling attention to the difference between the United States and the Old World. For even as they constructed these vast museums, Americans saw Europeans as their opposites. In fiction, foreign policy, and politics, Americans celebrated their exceptionalism, their radical innocence, their escape from European culture. In saying they were not Europeans, Americans tried to come to terms with their new civilization.

This book began by examining how Europeans imagined America; it ends with some contradictions Americans use to imagine themselves.

| | | |
|---|---|---|
| Individualism | vs. | communalism |
| equality | vs | hierarchy |
| regional | vs. | national |
| white | vs. | Black |
| pluralism | vs. | the melting pot |
| rural | vs. | urban |
| resistance to order | vs. | desire for mechanical perfection |
| pastoralism | vs. | technological solutions |
| timelessness | vs. | "time is money" |
| inner-directed | vs. | other-directed |
| the future | vs. | the "exotic" past |
| America | vs. | Europe |

# Appendix I
# Declaration of Independence

WHEN in the Course of human Events, it becomes necessary for one People to dissolve the Political Bands which have connected them with another, and to assume among the Powers of the Earth, the separate and equal Station to which the Laws of Nature and of Nature's God entitle them, a decent Respect to the Opinions of Mankind requires that they should declare the Causes which impel them to the Separation.

WE hold these Truths to be self-evident, that all Men are created equal, that they are endowed by their Creator with certain unalienable Rights, that among these are Life, Liberty and the Pursuit of Happiness -- That to secure these Rights, Governments are instituted among Men, deriving their just Powers from the Consent of the Governed, that whenever any Form of Government becomes destructive of these Ends, it is the Right of the People to alter or to abolish it, and to institute new Government, laying its Foundation on such Principles, and organizing its Powers in such Form, as to them shall seem most likely to effect their Safety and Happiness. Prudence, indeed, will dictate that Governments long established should not be changed for light and transient Causes; and accordingly all Experience hath shewn, that Mankind are more disposed to suffer, while Evils are sufferable, than to right themselves by abolishing the Forms to which they are accustomed. But when a long Train of Abuses and Usurpations, pursuing invariably the same Object, evinces a Design to reduce them under absolute Despotism, it is their Right, it is their Duty, to throw off such Government, and to provide new Guards for their future Security. Such has been the patient Sufferance of these Colonies; and such is now the Necessity which constrains them to alter their former Systems of Government. The History of the present King of Great Britain is a History of repeated Injuries and Usurpations, all having in direct Object the Establishment of an absolute Tyranny over these States. To prove this, let Facts be submitted to a candid World.

HE has refused his Assent to Laws, the most wholesome and necessary for the public Good.

HE has forbidden his Governors to pass Laws of immediate and pressing Importance, unless suspended in their Operation till his Assent should be obtained; and when so suspended, he has utterly neglected to attend to them.

HE has refused to pass other Laws for the Accommodation of large Districts of People, unless those People would relinquish the Right of Representation in the Legislature, a Right inestimable to them, and formidable to Tyrants only.

HE has called together Legislative Bodies at Places unusual, uncomfortable, and distant from the Depository of their public Records, for the sole Purpose of fatiguing them into Compliance with his Measures.

HE has dissolved Representative Houses repeatedly, for opposing with manly Firmness his Invasions on the Rights of the People.

HE has refused for a long Time, after such Dissolutions, to cause others to be elected; whereby the Legislative Powers, incapable of Annihilation, have returned to the People at large for their exercise; the State remaining in the mean time exposed to all the Dangers of Invasion from without, and the Convulsions within.

HE has endeavoured to prevent the Population of these States; for that Purpose obstructing the Laws for Naturalization of Foreigners; refusing to pass others to encourage their Migrations hither, and raising the Conditions of new Appropriations of Lands.

HE has obstructed the Administration of Justice, by refusing his Assent to Laws for establishing Judiciary Powers.

HE has made Judges dependent on his Will alone, for the Tenure of their Offices, and the Amount and Payment of their Salaries.

HE has erected a Multitude of new Offices, and sent hither Swarms of Officers to harrass our People, and eat out their Substance.

HE has kept among us, in Times of Peace, Standing Armies, without the consent of our Legislatures.

HE has affected to render the Military independent of and superior to the Civil Power.

HE has combined with others to subject us to a Jurisdiction foreign to our Constitution, and unacknowledged by our Laws; giving his Assent to their Acts of pretended Legislation:

FOR quartering large Bodies of Armed Troops among us;

FOR protecting them, by a mock Trial, from Punishment for any Murders which they should commit on the Inhabitants of these States:

FOR cutting off our Trade with all Parts of the World:

FOR imposing Taxes on us without our Consent:

FOR depriving us, in many Cases, of the Benefits of Trial by Jury:

FOR transporting us beyond Seas to be tried for pretended Offences:

FOR abolishing the free System of English Laws in a neighbouring Province, establishing therein an arbitrary Government, and enlarging its

Boundaries, so as to render it at once an Example and fit Instrument for introducing the same absolute Rules into these Colonies:

FOR taking away our Charters, abolishing our most valuable Laws, and altering fundamentally the Forms of our Governments:

FOR suspending our own Legislatures, and declaring themselves invested with Power to legislate for us in all Cases whatsoever.

HE has abdicated Government here, by declaring us out of his Protection and waging War against us.

HE has plundered our Seas, ravaged our Coasts, burnt our Towns, and destroyed the Lives of our People.

HE is, at this Time, transporting large Armies of foreign Mercenaries to compleat the Works of Death, Desolation, and Tyranny, already begun with circumstances of Cruelty and Perfidy, scarcely paralleled in the most barbarous Ages, and totally unworthy the Head of a civilized Nation.

HE has constrained our fellow Citizens taken Captive on the high Seas to bear Arms against their Country, to become the Executioners of their Friends and Brethren, or to fall themselves by their Hands.

HE has excited domestic Insurrections amongst us, and has endeavoured to bring on the Inhabitants of our Frontiers, the merciless Indian Savages, whose known Rule of Warfare, is an undistinguished Destruction, of all Ages, Sexes and Conditions.

IN every stage of these Oppressions we have Petitioned for Redress in the most humble Terms: Our repeated Petitions have been answered only by repeated Injury. A Prince, whose Character is thus marked by every act which may define a Tyrant, is unfit to be the Ruler of a free People.

NOR have we been wanting in Attentions to our British Brethren. We have warned them from Time to Time of Attempts by their Legislature to extend an unwarrantable Jurisdiction over us. We have reminded them of the Circumstances of our Emigration and Settlement here. We have appealed to their native Justice and Magnanimity, and we have conjured them by the Ties of our common Kindred to disavow these Usurpations, which, would inevitably interrupt our Connections and Correspondence. They too have been deaf to the Voice of Justice and of Consanguinity. We must, therefore, acquiesce in the Necessity, which denounces our Separation, and hold them, as we hold the rest of Mankind, Enemies in War, in Peace, Friends.

WE, therefore, the Representatives of the UNITED STATES OF AMERICA, in GENERAL CONGRESS, Assembled, appealing to the Supreme Judge of the World for the Rectitude of our Intentions, do, in the Name, and by Authority of the good People of these Colonies, solemnly Publish and Declare, That these United Colonies are, and of Right ought to be,

FREE AND INDEPENDENT STATES; that they are absolved from all Allegiance to the British Crown, and that all political Connection between them and the State of Great-Britain, is and ought to be totally dissolved; and that as FREE AND INDEPENDENT STATES, they have full Power to levy War, conclude Peace, contract Alliances, establish Commerce, and to do all other Acts and Things which INDEPENDENT STATES may of right do. And for the support of this Declaration, with a firm Reliance on the Protection of divine Providence, we mutually pledge to each other our Lives, our Fortunes, and our sacred Honor.

*[Signed by John Hancock, President of the Congress,*
*and by representatives of the several states.]*

# Appendix 2
# Constitution of the United States

We the people of the United States, in order to form a more perfect union, establish justice, insure domestic tranquility, provide for the common defense, promote the general welfare, and secure the blessings of liberty to ourselves and our posterity, do ordain and establish this Constitution for the United States of America.

## Article I

Section 1. All legislative powers herein granted shall be vested in a Congress of the United States, which shall consist of a Senate and House of Representatives.

Section 2. The House of Representatives shall be composed of members chosen every second year by the people of the several states, and the electors in each state shall have the qualifications requisite for electors of the most numerous branch of the state legislature.

No person shall be a Representative who shall not have attained to the age of twenty five years, and been seven years a citizen of the United States, and who shall not, when elected, be an inhabitant of that state in which he shall be chosen. Representatives and direct taxes shall be apportioned among the several states which may be included within this union, according to their respective numbers, which shall be determined by adding to the whole number of free persons, including those bound to service for a term of years, and excluding Indians not taxed, three fifths of all other Persons. The actual Enumeration shall be made within three years after the first meeting of the Congress of the United States, and within every subsequent term of ten years, in such manner as they shall by law direct. The number of Representatives shall not exceed one for every thirty thousand, but each state shall have at least one Representative; and until such enumeration shall be made, the state of New Hampshire shall be entitled to chuse three, Massachusetts eight, Rhode Island and Providence Plantations one, Connecticut five, New York six, New Jersey four, Pennsylvania eight,

Delaware one, Maryland six, Virginia ten, North Carolina five, South Carolina five, and Georgia three.

When vacancies happen in the Representation from any state, the executive authority thereof shall issue writs of election to fill such vacancies. The House of Representatives shall choose their speaker and other officers; and shall have the sole power of impeachment.

Section 3. The Senate of the United States shall be composed of two Senators from each state, chosen by the legislature thereof, for six years; and each Senator shall have one vote. Immediately after they shall be assembled in consequence of the first election, they shall be divided as equally as may be into three classes. The seats of the Senators of the first class shall be vacated at the expiration of the second year, of the second class at the expiration of the fourth year, and the third class at the expiration of the sixth year, so that one third may be chosen every second year; and if vacancies happen by resignation, or otherwise, during the recess of the legislature of any state, the executive thereof may make temporary appointments until the next meeting of the legislature, which shall then fill such vacancies. No person shall be a Senator who shall not have attained to the age of thirty years, and been nine years a citizen of the United States and who shall not, when elected, be an inhabitant of that state for which he shall be chosen.

The Vice President of the United States shall be President of the Senate, but shall have no vote, unless they be equally divided. The Senate shall choose their other officers, and also a President pro tempore, in the absence of the Vice President, or when he shall exercise the office of President of the United States.

The Senate shall have the sole power to try all impeachments. When sitting for that purpose, they shall be on oath or affirmation. When the President of the United States is tried, the Chief Justice shall preside. And no person shall be convicted without the concurrence of two thirds of the members present.

Judgment in cases of impeachment shall not extend further than to removal from office, and disqualification to hold and enjoy any office of honor, trust or profit under the United States: but the party convicted shall nevertheless be liable and subject to indictment, trial, judgment and punishment, according to law.

Section 4. The times, places and manner of holding elections for Senators and Representatives shall be prescribed in each state by the legislature thereof; but the Congress may at any time by law make or alter such regulations, except as to the places of choosing Senators. The Congress shall assemble at least once in every year, and such meeting shall be on the first Monday in December, unless they shall by law appoint a different day.

Section 5. Each House shall be the judge of the elections, returns and qualifications of its own members, and a majority of each shall constitute a quorum to do business; but a smaller number may adjourn from day to day, and may be authorized to compel the attendance of absent members, in such manner, and under such penalties as each House may provide.

Each House may determine the rules of its proceedings, punish its members for disorderly behavior, and, with the concurrence of two thirds, expel a member.

Each House shall keep a journal of its proceedings, and from time to time publish the same, excepting such parts as may in their judgment require secrecy; and the yeas and nays of the members of either House on any question shall, at the desire of one fifth of those present, be entered on the journal.

Neither House, during the session of Congress, shall, without the consent of the other, adjourn for more than three days, nor to any other place than that in which the two Houses shall be sitting.

Section 6. The Senators and Representatives shall receive a compensation for their services, to be ascertained by law, and paid out of the treasury of the United States. They shall in all cases, except treason, felony and breach of the peace, be privileged from arrest during their attendance at the session of their respective Houses, and in going to and returning from the same; and for any speech or debate in either House, they shall not be questioned in any other place.

No Senator or Representative shall, during the time for which he was elected, be appointed to any civil office under the authority of the United States, which shall have been created, or the emoluments whereof shall have been increased during such time: and no person holding any office under the United States, shall be a member of either House during his continuance in office.

Section 7. All bills for raising revenue shall originate in the House of Representatives; but the Senate may propose or concur with amendments as on other Bills.

Every bill which shall have passed the House of Representatives and the Senate, shall, before it become a law, be presented to the President of the United States; if he approve he shall sign it, but if not he shall return it, with his objections to that House in which it shall have originated, who shall enter the objections at large on their journal, and proceed to reconsider it. If after such reconsideration two thirds of that House shall agree to pass the bill, it shall be sent, together with the objections, to the other House, by which it shall likewise be reconsidered, and if approved by two thirds of that House, it shall become a law. But in all such cases the votes of both Houses shall be determined by yeas and nays, and the names of the persons voting for and against the bill shall be entered on the journal of each House respectively. If any bill shall not be returned by the President within ten days (Sundays excepted) after it shall have been presented to him, the same shall be a law, in like manner as if he had signed it, unless the Congress by their adjournment prevent its return, in which case it shall not be a law.

Every order, resolution, or vote to which the concurrence of the Senate and House of Representatives may be necessary (except on a question of adjournment) shall be presented to the President of the United States; and before the same shall take effect, shall be approved by him, or being disapproved by him, shall be repassed by two thirds of the Senate and House of Representatives, according to the rules and limitations prescribed in the case of a bill.

Section 8. The Congress shall have power to lay and collect taxes, duties, imposts and excises, to pay the debts and provide for the common defense and general welfare of the United States; but all duties, imposts and excises shall be uniform throughout the United States;

To borrow money on the credit of the United States;

To regulate commerce with foreign nations, and among the several states, and with the Indian tribes;

To establish a uniform rule of naturalization, and uniform laws on the subject of bankruptcies throughout the United States;

To coin money, regulate the value thereof, and of foreign coin, and fix the standard of weights and measures;

To provide for the punishment of counterfeiting the securities and current coin of the United States;

To establish post offices and post roads;

To promote the progress of science and useful arts, by securing for limited times to authors and inventors the exclusive right to their respective writings and discoveries;

To constitute tribunals inferior to the Supreme Court;

To define and punish piracies and felonies committed on the high seas, and offenses against the law of nations;

To declare war, grant letters of marque and reprisal, and make rules concerning captures on land and water;

To raise and support armies, but no appropriation of money to that use shall be for a longer term than two years;

To provide and maintain a navy;

To make rules for the government and regulation of the land and naval forces;

To provide for calling forth the militia to execute the laws of the union, suppress insurrections and repel invasions;

To provide for organizing, arming, and disciplining, the militia, and for governing such part of them as may be employed in the service of the United States, reserving to the states respectively, the appointment of the officers, and the authority of training the militia according to the discipline prescribed by Congress;

To exercise exclusive legislation in all cases whatsoever, over such District (not exceeding ten miles square) as may, by cession of particular states, and the acceptance of Congress, become the seat of the government of the United States, and to exercise like authority over all places purchased by the consent of the legislature of the state in which the same shall be, for the erection of forts, magazines, arsenals, dockyards, and other needful buildings; And

To make all laws which shall be necessary and proper for carrying into execution the foregoing powers, and all other powers vested by this Constitution in the government of the United States, or in any department or officer thereof.

Section 9. The migration or importation of such persons as any of the states now existing shall think proper to admit, shall not be prohibited by the Congress prior to the year one thousand eight hundred and eight, but a tax or duty may be imposed on such importation, not exceeding ten dollars for each person.

The privilege of the writ of *habeas corpus* shall not be suspended, unless when in cases of rebellion or invasion the public safety may require it.

No bill of attainder or ex post facto Law shall be passed.

No capitation, or other direct, tax shall be laid, unless in proportion to the census or enumeration herein before directed to be taken.

No tax or duty shall be laid on articles exported from any state.

No preference shall be given by any regulation of commerce or revenue to the ports of one state over those of another: nor shall vessels bound to, or from, one state, be obliged to enter, clear or pay duties in another.

No money shall be drawn from the treasury, but in consequence of appropriations made by law; and a regular statement and account of receipts and expenditures of all public money shall be published from time to time.

No title of nobility shall be granted by the United States: and no person holding any office of profit or trust under them, shall, without the consent of the Congress, accept of any present, emolument, office, or title, of any kind whatever, from any king, prince, or foreign state.

Section 10. No state shall enter into any treaty, alliance, or confederation; grant letters of marque and reprisal; coin money; emit bills of credit; make anything but gold and silver coin a tender in payment of debts; pass any bill of attainder, ex post facto law, or law impairing the obligation of contracts, or grant any title of nobility.

No state shall, without the consent of the Congress, lay any imposts or duties on imports or exports, except what may be absolutely necessary for executing its inspection laws: and the net produce of all duties and imposts, laid by any state on imports or exports, shall be for the use of the treasury of the United States; and all such laws shall be subject to the revision and control of the Congress.

No state shall, without the consent of Congress, lay any duty of tonnage, keep troops, or ships of war in time of peace, enter into any agreement or compact with another state, or with a foreign power, or engage in war, unless actually invaded, or in such imminent danger as will not admit of delay.

## Article II

Section 1. The executive power shall be vested in a President of the United States of America. He shall hold his office during the term of four years, and, together with the Vice President, chosen for the same term, be elected, as follows:

Each state shall appoint, in such manner as the Legislature thereof may direct, a number of electors, equal to the whole number of Senators and Representatives to which the State may be entitled in the Congress: but no Senator or Representative, or person holding an office of trust or profit under the United States, shall be appointed an elector.

The electors shall meet in their respective states, and vote by ballot for two persons, of whom one at least shall not be an inhabitant of the same state with themselves. And they shall make a list of all the persons voted for, and of the number of votes for each; which list they shall sign and certify, and transmit sealed to the seat of the government of the United States, directed to the President of the Senate. The President of the Senate shall, in the presence of the Senate and House of Representatives, open all the certificates, and the votes shall then be counted. The person having the greatest number of votes shall be the President, if such number be a majority of the whole number of electors appointed; and if there be more than one who have such majority, and have an equal number of votes, then the House of Representatives shall immediately choose by ballot one of them for President; and if no person have a majority, then from the five highest on the list the said House shall in like manner choose the President. But in choosing the President, the votes shall be taken by States, the representation from each state having one vote; A quorum for this purpose shall consist of a member or members from two thirds of the states, and a majority of all the states shall be necessary to a choice. In every case, after the choice of the President, the person having the greatest number of votes of the electors shall be the Vice President. But if there should remain two or more who have equal votes, the Senate shall choose from them by ballot the Vice President.

The Congress may determine the time of choosing the electors, and the day on which they shall give their votes; which day shall be the same throughout the United States.

No person except a natural born citizen, or a citizen of the United States at the time of the adoption of this Constitution, shall be eligible to the office of President; neither shall any person be eligible to that office who shall not have attained to the age of thirty five years, and been fourteen years a resident within the United States.

In case of the removal of the President from office, or of his death, resignation, or inability to discharge the powers and duties of the said office, the same shall devolve on the Vice President, and the Congress may by law provide for the case of removal, death, resignation or inability, both of the President and Vice President, declaring what officer shall then act as President, and such officer shall act accordingly, until the disability be removed, or a President shall be elected.

The President shall, at stated times, receive for his services, a compensation, which shall neither be increased nor diminished during the period for which he shall have been elected, and he shall not receive within that period any other emolument from the United States, or any of them.

Before he enter on the execution of his office, he shall take the following oath or affirmation:--"I do solemnly swear (or affirm) that I will faithfully execute the office of President of the United States, and will to the best of my ability, preserve, protect and defend the Constitution of the United States."

Section 2. The President shall be commander in chief of the Army and Navy of the United States, and of the militia of the several states, when called into the actual service of the United States; he may require the opinion, in writing, of the principal officer in each of the executive departments, upon any subject relating to the duties of their respective offices, and he shall have power to grant reprieves and pardons for offenses against the United States, except in cases of impeachment.

He shall have power, by and with the advice and consent of the Senate, to make treaties, provided two thirds of the Senators present concur; and he shall nominate, and by and with the advice and consent of the Senate, shall appoint ambassadors, other public ministers and consuls, judges of the Supreme Court, and all other officers of the United States, whose appointments are not herein otherwise provided for, and which shall be established by law: but the Congress may by law vest the appointment of such inferior officers, as they think proper, in the President alone, in the courts of law, or in the heads of departments.

The President shall have power to fill up all vacancies that may happen during the recess of the Senate, by granting commissions which shall expire at the end of their next session.

Section 3. He shall from time to time give to the Congress information of the state of the union, and recommend to their consideration such measures as he shall judge necessary and expedient; he may, on extraordinary occasions, convene both Houses, or either of them, and in case of disagreement between them, with respect to the time of adjournment, he may adjourn them to such time as he shall think proper; he shall receive ambassadors and other public ministers; he shall take care that the laws be faithfully executed, and shall commission all the officers of the United States.

Section 4. The President, Vice President and all civil officers of the United States, shall be removed from office on impeachment for, and conviction of, treason, bribery, or other high crimes and misdemeanors.

## Article III

Section 1. The judicial power of the United States, shall be vested in one Supreme Court, and in such inferior courts as the Congress may from time to time ordain and establish. The judges, both of the supreme and inferior courts, shall hold their offices during good behaviour, and shall, at stated times, receive for their services, a compensation, which shall not be diminished during their continuance in office.

Section 2. The judicial power shall extend to all cases, in law and equity, arising under this Constitution, the laws of the United States, and treaties made, or which shall be made, under their authority;--to all cases affecting ambassadors, other public ministers and consuls;--to all cases of admiralty and maritime jurisdiction;--to controversies to which the United States shall be a party;--to controversies between two or more states;--between a state and citizens of another state;-- between citizens of different states;--between citizens of the same state claiming lands under grants of different states, and between a state, or the citizens thereof, and foreign states, citizens or subjects. 

In all cases affecting ambassadors, other public ministers and consuls, and those in which a state shall be party, the Supreme Court shall have original jurisdiction. In all the other cases before mentioned, the Supreme Court shall have appellate jurisdiction, both as to law and fact, with such exceptions, and under such regulations as the Congress shall make.

The trial of all crimes, except in cases of impeachment, shall be by jury; and such trial shall be held in the state where the said crimes shall have been committed; but when not committed within any state, the trial shall be at such place or places as the Congress may by law have directed.

Section 3. Treason against the United States, shall consist only in levying war against them, or in adhering to their enemies, giving them aid and comfort. No person shall be convicted of treason unless on the testimony of two witnesses to the same overt act, or on confession in open court.

The Congress shall have power to declare the punishment of treason, but no attainder of treason shall work corruption of blood, or forfeiture except during the life of the person attainted.

## Article IV

Section 1. Full faith and credit shall be given in each state to the public acts, records, and judicial proceedings of every other state. And the Congress may by general laws prescribe the manner in which such acts, records, and proceedings shall be proved, and the effect thereof.

Section 2. The citizens of each state shall be entitled to all privileges and immunities of citizens in the several states.

A person charged in any state with treason, felony, or other crime, who shall flee from justice, and be found in another state, shall on demand of the executive authority of the state from which he fled, be delivered up, to be removed to the state having jurisdiction of the crime.

No person held to service or labor in one state, under the laws thereof, escaping into another, shall, in consequence of any law or regulation therein, be discharged from such service or labor, but shall be delivered up on claim of the party to whom such service or labor may be due.

Section 3. New states may be admitted by the Congress into this union; but no new states shall be formed or erected within the jurisdiction of any other state; nor any state be formed by the junction of two or more states, or parts of states, without the consent of the legislatures of the states concerned as well as of the Congress.

The Congress shall have power to dispose of and make all needful rules and regulations respecting the territory or other property belonging to the United States; and nothing in this Constitution shall be so construed as to prejudice any claims of the United States, or of any particular state.

Section 4. The United States shall guarantee to every state in this union a republican form of government, and shall protect each of them against invasion; and on application of the legislature, or of the executive (when the legislature cannot be convened) against domestic violence.

## Article V

The Congress, whenever two thirds of both houses shall deem it necessary, shall propose amendments to this Constitution, or, on the application of the legislatures of two thirds of the several states, shall call a convention for proposing amendments, which, in either case, shall be valid to all intents and purposes, as part of this Constitution, when ratified by the legislatures of three fourths of the several states, or by conventions in three fourths thereof, as the one or the other mode of ratification may be proposed by the Congress; provided that no amendment which may be made prior to the year one thousand eight hundred and eight shall in any manner affect the first and fourth clauses in the ninth section of the first article; and that no state, without its consent, shall be deprived of its equal suffrage in the Senate.

## Article VI

All debts contracted and engagements entered into, before the adoption of this Constitution, shall be as valid against the United States under this Constitution, as under the Confederation.

This Constitution, and the laws of the United States which shall be made in pursuance thereof; and all treaties made, or which shall be made, under the authority of the United States, shall be the supreme law of the land; and the judges in every state shall be bound thereby, anything in the Constitution or laws of any State to the contrary notwithstanding.

The Senators and Representatives before mentioned, and the members of the several state legislatures, and all executive and judicial officers, both of the United States and of the several states, shall be bound by oath or affirmation, to support this Constitution; but no religious test shall ever be required as a qualification to any office or public trust under the United States.

## Article VII

The ratification of the conventions of nine states, shall be sufficient for the establishment of this Constitution between the states so ratifying the same.

Done in convention by the unanimous consent of the states present the seventeenth day of September in the year of our Lord one thousand seven hundred and eighty seven and of the independence of the United States of America the twelfth. In witness whereof We have hereunto subscribed our Names,

G. Washington-President and deputy from Virginia
(there followed signatures of 38 representatives from the other states)

**Amendments** (1-10 were all passed together in the 1790s, and they and are usually called **The Bill of Rights**)

Resolved, by the Senate and House of Representatives of the United States of America, in Congress assembled, two-thirds of both Houses concurring, that the following articles be proposed to the Legislatures of the several States, as amendments to the Constitution of the United States; all or any of which articles, when ratified by three-fourths of the said Legislatures, to be valid to all intents and purposes as part of the said Constitution, namely:

Amendment I
Congress shall make no law respecting an establishment of religion, or prohibiting the free exercise thereof; or abridging the freedom of speech, or of the press; or the right of the people peaceably to assemble, and to petition the government for a redress of grievances.

Amendment II

A well regulated militia being necessary to the security of a free state, the right of the people to keep and bear arms, shall not be infringed.

Amendment III

No soldier shall, in time of peace be quartered in any house, without the consent of the owner, nor in time of war, but in a manner to be prescribed by law.

Amendment IV

The right of the people to be secure in their persons, houses, papers, and effects, against unreasonable searches and seizures, shall not be violated, and no warrants shall issue, but upon probable cause, supported by oath or affirmation, and particularly describing the place to be searched, and the persons or things to be seized.

Amendment V

No person shall be held to answer for a capital, or otherwise infamous crime, unless on a presentment or indictment of a grand jury, except in cases arising in the land or naval forces, or in the militia, when in actual service in time of war or public danger; nor shall any person be subject for the same offense to be twice put in jeopardy of life or limb; nor shall be compelled in any criminal case to be a witness against himself, nor be deprived of life, liberty, or property, without due process of law; nor shall private property be taken for public use, without just compensation.

Amendment VI

In all criminal prosecutions, the accused shall enjoy the right to a speedy and public trial, by an impartial jury of the state and district wherein the crime shall have been committed, which district shall have been previously ascertained by law, and to be informed of the nature and cause of the accusation; to be confronted with the witnesses against him; to have compulsory process for obtaining witnesses in his favor, and to have the assistance of counsel for his defense.

Amendment VII

In suits at common law, where the value in controversy shall exceed twenty dollars, the right of trial by jury shall be preserved, and no fact tried by a jury, shall be otherwise reexamined in any court of the United States, than according to the rules of the common law.

Amendment VIII

Excessive bail shall not be required, nor excessive fines imposed, nor cruel and unusual punishments inflicted.

Amendment IX

The enumeration in the Constitution, of certain rights, shall not be construed to deny or disparage others retained by the people.

Amendment X

The powers not delegated to the United States by the Constitution, nor prohibited by it to the states, are reserved to the states respectively, or to the people.

Amendment XI (1798)

The judicial power of the United States shall not be construed to extend to any suit in law or equity, commenced or prosecuted against one of the United States by citizens of another state, or by citizens or subjects of any foreign state.

Amendment XII (1804)

The electors shall meet in their respective states and vote by ballot for President and Vice-President, one of whom, at least, shall not be an inhabitant of the same state with themselves; they shall name in their ballots the person voted for as President, and in distinct ballots the person voted for as Vice President, and they shall make distinct lists of all persons voted for as President, and of all persons voted for as Vice-President, and of the number of votes for each, which lists they shall sign and certify, and transmit sealed to the seat of the government of the United States, directed to the President of the Senate;--The President of the Senate shall, in the presence of the Senate and House of Representatives, open all the certificates and the votes shall then be counted;--the person having the greatest number of votes for President, shall be the President, if such number be a majority of the whole number of electors appointed; and if no person have such majority, then from the persons having the highest numbers not exceeding three on the list of those voted for as President, the House of Representatives shall choose immediately, by ballot, the President. But in choosing the President, the votes shall be taken by states, the representation from each state having one vote; a quorum for this purpose shall consist of a member or members from two-thirds of the states, and a majority of all the states shall be necessary to a choice. And if the House of Representatives shall not choose a President whenever the right of choice shall devolve upon them, before the fourth day of March next following, then the Vice-President shall act as President, as in the case of the death or other constitutional disability of the President. The person having the greatest number of votes as Vice-President, shall be the Vice-President, if such number be a majority of the whole number of electors appointed, and if no person have a majority, then from the two highest numbers on the list, the Senate shall choose the Vice-President; a quorum for the purpose shall consist of two-thirds of the whole number of Senators, and a majority of the whole number shall be necessary to a choice. But no person constitutionally ineligible to the office of President shall be eligible to that of Vice-President of the United States.

Amendment XIII (1865)

Section 1. Neither slavery nor involuntary servitude, except as a punishment for crime whereof the party shall have been duly convicted, shall exist within the United States, or any place subject to their jurisdiction.

Section 2. Congress shall have power to enforce this article by appropriate legislation.

Amendment XIV (1868)

Section 1. All persons born or naturalized in the United States, and subject to the jurisdiction thereof, are citizens of the United States and of the state wherein they reside. No state shall make or enforce any law which shall abridge the privileges or immunities of citizens of the United States; nor shall any state deprive any person of life, liberty, or property, without due process of law; nor deny to any person within its jurisdiction the equal protection of the laws.

Section 2. Representatives shall be apportioned among the several states according to their respective numbers, counting the whole number of persons in each state, excluding Indians not taxed. But when the right to vote at any election for the choice of electors for President and Vice President of the United States, Representatives in Congress, the executive and judicial officers of a state, or the members of the legislature thereof, is denied to any of the male inhabitants of such state, being twenty-one years of age, and citizens of the United States, or in any way abridged, except for participation in rebellion, or other crime, the basis of representation therein shall be reduced in the proportion which the number of such male citizens shall bear to the whole number of male citizens twenty-one years of age in such state.

Section 3. No person shall be a Senator or Representative in Congress, or elector of President and Vice President, or hold any office, civil or military, under the United States, or under any state, who, having previously taken an oath, as a member of Congress, or as an officer of the United States, or as a member of any state legislature, or as an executive or judicial officer of any state, to support the Constitution of the United States, shall have engaged in insurrection or rebellion against the same, or given aid or comfort to the enemies thereof. But Congress may by a vote of two-thirds of each House, remove such disability.

Section 4. The validity of the public debt of the United States, authorized by law, including debts incurred for payment of pensions and bounties for services in suppressing insurrection or rebellion, shall not be questioned. But neither the United States nor any state shall assume or pay any debt or obligation incurred in aid of insurrection or rebellion against the United States, or any claim for the loss or emancipation of any slave; but all such debts, obligations and claims shall be held illegal and void.

Section 5. The Congress shall have power to enforce, by appropriate legislation, the provisions of this article.

Amendment XV (1870)

Section 1. The right of citizens of the United States to vote shall not be denied or abridged by the United States or by any state on account of race, color, or previous condition of servitude.

Section 2. The Congress shall have power to enforce this article by appropriate legislation.

Amendment XVI (1913)

The Congress shall have power to lay and collect taxes on incomes, from whatever source derived, without apportionment among the several states, and without regard to any census of enumeration.

Amendment XVII (1913)

The Senate of the United States shall be composed of two Senators from each state, elected by the people thereof, for six years; and each Senator shall have one vote. The electors in each state shall have the qualifications requisite for electors of the most numerous branch of the state legislatures. When vacancies happen in the representation of any state in the Senate, the executive authority of such state shall issue writs of election to fill such vacancies: Provided, that the legislature of any state may empower the executive thereof to make temporary appointments until the people fill the vacancies by election as the legislature may direct. This amendment shall not be so construed as to affect the election or term of any Senator chosen before it becomes valid as part of the Constitution.

Amendment XVIII (1919)

Section 1. After one year from the ratification of this article the manufacture, sale, or transportation of intoxicating liquors within, the importation thereof into, or the exportation thereof from the United States and all territory subject to the jurisdiction thereof for beverage purposes is hereby prohibited.

Section 2. The Congress and the several states shall have concurrent power to enforce this article by appropriate legislation.

Section 3. This article shall be inoperative unless it shall have been ratified as an amendment to the Constitution by the legislatures of the several states, as provided in the Constitution, within seven years from the date of the submission hereof to the states by the Congress.

Amendment XIX (1920)

The right of citizens of the United States to vote shall not be denied or abridged by the United States or by any state on account of sex. Congress shall have power to enforce this article by appropriate legislation.

Amendment XX (1933)

Section 1. The terms of the President and Vice President shall end at noon on the 20th day of January, and the terms of Senators and Representatives at noon on the 3d day of January, of the years in which such terms would have ended if this article had not been ratified; and the terms of their successors shall then begin.

Section 2. The Congress shall assemble at least once in every year, and such meeting shall begin at noon on the 3d day of January, unless they shall by law appoint a different day.

Section 3. If, at the time fixed for the beginning of the term of the President, the President elect shall have died, the Vice President elect shall become President. If a President shall not have been chosen before the time fixed for the beginning of his term, or if the President elect shall have failed to qualify, then the Vice President elect shall act as President until a President shall have qualified; and the Congress may by law provide for the case wherein neither a President elect nor a Vice President elect shall have qualified, declaring who shall then act as President, or the manner in which one who is to act shall be selected, and such person shall act accordingly until a President or Vice President shall have qualified.

Section 4. The Congress may by law provide for the case of the death of any of the persons from whom the House of Representatives may choose a President whenever the right of choice shall have devolved upon them, and for the case of the death of any of the persons from whom the Senate may choose a Vice President whenever the right of choice shall have devolved upon them.

Section 5. Sections 1 and 2 shall take effect on the 15th day of October following the ratification of this article.

Section 6. This article shall be inoperative unless it shall have been ratified as an amendment to the Constitution by the legislatures of three-fourths of the several states within seven years from the date of its submission.

## Amendment XXI (1933)

Section 1. The eighteenth article of amendment to the Constitution of the United States is hereby repealed.

Section 2. The transportation or importation into any state, territory, or possession of the United States for delivery or use therein of intoxicating liquors, in violation of the laws thereof, is hereby prohibited.

Section 3. This article shall be inoperative unless it shall have been ratified as an amendment to the Constitution by conventions in the several states, as provided in the Constitution, within seven years from the date of the submission hereof to the states by the Congress.

## Amendment XXII (1951)

Section 1. No person shall be elected to the office of the President more than twice, and no person who has held the office of President, or acted as President, for more than two years of a term to which some other person was elected President shall be elected to the office of the President more than once. But this article shall not apply to any person holding the office of President when this article was proposed by the Congress, and shall not prevent any person who may be holding the office of President, or acting as President, during the term within which this article becomes operative from holding the office of President or acting as President during the remainder of such term.

Section 2. This article shall be inoperative unless it shall have been ratified as an amendment to the Constitution by the legislatures of three-fourths of the several states within seven years from the date of its submission to the states by the Congress.

## Amendment XXIII (1961)

Section 1. The District constituting the seat of government of the United States shall appoint in such manner as the Congress may direct: A number of electors of President and Vice President equal to the whole number of Senators and Representatives in Congress to which the District would be entitled if it were a state, but in no event more than the least populous state; they shall be in addition to those appointed by the states, but they shall be considered, for the purposes of the election of President and Vice President, to be electors appointed by a state; and they shall meet in the District and perform such duties as provided by the twelfth article of amendment.

Section 2. The Congress shall have power to enforce this article by appropriate legislation.

Amendment XXIV (1964)

Section 1. The right of citizens of the United States to vote in any primary or other election for President or Vice President, for electors for President or Vice President, or for Senator or Representative in Congress, shall not be denied or abridged by the United States or any state by reason of failure to pay any poll tax or other tax.

Section 2. The Congress shall have power to enforce this article by appropriate legislation.

Amendment XXV (1967)

Section 1. In case of the removal of the President from office or of his death or resignation, the Vice President shall become President.

Section 2. Whenever there is a vacancy in the office of the Vice President, the President shall nominate a Vice President who shall take office upon confirmation by a majority vote of both Houses of Congress.

Section 3. Whenever the President transmits to the President pro tempore of the Senate and the Speaker of the House of Representatives his written declaration that he is unable to discharge the powers and duties of his office, and until he transmits to them a written declaration to the contrary, such powers and duties shall be discharged by the Vice President as Acting President.

Section 4. Whenever the Vice President and a majority of either the principal officers of the executive departments or of such other body as Congress may by law provide, transmit to the President pro tempore of the Senate and the Speaker of the House of Representatives their written declaration that the President is unable to discharge the powers and duties of his office, the Vice President shall immediately assume the powers and duties of the office as Acting President.

Thereafter, when the President transmits to the President pro tempore of the Senate and the Speaker of the House of Representatives his written declaration that no inability exists, he shall resume the powers and duties of his office unless the Vice President and a majority of either the principal officers of the executive department or of such other body as Congress may by law provide, transmit within four days to the President pro tempore of the Senate and the Speaker of the House of Representatives their written declaration that the President is unable to discharge the powers and duties of his office. Thereupon Congress shall decide the issue, assembling within forty-eight hours for that purpose if not in session. If the Congress, within twenty-one days after receipt of the latter written declaration, or, if Congress is not in session, within twenty-one days after Congress is required to assemble, determines by two-thirds vote of both Houses that the President is unable to discharge the powers and duties of his office, the Vice President shall continue to discharge the same as Acting President; otherwise, the President shall resume the powers and duties of his office.

Amendment XXVI (1971)

Section 1. The right of citizens of the United States, who are 18 years of age or older, to vote, shall not be denied or abridged by the United States or any state on account of age.

Section 2. The Congress shall have the power to enforce this article by appropriate legislation.

Amendment XXVII (1992)

No law varying the compensation for the services of the Senators and Representatives shall take effect until an election of Representatives shall have intervened.

# Appendix 3
# Presidents of the United States, 1789-

George Washington (1789–1797)
John Adams (1797–1801)
Thomas Jefferson (1801–1809)
James Madison (1809–1817)
James Monroe (1817–1825)
John Quincy Adams (1825–1829)
Andrew Jackson (1829–1837)
Martin Van Buren (1837–1841)
William Henry Harrison (1841)
John Tyler (1841–1845)
James Polk (1845–1849)
Zachary Taylor (1849–1850)
Millard Fillmore (1850–1853)
Franklin Pierce (1853–1857)
James Buchanan (1857–1861)
Abraham Lincoln (1861–1865)
Andrew Johnson (1865–1869)
Ulysses S. Grant (1869–1877)
Rutherford B. Hayes (1877–1881)
James A. Garfield (1881)
Chester A. Arthur (1881–1885)
Grover Cleveland (1885–1889)

Benjamin Harrison (1889–1893)
Grover Cleveland (1893–1897)
William McKinley (1897–1901)
Theodore Roosevelt (1901–1909)
William H. Taft (1909–1913)
Woodrow Wilson (1913–1921)
Warren Harding (1921–1923)
Calvin Coolidge (1923–1929)
Herbert Hoover (1929–1933)
Franklin D. Roosevelt (1933–1945)
Harry S. Truman (1945–1953)
Dwight D. Eisenhower (1953–1961)
John F. Kennedy (1961–1963)
Lyndon B. Johnson (1963–1969)
Richard M. Nixon (1969–1974)
Gerald R. Ford (1974–1977)
Jimmy Carter (1977–1981)
Ronald W. Reagan (1981–1989)
George Bush (1989–1993)
William Clinton (1993–2001)
George W. Bush (2001- )

# Reference Guide

For detailed bibliographies see Internet sites listed in the following section.

Appiah, Kwame Anthony and Henry Louis Gates, Jr. (eds.), *Africana : The Encyclopedia of the African and African American Experience*, (Basic Civitas Books, 1999).

Commager, Henry Steele, *Documents of American History* (Prentice Hall, 1979).

Duchak, Alicia, *A-Z of Modern America* (Routledge, 1999).

Elliott, Emory, ed., *Columbia Literary History of the United States* (Columbia University Press, 1988).

Faragher, John M. (ed.) *The American Heritage Encyclopedia of American History* (Henry Holt, 1998).

Foner, Eric and John A. Garraty (eds.), *The Reader's Companion to American History* (Houghton Mifflin, 1991).

Inge, Thomas, (ed.), *Handbook of American Popular Culture* (Greenwood, 1989).

Johnson, (ed.), Thomas H., *The Oxford Companion to American History* (Oxford University Press, 1966).

Library of Congress, *Guide to the Study of the United States of America* (U.S. Government Printing Office 1960, supplement, 1976).

Morris, Richard B., (ed.), *Encyclopedia of American History* (Harper/Collins, 1996).

Nye, David E., Carl Pedersen and Niels Thorsen (eds.), *American Studies: A Source Book* (Akademisk Forlag, 1994).

Puchra, Francis Paul, *Handbook for Research in American History* (Nebraska University Press, 1994).

Rooney, John F., *This Remarkable Continent: An Atlas of the United States* (Texas A. M. University Press, 1982).

*Statistical Abstract of the United States* Washington, D. C.: United States Government Printing Office. [Issued every year.]

Thomas G. Patterson and Dennis Merrill (eds.), *Major Problems in American Foreign Relations* (D. C. Heath, 1995).

Vile, M. J. C., *Politics in the USA*, 5th ed. (Routledge, 1999).

Walker, Robert H., *Sources for American Studies* (Greenwood Press, 1983).

Wattenberg, Ben, *The Statistical History of the United States* (Basic Books, 1976).